TEACHING EDUCABLE
MENTALLY RETARDED CHILDREN

TEACHING EDUCABLE MENTALLY RETARDED CHILDREN

100811

SECOND EDITION

OLIVER P. KOLSTOE
University of Northern Colorado
Greeley, Colorado

HOLT, RINEHART AND WINSTON
New York   Chicago   San Francisco   Atlanta
Dallas   Montreal   Toronto   London   Sydney

Library of Congress Cataloging in Publication Data

Kolstoe, Oliver P.
    Teaching educable mentally retarded children.

    Includes bibliographical references and index.
    1. Mentally handicapped children—Education.
I. Title. [DNLM: 1. Education of mentally re-
tarded. LC4601 K85t]
LC4661.K576 1976   371.9′282   75-23456
ISBN 0-03-089724-6

PREFACE

Over the years, practices in educational programs for the mentally retarded have exhibited a diversity which probably reflects the particular conceptualization of the condition accepted by the teachers involved. Even in the same school system, teachers of different age groups may have startling differences in their programs because each sees mental retardation differently. The result of this diversity has been confusion in the goals and subsequent lack of articulation between one level of program and the next.

This book uses a conceptualization of the condition which combines a neurophysiological theory with a behavioral theory in order to secure a consistent frame of reference for teachers to use. It then ties methods and materials to specific behavioral outcomes consistent with the goal of developing an adult who has acceptable skills for work and independent living.

The translation of theory into practice provides an internal consistency for the program and assures that practices at one level are related to those of the next level. Whether this approach is valid, only history can decide. Whether the suggestions are feasible, only teachers can decide. The real test of any system, however, is the degree to

v

which it contributes to the end of producing self-managing adults. Such a determination must await the verdict of research.

The decision to develop a total program was made with the full cognizance of recent attempts to subsume mental retardation under classifications of "learning disability," "educational handicap," and "functional retardation." Although these terms are not precisely equivalent, they carry the common denominator of implying that intensive educational intervention of a specific nature will remove the learning handicap. Such a contention may be a reality, but it has not yet been conclusively demonstrated. Thus the comprehensiveness of the program presented in this book can be interpreted as reflecting this writer's concern that various short-term approaches may not prove as therapeutically effective as we may wish. If they do not, it would seem prudent to plan for long-term instructional attention on the premise that mental retardation may, indeed, represent a chronic condition.

Such a point of view is not intended as a pessimistic commentary. Research evidence would lead instead to a quite optimistic feeling about what a good program can accomplish. But the optimism is tempered by the realization that many years of concerted effort may be required to influence effectively the life style of retarded youngsters. The plan of this book allows for innovative efforts within the framework of such a long-term program.

As is usual, no author is unaided. What has evolved into the program presented in this book has been influenced by many people who deserve recognition. Dr. Tony D. Vaughan, his students, and staff developed the original outcomes list, which in modified form makes up the framework of the book. William S. Wright read and criticized the manuscript, helped in the evaluation of specific materials, and has been a consistent source of ideas and encouragement. Dr. Charles Forgnone helped quite measurably in clarifying the conceptualization of mental retardation and provided a sounding board for ideas. I am grateful to Bertha Smith for valuable materials suggestions and to Willia Hintergardt and Jan Green for typing the manuscript. Throughout the revision of the manuscript, colleagues and students have provided criticism and encouragement in abundance. Both were gratefully accepted, but special thanks go to Dr. Wilbur Millslagle, William Cain, and Dr. Neil Henderson and his staff.

Greeley, Colorado   *Oliver P. Kolstoe*
August 1975

CONTENTS

Preface   v

Part I   Objectives and Organization   1

Chapter 1   The Learner   3

   Introduction   3
   The Nature of Mental Retardation   6
   Toward a Clarification of the Concept of Mental Retardation   15
   Characteristics of the Mentally Retarded   20
   Theories of Retardation   21
   A Definition of Mental Retardation   24
   Principles of Presentation   26

Chapter 2   The Objectives   28

   Need for Intervention   28
   Goals of Education   32
   The Program   36
   Instructional Outcomes   38
   Preschool Program   41

Primary Program   42
Intermediate Program   42
Prevocational Program   42
Vocational Program   43
Book Plan   43

Chapter 3   The Organization   46

Program Delivery   46
Identification   57
Diagnosis   58
Services Assignment   59
Grouping for Services   62
Instructional Methods   67
Individual Programs of Instruction   71
Learning Paradigm   81

Part II   Methods and Materials   83

Chapter 4   Communication Skills   85

Oral Communication   85
Listening Skills   91
Written Communication   93
Reading   100
Developmental Approaches   113

Chapter 5   Arithmetic Skills   119

Arithmetic Facts and Processes   120
Money   121
Time   123
Measurement   125
Teaching Arithmetic   126
Teaching Money   136
Teaching Time   137
Teaching Measurement   138
Arithmetic Diagnosis   139

Chapter 6   Social Competencies   142

The Self   144
In the School   146
The Home, Neighborhood, and Community   149
Teaching Social Competencies   151

Chapter 7   Motor Skills and Recreation   156

   Motor Skills   156
   Motor and Recreational Skills   160
   Teaching Mobility   163
   Recreation   167

Chapter 8   Esthetics   171

   Art   173
   Outcomes   177
   Music   179
   Implementing Art and Music   182

Chapter 9   Health and Safety   184

   Teaching Health   188
   Safety   191
   Teaching Safety   194

Chapter 10   Vocational Competencies   197

   Initial Work Experiences   205
   Work Tryout   207
   Permanent Placement   207
   Analysis of Occupation and Job Finding   208
   Developing the Individual for
      Occupational Placement and Job Retention   211

Part III   Units of Instruction   216

Chapter 11   Preschool, Primary, and Inter-
             mediate Units of Instruction   217

   Preschool Level—The Home   224
   Primary Level—The Neighborhood   229
   Intermediate Level—City, Region, and State   235

Chapter 12   Prevocational and Vocational Units   239

   Prevocational Level   239
   Vocational Level   249

Part IV   Summary   258

Chapter 13   Summary and Projection   259

   Projection   263

Appendix 269

Communications Skills	269
Arithmetic	275
Social Competencies	280
Motor and Recreational Skills	285
Esthetics	288
Health	290
Safety	293
Vocational Competencies	296

Index   301

Part I

OBJECTIVES AND ORGANIZATION

CHAPTER 1

The Learner

Introduction

The history of civilization is a continuing story of man's efforts to adapt to the demands of the environment he lives in. In every culture, those persons who do not seem able to achieve a reasonable level of adequacy in their adaptive behavior are given some special consideration. The focus of the consideration may be dictated by a variety of motives—political, economic, spiritual, or some combination of these societal needs, but inadequacy is never ignored.

Mental retardation as a departure from adequacy in intellectual, social, physical, psychological, medical, and educational areas has generated a venerable record of efforts to deal with the condition. Not all of the history has been a tribute to man's capacity for humanitarian accommodation, but the present era is a wondrous improvement over practices of the past. The eras of extermination, ridicule, asylum, and education document a steady but painfully slow change in the concern of western society for these handicapped citizens. It is difficult to find very much concern for the welfare of the individual in a policy of extermination. Similarly, the era of ridicule had its savage side, but allowing the handicapped to participate with other nonhandicapped people, even within the restrictions of a circumscribed role, widened their social horizons rather substantially. On the other hand, as the practice of providing asylum became widespread, it certainly documented a recognition of the right to life of the handicapped albeit a life of segregation from the ongoing activities of the rest of society. In the 1790s or early 1800s the era of education began, which expanded the opportunities for the retarded and reflected a degree of tolerance and understanding hitherto unparalleled. Yet full participation (subject only to their own limitations and interests) in the societies in which they live has only recently been possible. Universal humanitarian efforts to provide opportunities afforded to every citizen are so recent as to be scarcely noticeable until after World War II and, although services to the handicapped have increased significantly since then, anything approaching equal opportunity did not exist until after the right to education lawsuit of *The Pennsylvania Association for Retarded Children* v. *The Commonwealth of Pennsylvania* in 1971. The lawsuit was brought on by the failure of the public schools in Pennsylvania to provide educational opportunities for rather severely mentally retarded children that would be appropriate to their abilities and needs. The court ruling in favor of the children prompted a host of other states to reexamine the educational opportunities available to the mentally retarded in their areas and to enact legislation mandating educational opportunities for the handicapped where only permissive legislation had existed before.

This movement toward increased educational opportunities had a companion movement in other social areas. Lawsuits to ensure educational and occupational opportunities for racial and ethnic minorities became centered in affirmative action programs which touched any company or institution that did business with government agencies or used federal funds. Since nearly every level of government is likely to have a project of some kind that is somewhat supported by federal funds, the positive action of employing a percentage of minorities equal to their representation in the local population became a fact of life. Handicapped individuals shared in this movement, including its advantages of increased employment opportunities. At the same time, Blatt called attention to the almost inhuman conditions that existed in some institutions for the mentally retarded in Massachusetts and New York. This set off a series of similar investigations in other parts of the country. Since conditions similar to those described by Blatt were found to be widespread, cries for corrective measures soon became a concerted movement for changing institutional practices to more humane efforts.

The focus for this movement found itself in a practice that came to be called "normalization." The principle had its roots in the work of Nirja in Sweden, but was first articulated in this country in the 1969 Report of the President's Panel on Mental Retardation. In a kind of declaration of rights for the retarded, the report contended that every human being had the right to a free choice of where he would live, work, and learn, so long as he did not constitute a threat to the rights of other people. In short, the principle of normalization upheld the right of the retarded to have a life style as close to normal as possible.

The ushering in of the era of normalization provided a fundamental change in the treatment of the retarded. As each preceding change reflected a shift in the way individuals called retarded have been treated by society, the story line has led in the direction of gradual recognition of a greater degree of capability of each generation. The Era of Education recognized that the retarded could learn; the Era of Normalization recognized that the retarded could be self-managing adults. Fundamentally, it assures individuals who are mentally retarded those rights guaranteed any other citizen subject only to the test of performance. In the past, opportunities for the retarded to even try to live lives of simple human dignity were severely restricted. With the idea of normalization as a guiding principle, the chances to be human have increased enormously.

Just how this change has come about may not be immediately clear, but it is clear that increased knowledge of the condition has been a significant factor. Since 1945, the literature and services in the field have expanded at an almost geometric rate. Its truly heartening trend, however, has been not only the quantity of effort, but also the quality of effort and the diversity of professional specialties which are contributing.

While the focus of each profession reflects the unique concern of that specialty, all attempts carry the common story thread of making it possible for the mentally retarded to adapt successfully to societal demands. Some professions have attended to the task of modifying the behavior of the retarded. Education, in particular, has been concerned with developing methods, materials, techniques, and procedures which effect behavior modifications, and result in more adequate adaptive behavior for the retarded. In this effort, two points of concern are critical: one is an understanding of the nature and consequences of mental retardation, and a second is an understanding of the behaviors, values, knowledges, and skills required for adequate functioning in society.

The mission of this book is, first, to provide a conceptualization of mental retardation upon which educational programs can rest; second, to specify the minimum behavior outcomes required for adequate adaptive behavior; and third, to present an educational program which provides for the systematic development of those specified behavioral outcomes.

The Nature of Mental Retardation

Classifying the Mentally Retarded

As more and more people of different professional specializations attend to the condition, it is inevitable that each should formulate the problem in somewhat different terms. As a result, recent literature contains a bewildering variety of labels, each reflecting the purpose and professional background of the investigator or commentator.

Since the British workers of the early 1900s had no psychometric devices, it is quite understandable that they should describe the condition in levels of behavior which were identifiable to a casual observer.[1] At the most severe level, they classified idiots (from the Greek word *idios*—literally, "one who stands alone"). The behavior associated with this level was "one who cannot protect himself from the ordinary hazards of life." The imbecile, by implication, can recognize and avoid obvious hazards, but is incapable of managing his own affairs. The feeble-minded or moron (so named by American psychologists) is characterized as one who can manage himself and his affairs, but displays "foolish" behavior. Such descriptions have great utility for dividing the retarded into groups that need different kinds of training and care, but the overlap between groups is great, the distinction between categories is vague, and it is nearly impossible to identify accurately the degree of retardation while the individual is still young.

Clearly, a system for identifying the retarded was needed that was fast and accurate, which would provide for both classifying and predicting, and which could be used with people at all ages. Such a system was provided by the test developed by Binet and Simon in Paris, about 1900.[2] Subsequent revisions of the test by Terman and his colleagues at Stanford University in 1916, 1937, and 1960 provided an

---

[1] See J. E. Wallace Wallin, *The Education of Handicapped Children* (Boston: Houghton Mifflin Company, 1924).

[2] Alfred Binet and Theodore Simon, *The Development of Intelligence in Children* (Baltimore: The Williams & Wilkins Co., 1916).

instrument that met these criteria.[3] By using tasks appropriate for different age groups, it became possible to compare children with their peers in an accurate manner. "Normalcy" was operationally defined as performance equal to one's peers. In a similar manner, performance equivalent to that of older children defined superior children, and performance similar to that of younger children identified the subnormal. Since Binet and subsequent test developers believed the tasks required "intelligence" for successful performance, the tests became known as "tests of intelligence," and mental retardation became defined as subnormal intellectual functioning.

Unfortunately, the performances on the tests not only classified the youngsters, but also the content of the tests was used to describe their condition. The retarded not only were defined as falling in the lower 3 percent of the population, but they were then described as being poor in memory, sequencing, and detecting likenesses and differences. They possessed limited information, and showed inferior comprehension—tasks measured by the test itself.

From the scientific viewpoint, this has become a classic example of circular reasoning. Yet the contribution of psychometric devices was enormous. Workers in the field now had an instrument that could be used for identifying, classifying, and predicting while the child was still young enough to profit from intervention techniques.

By reference to the percentage of children in the standardization group who obtained different scores on the test, mental retardation became the term assigned a youngster whose intelligence quotient (IQ) fell in the lowest 3 percent of the range of the possible scores. Classification into groups according to severity became more precise, and a standard of performance came into general use. An IQ of from 50 to 70 classified the morons, 25 to 50 classified the imbeciles, and below 25, the idiots. Further, morons could be expected to develop to a mental age of about 9, imbeciles to about 5, and idiots to about 2. By inference, the behavior distinctions of the three groups offered by the British Royal Commission were not only retained, but were rendered more useful because it was now possible to predict, with some accuracy, the probable level of social maturity that would be achieved by an individual while he was still very young. In essence, training and care plans could be initiated early in the child's life with considerable confidence that the plans would be realistic.

The psychometric movement had, as a consequence, the focusing

---

[3] Lewis M. Terman and Maud A. Merrill, *Stanford-Binet Intelligence Scale*, Manual for the Third Revision, Form L-M (Boston: Houghton Mifflin Company, 1960).

of professional attention on retarded children. It was felt, for example, that perhaps concerted training efforts with young children could ameliorate or even cure the condition. Child development specialists, including pediatricians, were attracted to a field of study previously believed to be unworthy of their efforts and concern because of the futility of expecting possible improvements.

With increased attention came increased knowledge. One of the early discoveries was that the classification, "mental retardation," embraced a group that was more different than alike—more hetero-geneous than homogeneous. As a consequence, many workers attended to the various causes of the condition. The etiology controversy has centered not so much on the fact that there are many different causes that affect development before, during, or at any time after birth, but rather on whether the different causes have significant learning or behavior consequences. In deference to this possibility, Strauss and his co-workers added two more terms: *endogenous* and *exogenous*.[4] (The genesis or beginning of the retardation is within the individual—*endo*, or outside the individual—*exo*.) No assumption is made as to severity, but controversy still rages over whether different teaching techniques are more effective with endogenous children or exogenous ones. At present, the findings can only be termed equivocal.[5] No clear evidence exists for prescribing educational practices based on the cause of the condition. Rather, it appears that education must be concerned with the inadequate characteristics of each individual since these are not necessarily determined by the etiology of the condition.

This same etiology conflict has given rise to other terms that permeate the literature. "Mental deficiency" has been used to classify those individuals who are presumed to be subnormal only in the degree of mental ability, while "mentally defective" has been used to identify those individuals who differ not only in ability but also in the extent of their thought processes. Likewise, some workers in the area have used "mental defective" as a term that is synonymous with some brain damage or pathology. Thus "exogenous," "mental defective," and "brain damaged" have sometimes been used interchangeably, while "mental deficiency," "mental retardation," and "endogenous" are some-times used synonymously. Regardless of the terms used, it still re-

---

[4] Alfred A. Strauss and Laura E. Lehtinen, *Psychopathology and Education of the Brain-Injured Child*, Vol. 2: *Progress in Theory and Clinic* (New York: Grune & Stratton, Inc., 1955).

[5] See W. Cruickshank, *A Teaching Method for Brain Injured and Hyperactive Children* (Syracuse: Syracuse University Press, 1961).

mains to be demonstrated that etiology has significant implications for education.

Educators who daily faced the problem of providing suitable educational tasks for the mentally retarded soon needed a terminology which had educational implications. These they found in a system presented by Kirk and Johnson in 1951.[6] Tying the terms to probable ability to cope with academic requirements, these authors also distinguished between a "difference" and a "handicap." Taking a lead from the *49th Yearbook of the National Society for the Study of Education*, prepared by a committee chaired by Kirk, the 1951 book by Kirk and Johnson defined a disability as a deviation from the average, and a handicap as the degree to which this deviation could be expected to interfere with some activity.[7] In the case of mental retardation, the low IQ identified the degree of deviation from the average. The extent to which the deviation constituted a handicap to adequate achievement is a value judgment based on the relationship of IQ to academic achievement and the kinds of demands represented in particular schools. An IQ of 70, for example, is a greater handicap in a school where the average IQ is 125 than it would be in a school where the average IQ is 95. In most schools, the typical IQ can be expected to be about 100. Thus, an IQ of below 85 can be expected to be a significant handicap to academic achievement, and in a more or less orderly manner, the lower the IQ the greater the handicap.

Kirk and Johnson avoided sharply defined categories and rigid lines of demarcation. Instead, they suggested ranges which allowed a good deal of overlap between levels of retardation. They added four new terms to the lexicon: *slow learners, educable mentally handicapped, trainable mentally handicapped,* and *totally dependent children.*

Slow learners were described by Kirk in 1962[8] as children who could be expected to achieve a moderate degree of academic success, although at a slower rate than average children. These children can be educated in the regular grades, do not need special class placement, and can be expected to become self-supporting, independent, and socially adjusted adults.

The educable mentally handicapped (EMH) child is a youngster

[6] Samuel A. Kirk and G. Orville Johnson, *Educating the Retarded Child* (Boston: Houghton Mifflin Company, 1951).

[7] "The Education of Exceptional Children," Part II of the *National Society for the Study of Education, 49th Yearbook* (Chicago: University of Chicago Press, 1950).

[8] Samuel A. Kirk, *Educating Exceptional Children* (Boston: Houghton Mifflin Company, 1962).

who, because of slow mental development, is unable to profit in any degree from the program in the regular classroom, but has the following potentialities for development:

1. minimum educability in reading, writing, spelling, arithmetic, and so forth
2. capacity for social adjustment to a point where he can get along independently in the community
3. minimum occupational adequacy such that he can later support himself partially or totally at a marginal level[9]

The trainable mentally handicapped (TMH) child is one who is so subnormal in intelligence that he is unable to profit from classes for educable mentally handicapped children, but has potentialities in these areas:

1. learning self-care in activities such as eating, dressing, undressing, toileting, and sleeping
2. learning to adjust in the home or neighborhood, though not the total community
3. learning economic usefulness in the home, a sheltered workshop, or an institution[10]

Kirk described the totally dependent child as "one who, because of markedly subnormal intelligence, is unable to be trained in self-care, socialization, or economic usefulness." He needs continuing care and supervision for his survival.

No IQ figures were attached to these categories by Kirk and Johnson, since a deviation from average is not synonymous with a handicap. However, many school systems have bowed to the administrative expedient of not distinguishing between a disability and a handicap, and have assigned IQ ranges to the categories as follows:

Slow Learner—70 or 75 to 90 or 95
EMH   —50 to 75 or 80
TMH   —25 or 30 to 50
Dependent — 0 to 25 or 30

The Kirk and Johnson categories are perhaps more widely used and accepted than any others, yet they are primarily designed for educators.

---

[9] Kirk, *Educating Exceptional Children.*
[10] Kirk, *Educating Exceptional Children.*

In an attempt to provide a general terminology that could be used by all professional groups, the American Association on Mental Deficiency appointed a subcommittee on nomenclature which reported in 1959.[11] The manual developed by the committee used mental retardation to apply to all degrees of subnormal mental functioning and identified five levels: borderline, mild, moderate, severe, and profound. They then tied the labels to standard deviations so that the categories would be: borderline, 85–70; mild, 70–55; moderate, 55–40; severe, 40–25; profound, below 25. The President's Panel Report of 1962 modified the AAMD report and assigned categories and ranges as follows: mild, 70–50; moderate, 50–35; severe, 35–20; profound, 20 and below.[12]

Any system of classification should be evaluated on the basis of its usefulness for whatever purpose it was designed. The behavior system of moron, imbecile, and idiot was useful because it distinguished between levels of behavior which could be identified by observation. This was necessary because no tests existed at that time.

The psychometric system was useful because it provided an IQ—a ratio between mental age and chronological age—that was understandable, easy to obtain, and that provided a method of arranging the children in the order of the size of the IQ, from low to high, in a convenient manner. As a dividend, it subsequently provided for prediction.

Classifications by cause are not very useful to educators. A classification of "exogenous" is possible only when specific causes of pathology or syndromes are detected. A classification of "endogenous" is made when no evidence of outside causation can be found. Exogenous classification is made on the presence of symptoms, endogenous on the absence of them. This is a splendid example of negative assignment and it violates the basic scientific classification principle of identity. Furthermore, there is insufficient evidence that even if the classifications were possible and valid, this kind of distinction has implications for education. So far the research has not been very convincing.[13]

The educational classification system has been useful in that educa-

---

[11] Rick F. Heber, "A Manual on Terminology and Classification in Mental Retardation," *American Journal of Mental Deficiency*, monograph supplement, LXIV (September 1961).

[12] President's Panel on Mental Retardation, *A Proposed Program for National Action to Combat Mental Retardation* (Washington, D.C.: Government Printing Office, 1962).

[13] Roger M. Frey, "Reading Behavior of Public School Brain-Injured and Non-Brain-Injured Children of Average and Retarded Mental Development," unpublished doctoral dissertation, University of Illinois, 1961.

tional programs have been developed which are suitable for various degrees of retardation: total care for the dependent; behavior training in self-help, socialization, and economic usefulness—but no academics —for the trainable; and academics, independent living, and vocational skills for the educable. Furthermore, through experience, the classification levels have been tied to both IQ and mental age.

The IQ has been used to indicate the rate of mental development, and the mental age has shown the level of development. This was based on the assumption that if an individual earned an IQ of 50, this was half of average. Therefore for each year he lived he was assumed to be learning only half as fast as average children. Likewise if his IQ was 75, he was believed to be capable of learning at a rate equal only to three-fourths of that of an average child. No research data have been offered to substantiate the rate of learning of the mentally retarded, yet the statement has been widely accepted as an established characteristic, important enough to govern the amount of material that should be included in the curriculum for the mentally retarded. The mental age as an indicator of the level of mental ability, on the other hand, has been demonstrated to be a useful index.[14] A ten-year-old child with an earned IQ of 75 would have a mental age of about seven and a half:

$$(CA \times IQ)/100 = MA; \quad (10 \times 75)/100 = 7\frac{1}{2}.$$

By applying the mental age to grade level equivalent, we see that the child could be expected to understand ideas and materials approximately equal to those understood by children in about the second grade in school. Since most children show a readiness for learning to read at about age six, the child with the 75 IQ would have to reach a chronological age of about eight—about the same age as a third grader —before he could be expected to read. This same child could develop to a mental age of about nine or ten when he reaches a chronological age of eighteen or nineteen years. (One of the peculiarities of mental measurement is that of using a CA of no more than 13 for adults.) The academic achievement in reading, writing, and arithmetic expected of a child with a mental age of nine or ten would be about fourth or fifth grade level.

To the extent that there is a relationship between IQ and achievement, use of the IQ for determining the mental age level is justified. However, the relationship between IQ and achievement is far from

---

[14] cf. Oliver P. Kolstoe, *Mental Retardation: An Educational Viewpoint* (New York: Holt, Rinehart and Winston, 1972), p. 158.

perfect. Furthermore, the relationship between the IQ and social or vocational adjustment is even more limited. Thus the IQ as a predictor of probable achievement in academics is fairly useful (roughly a correlation coefficient of .50 to .70), but the accuracy of the prediction of social or vocational adjustment approaches zero.[15]

Given these inadequacies of the IQ and MA, it is still necessary to find some guides for educational purposes. Because the mental ages of these youngsters are lower than their chronological ages, they are usually conspicuous for their inability to learn to read at the same age as their nonretarded peers. This lack of achievement is ordinarily interpreted as a deficiency in adaptive behavior. Thus a useful method of classification that will allow us to try to deal with the educational problem in a realistic manner is to combine the psychometric, educational, and AAMD (American Association on Mental Deficiency) systems. The use of "mental retardation" as a generic term to encompass all levels of subnormal intellectual functioning provides a useful, nonspecific term that characterizes the entire range of individuals who earn scores significantly below average on tests that yield an IQ, and whose poor performance cannot be attributed to sensory disability (poor vision or hearing) or emotional problems. The use of the term "adaptive behavior" from the AAMD system makes it possible to distinguish between a deviation and a handicap, since adaptive behavior implies that an individual is required to adapt to something.

Particularly at the beginning levels in school, learning to read is the primary adaptive behavior requirement but there are other demands, which differ with the child's age. The young child is expected to master the development patterns of self-help skills of young children in the home and the adult is expected to cope with problems of employment and self-maintenance in the community. Thus, it is possible to judge that a youngster who falls in the lowest 15 percent of the population in IQ (roughly 1 standard deviation or more below the mean) will probably also show some inadequacies in maturation, academics, vocational competencies, and self-management. Furthermore, it is fairly safe to predict that the lower his IQ, the greater will be his other inadequacies; in other words, the more serious will be his problems of adapting to the demands of his environment.

Past practices in many states employed IQ scores almost exclusively as the criterion to identify the condition of mental retardation.

[15] Oliver P. Kolstoe and Roger M. Frey, *A High School Work–Study Program for the Mentally Subnormal Student* (Carbondale, Ill.: Southern Illinois University Press, 1965).

The exact cut-off score varied from state to state and even from one locality to another, but the range usually included scores between 50 and 85 IQ. These scores corresponded to from one to three standard deviations below the mean and encompassed about 15 percent of the population. This kind of identification would be acceptable if the distinction between a deviation from average and a handicap, as proposed by Kirk, was carefully observed. Another way of considering the problem would be to use the AAMD system and seek evidence of a low IQ coupled with poor adaptive behavior. Unfortunately, many children from minority racial or ethnic backgrounds have been identified as mentally retarded on very tenuous evidence of either low IQ or poor adaptive behavior. Mercer, for instance, reported finding three times more blacks and two times more Chicanos in special education programs than their percentage representation in the population in general.[16] The explanation of this unequal representation has been laid on the doorstep of the improper use of tests that yield an IQ and the lack of adequate methods of assessing adaptive behavior.

To correct the practices, California passed a law in 1971,[17] which stipulated that every child who was being considered for special education services because of suspected mental retardation was to be tested with a psychological test in his natural language, preferably given by a psychometrician of the child's same racial or ethnic background. At the same time, the cut-off IQ score for inclusion was pegged at 70 rather than 85. This has had the effect of reducing the size of the potential candidates for services from 16 percent to about 2.5 percent, and simultaneously made it virtually unnecessary to differentiate between a deviation and a handicap since the score of two standard deviations below the mean is all the evidence needed to qualify for special education help. As an increasing number of states began to follow the California example, an IQ range of from 40 to 70 has come to be considered the parameter which identifies the child who is mentally retarded at the educable level. This is still a range of two standard deviations but it includes those children of even less ability than many youngsters who were included in programs in the past. With this change in the criteria for classifying children for special education services has come another problem and that is what to do with children who earn IQ scores above 70. At present no simple answer to the question has been presented

[16] Jane Mercer, "Sociocultural Factors in Labeling Mental Retardates," *Peabody Journal of Education*, 48 (1971), 188–205.

[17] California Education Code 6902.085, *West's California Legislative Service* (St. Paul: West Publishing, 1971).

and the practice has been to assign the youngsters to resource rooms for remedial or compensatory instruction. In many places they are labeled educationally handicapped as distinguished from mentally retarded. However, since tests that yield an IQ are used as a basis for identifying the condition with no consideration for the presence of poor adaptive behavior, the practice is at best questionable. Nevertheless, some kind of resolution of the problem must be made if we are to provide sound programs for either group.

Toward a Clarification of the Concept of Mental Retardation

As more professionals have become concerned with the condition, more and more definitions have appeared in the literature. These have been very well examined by Clausen[18] and by Jordan.[19] Both of these scholars have called attention to the intent of the authors of the definitions and, especially, to the fact that the definitions are intended to be useful to people in various persuasions—psychology, sociology, medicine, and education. Jordan classifies definitions by function into fourteen types running from synoptic to phylogenetic. He then discusses the nature of a definition as a statement which: (1) orders the data; (2) has exclusivity; (3) provides a causal explanation; (4) allows for prediction; and (5) relates the condition to normalcy. Jordan concludes that none of the definitions offered meets the five criteria of a definition. With this, he contends that mental retardation is not yet defined. Clausen also rejects most definitions offered by previous writers, but, unlike Jordan, proposes to accept a psychometric definition (in lieu of any reasonable alternative) of mental retardation as a condition of subaverage intellectual functioning revealed by a low score on a test which yields an IQ. He stresses that it is a condition as opposed to a disease. If this is accepted, then it is also necessary to accept our present intelligence tests as operational definitions of intelligence. Thus, intelligence is what intelligence tests measure, and mental retardation is less than average of whatever is contained in intelligence tests. Before such a proposal can be accepted, it would seem important to examine briefly the development of notions of intelligence as they relate to the condition of mental retardation.

[18] Johs Clausen, "Mental Deficiency—Development of a Concept," *American Journal of Mental Deficiency*, LXXI (March 1967), 727–745.

[19] Thomas E. Jordan, *The Mentally Retarded*, 2d ed. (Columbus, Ohio: Charles E. Merrill Books, Inc., 1966).

Sensory Deficiency

The first recorded speculation of the nature of intelligence as it relates to mental retardation apparently appears in the often-referred-to writings of Itard.[20] This French physician believed that the mind was a blank paper to be written on by experience. We may interpret this to mean that Itard believed that all persons were born with equal intellectual potential. Those who later demonstrated superior intellectual performance were those persons who had superior experiences in their formative years. The mentally retarded, therefore, would be those persons who had few or inferior developmental experiences. Seguin believed, as Itard did, that the capacity of the mind for development was equal in all newborn, but that the nerves which transmit sensory messages to the brain were deficient or inefficient in some individuals, thus preventing the experiences from being effectively transmitted.[21] Thus, a person could be mentally retarded despite rich experiences, simply because the sensations failed to reach the brain in sufficient number or intensity to develop adequate intellectual behavior.

Neither of these pioneer workers speculated on the specific nature of intelligence. They apparently were concerned only with the explanation of why children of seemingly equal potential did not grow up to demonstrate equal intellectual performance, and they agreed on sensory deficiency as the reason.

Psychometric Performance

The development of the Binet-Simon mental age scale provided the first operational definition of intelligence.[22] This test, and the revisions and development offered by Terman and Merrill and their associates at Stanford University provided an impetus to psychologists to reexamine intelligence from many points of view.[23] Workers, principally in child psychology, educational psychology, and psychometrics, have provided evidence and proposed theories in abundance. Underlying the Binet test was the notion that problem-solving behavior was dependent upon something called intelligence. This was challenged

---

20 J. M. Itard, *The Wild Boy of Averyron* (New York: Appleton-Century-Crofts, 1932).

21 Edward Seguin, *Idiocy and Its Treatment by the Physiological Methods* (New York: Bureau of Publications, Teachers College, Columbia University, 1907).

22 Binet and Simon, *The Development of Intelligence in Children.*

23 Terman and Merrill, *Stanford-Binet Intelligence Scale.*

by Spearman, in England, who conceded a general factor called intelligence, but who also believed that there were specific kinds of intelligence possessed by some people.[24] Thurstone extended the work of Spearman through the statistical tool of factor analysis and announced that there were five principal intellectual functions—space, number, word fluency, memory, and reasoning—which made up intelligence.[25] Getzels and Jackson[26] popularized the notion that creative thought was an intellectual function and that it was measured only minimally by intelligence tests, although they borrowed the notion of creative thought from Guilford.[27]

Guilford and his associates have constructed a model of the structure of intellect. They held that intelligence was made up of five intellectual operations—cognition, memory, divergent thinking, convergent thinking, and evaluative thinking. These may use the contents —figures, semantics, symbols, or behavior—to produce units, classes, relations, systems, transformations, and implications. Guilford's model of operations, contents, and products is a three-dimensional one that contains five operations using four different contents to produce six different kinds of products, totalling 120 possible cells. This is the most comprehensive theory of the structure of intellect, and seems to account for every known intellectual function. It does not, however, account for differences in intelligence among individuals and, therefore, does not explain the condition of mental retardation.

Developmental Concepts

Piaget and his associates have identified stages in the development of thought processes in normal children.[28] Essentially, Piaget has dealt with his own equivalents of Guilford's operations, but has not accounted for contents or products. His stages, however, are pertinent to the condition of mental retardation.

---

[24] C. Spearman, *The Abilities of Man: Their Nature and Measurement* (New York: Crowell Collier and Macmillan, Inc., 1927).

[25] L. L. Thurstone, *Primary Mental Abilities* (Chicago: University of Chicago Press, 1938).

[26] Jacob W. Getzels and Phillip W. Jackson, *Creativity and Intelligence* (New York: John Wiley & Sons, Inc., 1962).

[27] J. P. Guilford, "Intelligence: 1965 Model," *American Psychologist*, XXI (January 1966), 20–26.

[28] J. H. Flavell, *The Developmental Psychology of Jean Piaget* (Van Nostrand Reinhold, Inc., 1963).

Piaget views all aspects of behavior as adaptive in which the organism assimilates elements of the environment for its own use, or accommodates itself to the demands and restrictions of the environment. This constant interaction is the process of adaptive behavior. The intellectual development of a child is seen by Piaget as an orderly progression through levels that can be identified by the thought processes that the child uses.

The first level is sensory-motor, in which the child responds to stimuli, first on an all-or-none basis and later on a selective basis. As he begins to select stimuli to which to respond, he begins to organize the world in terms of meaningful versus irrelevant stimuli and to use signs and symbols to represent the perceptions and concepts he learns. The sensory-motor stage is believed by Piaget to run from zero to about two years of age.

The development of conceptual intelligence runs from age 2 to adulthood and is identified by four substages, each characterized by the thought processes exhibited by the child in each stage.

Preconceptual thought is exhibited between the ages of 2 to 4 and is characterized by the beginning of symbolic thought. In this stage, the child reacts not just to the physical nature of stimuli, but to the meaning signified by the stimuli. Father waving "bye-bye," for example, evokes a reaction not just to the physical movement, but signifies that Daddy is going to leave—a common precipitator of a calamity response.

Intuitive thought is distinguished from preconceptual thought by more elaborate concepts, but each concept is largely based on a single salient characteristic. The intuitive stage is primarily egocentric in that the child apparently cannot adopt the viewpoint of others, and is not concerned with logic; cause and effect are based on the juxtaposition of elements, and justice, morality, reality, and the world are primitive and rigid. Typically, this stage is apparent between the ages of 4 and about 7.

The stage of concrete operations occurs at about the age of 7 and continues until about 11. The chief difference between this stage and the intuitive stage is the increasing ability of the child to classify according to general conceptual characteristics. In addition, the child displays the ability to order objects by more than one dimension—for example, size and weight—to use a cardinal number system, and to recognize the process of reversibility.

The final stage is that of formal operations and occurs sometime after the age of about 11 years. Piaget describes the thought processes of this stage as moving from the real to the possible, and casting possibilities as propositions for implications, conjunctions, identity, and disjunctions for the isolation of variables and identification of causal relations.

Flavell summarizes the behaviors in the different stages by saying:

> The preoperational child is the child of wonder: his cognition appears to us naive, impression bound, and poorly organized. There is an essential lawlessness about his world without, of course, this fact in any way entering his awareness to inhibit the zest and flights of fancy with which he approaches new situations. . . . The child of concrete operations can be caricatured as a sober and bookkeeperish organizer of the real and a distrustor of the subtle, the elusive, and the hypothetical. The adolescent has something of both. . . . Unlike the concrete-operational child he can soar; but also unlike the preoperational child, it is a controlled and planned soaring, solidly grounded in a bedrock of careful analysis and painstaking accommodation to detail.[29]

Comparison of Intelligence Measures

Throughout the various approaches to describing intelligence there is a discernible theme, and that is the assumption of the development or emergence of increasingly complex thought processes with increasing age (at least up to late adolescence). This theme is sometimes augmented with content (as, for example, the comprehension subtest of the Wechsler),[30] but often it is not. Thus the comparability of different tests is difficult to determine often because of the content of one test and the lack of content of another. Guilford's structure and Piaget's levels may be found to have a great deal in common because neither deals with a normative content in relation to particular ages or groups of youngsters. Indeed, it would appear that Guilford's operations of convergence, divergence, and evaluation are quite similar to the hypothetical thought of Piaget's stage of formal operations, but this has yet to be conclusively demonstrated.

The difficulty of drawing firm conclusions concerning intellectual behavior stems partly from the fact that some tests sample operations with little concern for content, while others sample content with no clear indication of which processes are necessary for successful performance. Those tests which purport to measure intelligence proceed to do so in quite different ways and therefore probably sample only certain aspects—apparently those that are related to success in an

[29] Flavell, *The Developmental Psychology of Jean Piaget*, p. 211.

[30] D. Wechsler, *Wechsler Intelligence Scale for Children: Manual* (New York: Psychological Corporation, 1949).

academic setting. A less ambiguous sampling would be representative of both clearly identified content and process, which allow normative comparison. The Wechsler scales do differentiate between Verbal and Performance IQ, but fall far short of the structure of intellect represented by Guilford's model.

It appears that mental retardation has been characterized by deficiencies in both intellectual content and processes. Unfortunately, as yet no tests exist that clearly sample both and provide a meaningful comparison with the performance of children carefully selected from the total population. Thus professionals have no alternative but to use tests that have been standardized on a representative sample of the population and so have normative data that can be used for comparison, such as the Binet and Wechsler tests. Mental retardation becomes a suspected condition when a child earns an IQ score of about 70 or below (two standard deviations below the mean) and his performance on the test is judged not to have been significantly lowered by sensory deficit, emotional problems, language deficiencies, or acculturation. The tests, as Clausen suggests, have become the method for identifying the condition. Even if it is conceded that this is a legitimate way to identify the condition, this does not imply that it is either explained or defined. Detection, however, does allow investigators to examine behaviors and characteristics that accompany the condition and these concomitants can provide the basis for meaningful intervention.

Characteristics of the Mentally Retarded

Because of the lack of comparability between tests that purport to measure the same things, notions concerning the nature of mental retardation are difficult to infer from the analysis of test behavior itself. Fortunately, a considerable body of research has become available since 1955, which can help us understand the concomitants of the condition.[31]

Many of the descriptions emphasize the theme that retarded children are less adequate than their peers. Behaviorally, they have been found to do less well than nonretarded peers on a variety of learning tasks. They seem to have a limited ability to abstract, difficulty in understanding cause and effect, faulty concept formation,

---

[31] Harvey A. Stevens and Rick F. Heber (eds.), *Mental Retardation: A Review of Research* (Chicago: University of Chicago Press, 1964) and Norman R. Ellis (ed.), *Handbook of Mental Deficiency* (New York: McGraw-Hill, Inc. 1963).

imprecise perceptions, limited incidental learning, impoverished language, and difficulty in generalizing. Their thought processes can be described as concrete, discrete, unrelated, immediate, and obvious.

Academically the mentally retarded youngsters reach a stage of readiness for learning later than nonretarded children, and therefore teaching of academic subjects is often delayed until the readiness skills have been learned. Even when instruction does begin, mentally retarded youngsters are likely to have difficulty learning abstract concepts. In addition, they are typically deficient in self-teaching or auto-instruction. That is, while most youngsters can be counted on to practice skills or rehearse information until they have learned it, retarded children do not seem to show this same capability.

In the personal and social realms, mentally retarded youngsters show characteristics that are related to the kinds of environmental influences they face. For instance, when they are called upon to perform in areas that are too difficult for them to be successful in, they may exhibit a very low frustration tolerance. However, even in situations where they can cope adequately, their social and personal behaviors are more like that of younger children. As a result, they often appear to do things that demonstrate poor judgment. Their behavior often seems to be immature or foolish.

They also have a good number of rather positive characteristics, which can be capitalized on. They can deal quite effectively with concrete concepts in learning academic skills. They can learn to master motor tasks that involve fine as well as gross coordination movements. They can learn to get and hold jobs of some complexity, and they can learn to manage their daily lives well enough to be able to live independently in society. There is no legitimate reason for hand-wringing dismay about the future, but there is an obligation to develop and provide educational programs based on the best information available, and to continue to try to reconcile what is known about the condition with whatever theoretical positions seem able to accommodate the data.

Theories of Retardation

Sensory Deprivation

The first attempt to relate a theory to the condition of mental retardation appears to have been Itard's notion that the mind of a newborn infant was a blank paper to be written on by experience, and that mental retardation was a consequence of inappropriate or inferior

early sense experiences. Seguin also believed in the effect of sensations on intellectual development, but he conjectured that a deficient
peripheral or central nervous system might prevent the sensations
from reaching the brain; thus mental retardation could have an organic
pathology cause. Subsequent rejection of these theories because of
research in child development does not dim the brilliance of the
attempts made by Itard and Seguin in both practice and theory.

CNS Inefficiency

During the years between the 1850s and about 1950, while many
schools of psychology developed theories of learning and behavior, no
recorded attempt to explain mental retardation from a theoretical point
of view appeared until Benoit, in 1959, tried to relate the condition
to Hebb's theory of perceptual and conceptual neural organization.[32]
It was Hebb's theory that the impinging of a stimulus on a sense organ
activates a chain of cells, mostly in the upper portion of the central
nervous system, which he calls a "cell assembly."[33] Repeated excitation of the sense organ strengthens the intercellular bonds so that
stable perceptions are formed. Sequential perceptions are a series of
cell assemblies which through related excitation form a phase sequence (for example, walking or speaking grammatically), while associations are handled by phase cycles (the relating of stimuli to
previously learned perceptions). Benoit (1959) offers a definition of
mental retardation which states that:

> Mental retardation may be viewed as a deficit of intellectual function
> resulting from varied intrapersonal and/or extrapersonal determinants,
> but having as a common proximate cause a diminished efficiency of the
> central nervous system thus entailing a lessened general capacity for
> growth in perceptual and conceptual integration and consequently in en-
> vironmental adjustment.[34]

The definition offers an explanation of mental retardation that is
neurophysiological in character and that has neither been validated
nor rejected. It is, however, general and does not fully account for

[32] E. Paul Benoit, "Application of Hebb's Theory to Understanding the Learning Disability of Children with Mental Retardation," *The Training School Bulletin*, LVII (May
1960), 18–23.

[33] D. O. Hebb, *The Organization of Behavior* (New York: John Wiley & Sons, Inc.,
1949).

[34] See Benoit, "Application of Hebb's Theory."

the behavior of individuals, nor does it lend itself to an analysis of a possible relationship to theories of behavior. Thus a coupling of the neurophysiological theory with a behavioral theory might lead to a somewhat better understanding of the nature of mental retardation.

Subjective Behaviorism

Since the early 1900s the reflex arc has been considered by many behavioral psychologists as the controlling unit of behavior. In 1960, Miller, Galanter, and Pribram rejected the reflex arc on the grounds that it views human beings as machines, fails to account for mediation between stimulus and response, and that it cannot account for the initiation of action by an organism.[35] Miller, Galanter, and Pribram suggest instead that each individual develops an "image" of the world. The image is the sum total of the individual's perceptions, concepts, knowledge, values, needs, and feelings concerning the nature of reality. The image becomes the standard used by the individual to judge the current state of the world and his own relationship to all elements of the environment. Adaptive behavior is the way in which the individual responds to stimuli signals that come from the environment through the excitation of receptor sense organs. These sensations are compared with the standards of the image for congruity. When the incoming sensations are consistent with what the individual expects, the world is judged to be serene. However, if there is an incongruity between the incoming stimuli and the expectations of the individual, action is initiated to reduce the incongruity. The action is directed by plans that are judged by the organism to be able to reduce the incongruities between incoming stimuli and the standards or expectations.

The functional behavior mechanism employed by the organism is Test Operate Test Exit (TOTE), which is viewed as a feedback loop instead of a reflex arc. Incoming stimuli are tested for congruity against the expectations established by the individual. If an incongruity is detected, the organism acts (operates). The consequence of the action is again tested and if the incongruity is reduced or eliminated, the unit exits. Behavior is initiated because of the detection of incongruity between stimuli and expectation, but it is controlled by plans.

Plans evolve from the incongruity and are used by the organism to reduce incongruities between incoming stimuli and the standards of

---

[35] George Miller, Eugene Galanter, and Karl Pribram, *Plans and the Structure of Behavior* (New York: Holt, Rinehart and Winston, 1960); Guilford also has used essentially the same concept as a model for problem solving.

the organism. They control all of the behavior and may be simple and immediate or complex and continuing. Plans are subject to modification, alternation, or abandonment, depending upon the organism's evaluation of their utility or probable utility; but they depend, fundamentally, upon the sum total of the perception, knowledge, feeling, needs of the organism, and the thought processes possessed by the organism which can be used to evaluate the incoming stimuli. What a person knows and feels and how he thinks determines what he can or will do when called upon to act. Furthermore, what he knows and feels and how he thinks determines what he will react to, and what he reacts to, in turn, helps determine his standards of expectations.

In the context of the Miller, Galanter, and Pribram theory of subjective behaviorism, the concept of mental retardation comes into somewhat sharper focus, especially if subjective behaviorism is assumed to be dependent on Hebb's theory of cell assembly.

Given an individual with a diminished capacity for growth in perceptual and conceptual integration to begin with, the image of the mentally retarded child, from which his standards or expectancies stem, could be expected to be discrete, concrete, and unrelated—deficient in content and richness. Additionally, the thought processes available to assess incoming stimuli for the detection of incongruities would be limited.

A Definition of Mental Retardation

Although many definitions of mental retardation have been proposed, nearly all present some kind of learning problem as the basis of the condition. A departure from this view comes from the work of Piaget. For instance, Inhelder,[36] as reported by Stephens, studied the thought processes of mentally retarded children according to Piaget's levels. She found no retarded youngsters who demonstrated thought processes at the level of formal operations. The youngsters were apparently unable to cast possibilities as propositions to be speculated upon. Although Inhelder did not describe her population in terms of age, IQ, or etiology, this writer and one of his colleagues, using 16- to

[36] Will Beth Stephens, "Piaget and Inhelder—Application of Theory and Diagnostic Techniques to the Area of Mental Retardation," *Education and Training of the Mentally Retarded*, I (April 1966) 75–86; in addition, Bernard Farber, *Mental Retardation* (Boston: Houghton Mifflin Company, 1968), comes to the same conclusion and suggests that the inability to engage in propositional thought seriously interferes with the social adaptability of the mentally retarded.

19-year-old mentally retarded young adults were unable to find any evidence of convergent thinking at the formal level.[37] These young men had earned IQs of between 60 and 80 and were of essentially cultural-familial etiology. In addition, both Sweeter[38] and Sund failed in their efforts to teach mentally retarded children to develop hypotheses for science experiments. In none of this research was there any evidence that the youngsters examined could rise above the level of concrete operations in their thought levels. This research is far from definitive, but the often made observation that the achievement level in reading of most youngsters in the educable range seldom reaches fifth grade is consistent with the concrete operational level of thinking. Also, the often demonstrated lack of adequate foresight can be interpreted as another kind of validating information.

Acting on the hypothesis that the major problem exhibited by the mentally retarded is a limited capacity for using complex methods of thinking, which has a serious effect of interfering with the learning of these youngsters, it has been proposed that the focus of a definition is more properly on their problems of *thinking* than their problems of *learning.* Poor learning performance is an effect of the condition, but the condition itself is demonstrated by the restricted thought processes of the person, not just by his inefficient learning behavior. Mental retardation, therefore, seems to be characterized by deficient perceptions and concepts, and by thought processes that do not go beyond classifying by superordinate sets or ordering by two or three dimensions. The use of propositional thought seems impossible except in a most primitive form. Thus, we may conceptualize mental retardation as a diminished capacity for the formation of cell assemblies, intercellular and superordinate associations, which results in restricted standards for the formulation of plans needed for appropriate adapting behavior. Mental retardation then is defined as: *An arrest in thought processes at some level below Piaget's level of formal thought.*

Since no testing instruments currently exist which measure both intellectual content and processes in a precise manner, mental retardation is identified by a low score on an IQ test such as the Wechsler or Binet after the effects of sensory disability and emotional restrictions

[37] Oliver P. Kolstoe and Darvin Hirsch, "A Study of Convergent Thinking of Educable Mentally Retarded Males," *Exceptional Children,* 40 (1974), 292–293.

[38] Sweeter, William, "Discovery Oriented Instruction in Science Skills for Educable Mentally Retarded Children," unpublished doctoral dissertation, University of Northern Colorado, 1968; and also, Robert Sund, University of Northern Colorado, personal communication, 1975.

have been eliminated. Subnormal perceptions, concepts, and thought processes are the characteristics that identify mental retardation.

Using the foregoing conceptualization of mental retardation allows commentary on the condition hitherto not possible. The source of the condition is inadequate perceptual and conceptual organization and processing. Whether this stems from neural cells that are inefficient because of heredity, because of damage or destruction, or because of environmental deprivation is largely unimportant. It makes little difference whether the cause of the condition is poor diet, cultural deprivation, trauma, infection, or heredity; the intellectual functions of accepting information, organizing perceptions and concepts, storing, processing, using, and evaluating information are inadequate. Furthermore, they probably will continue to be inadequate throughout the lifetime of the individual. That is, mental retardation is probably a chronic condition. In our present state of knowledge, the tools needed to repair the inadequate functions do not appear to be available. To believe that some magic formula that will cure the inadequacy can be found in a technique, a method, a material, or some combination of these is a dangerous delusion. What can and must be done is to provide a training program that attends to all of the intellectual functions and that extends for the life span of the individual. The program should be presented in the most meaningful manner possible so the most adequate possible behaviors can be developed. This is the challenge of an educational program.

Principles of Presentation

In viewing mental retardation in this manner, the implications for educational programming became rather consistent. Since the adaptive behavior of the mentally retarded child depends upon his image of the world and the plans he develops to cope with incongruities between incoming stimuli and his expectancies, the nature of his image becomes the primary focus of attention. Because of his diminished capacity to form cell assemblies, it would seem most important to control the contact of the developing child with his environment, to enable him to form stable perceptions. In turn, the thought processes available to him are what he must use to evaluate the incoming stimuli, in order to formulate and initiate plans for adaptive behavior, and to evaluate the effectiveness of his actions in reducing or eliminating incongruities between incoming stimuli and his expectancies. These efforts must be framed in a program that will lead to adult behaviors adequate to societal demands.

Such a program must take into account the nature of mental re-tardation, the nature of the environment, and the probable future behavior desired for the recipient of the program. Specific considerations must be inherent in the manner in which learning tasks are presented:

1. The tasks should be uncomplicated. The new tasks should contain the fewest possible elements, and most of the elements should be familiar, so he has very few unknowns to learn.
2. The tasks should be brief. This assures that he will attend to the most important aspects of the tasks and not get lost in a sequence of inter-related events.
3. The tasks should be sequentially presented so the learner proceeds in a sequence of small steps, each one built upon previously learned tasks.
4. Each learning task should be the kind in which success is possible. One of the major problems to be overcome is that of failure proneness. This major deterrent to learning can be effectively reduced through success experiences.
5. Overlearning must be built into the lessons. Drills in game form seem to lessen the disinterest inherent in unimaginative drill.
6. Learning tasks should be applied to objects, problems, and situations in the learner's life environment. Unless the tasks are relevant, the learner has great difficulty in seeing their possible importance.

The following chapters identify the objectives, organization, tasks, and ways of developing those skills needed for independent living and vocational competence. They are based on the six principles in the previous paragraph and the conceptualization that precedes them.

CHAPTER 2

The Objectives

Need for Intervention

In a country that places such a high value on the rights of privacy of its citizens, it is probable that the actual number of mentally retarded citizens in the United States may never be known. Any efforts to identify these people would have to balance the good that would come out of the identification against the harm that an invasion of privacy could bring. However, if the mentally retarded are not identified, they cannot be given any substantial help. It is vital, therefore, to find a compromise that allows us to plan services for a realistic number of people who need help, but at the same time guards against the misuse of information that could be detrimental to the very ones we try to aid. Fortunately, surveys done in limited geographical areas both in this country and abroad have actually counted people, and these survey figures can be used to project estimates upon which service plans can be built with considerable confidence.[1]

[1] Bernard Farber, *Mental Retardation: Its Social Context and Social Consequences* (Boston: Houghton Mifflin Company, 1968). Chapters 3, 4, and 5 report the incidence and prevalence figure from widely varying sources. See also Ronald W. Conley, *The Economics of Mental Retardation* (Baltimore: *The Johns Hopkins Press*, 1973).

These estimates are consistent in identifying about 3 percent of the population as mentally retarded. In a total population of about 265 million the probable number of retarded persons would be approximately 7.9 million. Conley estimated the distribution of those between the ages of 4 and 19 in 1968–1970 to be 275,000 in institutions; 690,000 in special classes; 740,000 in regular classes; and 450,000 not in school. This simply means that a few more than one-fourth of the total number of mentally retarded are of school age and that about 1.5 million would need some kind of special educational help to be able to cope with school programs. Even the most generous estimates of current services concede that no more than about one-half of those youngsters eligible actually are being served.

This tells only part of the story. The costs for classes, according to Conley, are about twice the regular costs for the educable youngsters, three and a half times more for trainable, and nearly six times more for developmental day-care programs. Even in 1961 Kirk had indicated that about 2 billion dollars had been invested in institutions and nearly 200 million dollars were required each year to operate them.[2] Building costs continue to soar as do maintenance and training costs. Conley places the figure of actual expenditures at 4.7 billion dollars in 1970. Further, he places a figure of 7 billion dollars on the costs of social effects such as lack of production, welfare, and social services. The potential costs of mental retardation over the lifetime of these people, if not the actual costs, may be as high as several hundred billion dollars.

Happily, however, training does pay off. Each dollar invested in the preparation of the mild and moderately retarded returns at least 14 dollars in earnings, in spite of the fact that the actual earnings of the mildly retarded are only 86 percent of the average of their peers, and for the moderate and severely retarded the earnings are only 19 percent of the average of the nonretarded. Nonetheless, Findley found that those youngsters who had been through work-study programs would return the cost of their training programs in income tax alone in less than 10 years.[3]

Training also pays off in ways other than purely economic ones. Medical interventions have received great and deserved publicity. Many popular magazines have carried feature articles documenting the

[2] Samuel A. Kirk, *Educating Exceptional Children* (Boston: Houghton Mifflin Company, 1962), p. 115.

[3] William L. Findley, "A Follow-Up of the Financial Assets and Liabilities of Mentally Retarded Youth as Related to the Cost of Vocational Training in the Public Schools," unpublished doctoral dissertation, University of Northern Colorado, 1967.

effectiveness of surgical procedures in the prevention of mental retardation due to hydrocephaly.[4] Also, the use of diet control for phenylketonuria (PKU) and other metabolic deficiencies has undoubtedly prevented mental retardation in many children.[5]

The effects of educational intervention have not received quite as much public notice as medical successes, but these gains are no less dramatic and may be even more far-reaching because of their potential applicability to a much greater number of children.

One of the early attempts to improve the functioning of mentally retarded children was made by Skeels, Skodak, and Dye in 1930.[6] These investigators selected children below the age of three years who lived in an orphanage in Davenport, Iowa, The youngsters were matched for age, sex, and social background and divided into a control and an experimental group. The control group of 12 children remained in the orphanage. The 13 children in the experimental group were consigned to the care of middle-aged women in an institution for the retarded, and later were placed for adoption. In 1962, Skeels and Skodak were able to restudy their groups, who were then between 25 and 35 years old.

The results were most encouraging:

1. All the adults from the experimental group were found to be self-supporting; in the control group, about half were still in institutions and of those who were not, only one seemed to be making a reasonably good living.
2. Educational attainment in the experimental group averaged twelfth grade, with several going on to college; Educational attainment for the control group averaged third grade.
3. Total cost to the state from all causes averaged only 1,000 dollars for the experimental group; Total costs to the state for the control group ranged from 7,000 to 24,000 dollars, and gave every indication of rising much higher.

Kirk in 1958 reported on an intensive training program for children three to five years old.[7] Using three experimental and three contrast

---

[4] W. R. Vath, "Hydrocephalus: The Water That Kills," *Today's Health* XLI (May 1963), 52–53.

[5] "What is PKU Testing?" *Parent's Magazine*, XL (November 1965), 108.

[6] Harold Skeels and Marie Skodak, "Adult Status of Individuals Who Experienced Early Intervention," paper presented at the 90th convention of the American Association on Mental Deficiency, Chicago (May 1966); and Harold Skeel and H. B. Dye, "A Study of the Effects of Differential Stimulation in Mentally Retarded Children," *Proceedings of American Association on Mental Deficiency*, 44 (1939), 114–136.

[7] Samuel A. Kirk, *Early Education of the Mentally Retarded* (Urbana, Ill.: University of Illinois Press, 1958).

groups, he provided a rich and varied sense-training program for four years to children whose IQs were below 80. His findings are provocative because he started with children considerably older than those in the studies by either Heber and his colleagues or Skeels, et al., and because his was strictly a day-care educational program, not one in which home environment was altered. He reported that:

1. Seventy percent of the children in the experimental group raised their IQs by 10 points or more.
2. None of the children in the contrast groups improved in tested IQ.
3. The children in the experimental groups who made the most progress had no evidence of pathology and had relatively cooperative and accepting mothers.
   a. One boy raised his IQ from 50 to 113 and became a successful college student.
   b. One girl was the only child in a very large family to be successful in a program other than a class for the mentally retarded.

Even when educational programs are neither total nor started when the children are young, if they are appropriate, excellent results may be expected. Dinger, for example, studied 100 mentally retarded students four to five years after they had completed a work-study program at the high school level in Altoona, Pennsylvania.[8] The findings were fully as good as those of Skeels and Skodak and Kirk:

1. Eighty-five percent of the students were fully employed.
2. Fifty percent had jobs prior to graduation and 25 percent were employed within one year after graduation.
3. Forty-two percent were earning as much as or more than the beginning salaries of teachers in Pennsylvania.

In Milwaukee, starting in about 1967, Heber, Dever, and Conry began an intensive intervention program with families in which there was great likelihood that the children would be identified as mentally retarded once they reached school age.[9] The program identified 40 mothers residing in a slum tract in Milwaukee. These families had produced most of the children identified as mentally retarded in the

[8] J. C. Dinger, "Post-School Adjustment of Former Educable Retarded Pupils," *Exceptional Children*, XXVII (1961), 353–360.

[9] R. F. Heber, R. B. Dever, and J. Conry, "The Influence of Environmental and Genetic Variables on Intellectual Development," in H. J. Prehm, L. A. Hamerlynck, and J. E. Crasson (eds.), *Behavioral Research in Mental Retardation* (Eugene, Ore.: University of Oregon, 1968), also, Rick Heber, Howard Garber, Susan Harrington, Caroline Hoffman and Carol Falender, "Rehabilitation of Families at Risk for Mental Retardation," *Rehabilitation Research and Training Center in Mental Retardation*, Progress Report (December 1972), University of Wisconsin, Madison.

special education public school programs in previous years. The families were all black. The program consisted of three parts and started with newborn children of 20 families in the experimental group. During the first three or four months of the newborn child's life a specially trained woman worked directly with the child in a stimulation and "mothering" program. At the same time, the child's real mother was encouraged to improve her child-rearing and homemaking skills. After about 4 months, the child was enrolled in a child development center, and the mother was enrolled in a fairly formal program designed to teach her better child care and homemaking techniques. At the age of 66 months (about five and a half years), the mean IQ of the experimental group was 123, while the average IQ was only 92 for the control children. This study will not be final until the children become adults, but thus far it indicates a difference of 30 IQ points between the two groups, and there is every probability that as the children grow older, the gap will be even greater, with the youngsters in the control group continuing a downward trend in measured IQ.

Even though research data on the effects of nonmedical intervention are limited, it appears that attention to the development of the mentally retarded is warranted by the results. Furthermore, the earlier the intervention, the greater the gains. However, even if little attention is paid to the youngsters until they become adolescents, a good work-study program can be expected to materially affect good social adjustment. Educational intervention, whether begun early or late, appears to be an economic bargain and a humanitarian bonanza. However, the program would seem to be most effective if it is begun early, has realistic goals, is consonant with the characteristics of the learner, and is sequentially consistent.

Goals of Education

The National Education Association classifies: (1) economic efficiency; (2) worthy home membership; (3) worthy citizenship; and (4) self-realization as nearly all conceivable goals of education.[10] However, with mentally retarded youngsters, it would appear that unless some measure of economic efficiency can be achieved, all the other aims of education are unsupported. Economic efficiency, on the other hand, can make a substantial contribution to the other aims. For many re-

[10] Educational Policies Commission, *The Purposes of Education in American Democracy* (Washington, D.C.: National Education Association, 1938), p. 47.

tarded individuals, work success may actually be self-realization. That is, their sense of identity may be tied to the contribution they can make through their work. Similarly, they exercise good citizenship largely by not becoming burdens upon society, rather than by positive civic activities. Being worthy home members may depend upon their economic contribution or even upon so simple a fact as spending a major portion of their time at work, thus freeing the parents or guardians from the responsibility of total supervision. At a more independent level, most of the educable mentally retarded can be trained to be independent in their living and even maintain families of their own. Realistically, the goals of vocational competence and independent living are not only attainable, but once achieved will probably fulfill the aims of education enunciated by the NEA. The program of special education for the educable mentally retarded, therefore, should be the maximum development of the intellectual, personal, social, emotional, and motor skills necessary for vocational competence and independent living. To achieve these goals, it is necessary first to identify the specific skills and characteristics in each area—intellectual, personal, social, and motor —which are required for vocational competence and independent living in our society and then to arrange the learning environment in such a manner that the skills and characteristics are taught in a manner consistent with the learning abilities of the retarded.

Probably no final statement can ever be forthcoming concerning the skills and characteristics required to live successfully in this culture, primarily because society is characterized by constant change. That is, a definitive list which might accurately reflect the needs today will probably be outdated tomorrow by technological, sociological, and psychological change. There seems, however, no alternative other than to use the best current information available for curricular guidelines and to modify those guidelines as new and better information becomes available. If society is constantly changing, it seems only reasonable that curricula should also change.

Evidence concerning the kinds of skills and characteristics vital to vocational competence and independent living for the mentally retarded has been systematically catalogued by Cobb.[11] Although the research evidence is rather scarce, what has been accumulated is rather consistent, regardless of the source. Since the 1950 survey report by

[11] Henry Cobb, "The Predictive Assessment of the Adult Retarded for Social and Vocational Adjustment: A Review of Research," Part I, annotated bibliography (Vermillion, S. Dakota: Department of Psychology, University of South Dakota, 1966).

Michal-Smith identified four characteristics judged by personnel directors to be important for employees as: (1) should not tire on the job; (2) should avoid changes; (3) should follow orders; and (4) should exercise caution, these opinions have been verified and added to by other investigators.[12] Collman and Newlyn found that 52 percent of the mentally subnormal who were unable to hold jobs were discharged for character defects (unreliable on the job, late, sex offenses, rude, lazy); inefficiency, 22 percent; and temperamental instability, 10 percent.[13] Shotwell's 1948 report of the effect of social-emotional problems affecting employability is therefore confirmed.[14] Likewise, Beckham has added the personal qualities of congeniality, desire to please, getting along with others, obeying directions, and resourcefulness to the list of characteristics needed.[15] Warren has added the following: self-confidence, cooperation, cheerfulness, ability to accept criticism, ability to mix socially with other employees, ability to concentrate on assigned tasks, respect for superiors, initiative, and promptness.[16]

From our own investigations it is quite evident that above a 2.5 grade level in reading achievement, the actual achievement level does not appear to be critical.[17] Furthermore, the presence of an ancillary handicap does not seem to be important if the other desirable characteristics are present. However, the presence of work skills—persistence, dexterity, strength, coordination, and pacing—have been well identified as important by Peterson and Jones.[18]

IQ as a determinant for the extent of work performance has not

[12] H. Michal-Smith, "A Study of the Personal Characteristics Desirable for the Vocational Success of the Mentally Deficient," *American Journal of Mental Deficiency*, LV (1960), 139–143.

[13] R. D. Collman and D. Newlyn, "Employment Success of Mentally Dull and Intellectually Normal Ex-Pupils in England," *American Journal of Mental Deficiency*, LXI (1957), 484–490.

[14] A. Shotwell, "Effectiveness of Institutional Training of High Grade Mentally Defective Girls," *American Journal of Mental Deficiency*, LIII (1949), 432–440.

[15] A. S. Beckham, "Minimum Intelligence Levels for Several Occupations," *Personnel Journal*, IX (1930), 309–313.

[16] Fount G. Warren, "Ratings of Employed and Unemployed Mentally Handicapped Males on Personality and Work Factors," *American Journal of Mental Deficiency*, LXV (March 1961), 629–633.

[17] Oliver P. Kolstoe, "An Examination of Some Characteristics Which Discriminate between Employed and Not-Employed Mentally Retarded Males," *American Journal of Mental Deficiency*, LXVI (November 1961), 472–483.

[18] R. C. Peterson and E. M. Jones, *Guide to Jobs for the Mentally Retarded*, rev. ed. (Pittsburgh: American Institute for Research, 1964).

been well established. Reports of little relationship come from the findings of Tizard and O'Connor,[19] Clarke and Hermelin,[20] Saenger,[21] Rynbrandt,[22] and Kolstoe.[23] However, it is a common-sense observation that it takes more intelligence to be an atomic physicist than a ditch-digger. Such a relationship cannot be denied, but the range of jobs held by the retarded does not extend much beyond those of a semiskilled nature. The classification of jobs depends upon the amount of training required for the individual to perform the job, as well as the amount of responsibility he may have. Unskilled jobs require virtually no training and are performed under the direction of someone else. Representative jobs are those of a routine nature such as stocking a grocery store, general cleanup, gasoline station attendant, laborer on construction, dishwasher, housemaid, laundry worker, and assembly line station. Semiskilled jobs require some training and are usually performed without close supervision. Representative jobs are those of custodian, gasoline station mechanic, nurse's aide, laboratory assistant, carpenter's helper, some waitresses, and short-order cooks.[24] With such a restricted range, there is not much room for listing by order of complexity—they are all relatively simple. Thus it appears that the relationship of IQ to employability for the retarded is such that most of the retardates can perform a wide variety of simple jobs, but not many retarded individuals have been trained for jobs at a high level of complexity so there is not much of an opportunity to study that exact relationship. Another complicating factor is that the law of compensation may also be operating. For example, if a person is slow but also very accurate in his work, the accuracy may make him a desirable employee despite his slowness.

[19] J. Tizard and N. O'Connor, "The Employability of High Grade Mental Defectives," Part II, *American Journal of Mental Deficiency*, LV (1950), 144–157.

[20] A. D. B. Clarke and B. F. Hermelin, "Adult Imbiciles: Their Abilities and Trainability," *Lancet*, CCLXIX (1955), 337–339.

[21] G. Saenger, *The Adjustment of Severely Retarded Adults in the Community* (Albany: New York State Interdepartmental Health Resources Board, October 1957).

[22] D. M. Rynbrandt, "A Study of the Social-Economic Adjustment of People Who Have Attended the Auxiliary and Ungraded Classes of the Grand Rapids Public Schools," unpublished doctoral dissertation, Wayne State University, 1947.

[23] Kolstoe, "An Examination of Some Characteristics. . . ."

[24] Oliver P. Kolstoe and Roger M. Frey, *A High School Work Study Program for the Mentally Subnormal Student* (Carbondale, Ill.: Southern Illinois University Press, 1965) and Peterson and Jones, *Guide to Jobs for the Mentally Retarded* have fairly extensive lists of jobs which are being performed by retarded persons. The *Dictionary of Occupational Titles* of the U.S. Department of Labor lists virtually all jobs in these and other categories.

Findley, in his follow-up of graduates of work-study programs in four school systems, found both boys and girls to be living according to acceptable adult patterns.[25] In one system, for example, 65 percent of the girls were homemakers within one year after leaving school. Obviously this argues persuasively for providing training in domestic skills, child rearing, and family living as part of the secondary program. A second critical finding by Findley was that there was an equal likelihood of employment between an IQ range of 45 to 85, but the group between 45 and about 60 required more time for training, was more difficult to place, and earned less money than the 60 to 85 group. Thus, it appears that flexibility should be a key concept in programming at this level.

The Program

From the studies reviewed, it seems clear that every intervention attempt has been successful in some measure. From the point of view of providing the youngsters with those skills that make it possible for them to live independently and to work effectively, the literature is consistent in identifying the following as minimum essentials:

INTELLECTUAL CHARACTERISTICS
1. Academic achievement above 2.5 grade level in reading, language arts, and arithmetic
2. Thought processes at least at the level of grouping and ordering by more than one dimension, and command of the concept of evaluation
3. Oral language and listening skills sufficient to give and/or follow uncomplicated directions

PERSONAL CHARACTERISTICS
1. Acceptable habits of cleanliness, grooming, and health
2. Ability to inhibit reactions to stimuli to stem inappropriate outbursts
3. Self-management skills enabling appropriate choices based on probable consequences
4. Acceptable values involving loyalty, honesty, truthfulness, and dependability

SOCIAL CHARACTERISTICS
1. Ability to get along with peers
2. Ability to accept supervision

[25] William L. Findley, "A Follow-Up of the Financial Assets and Liabilities of Mentally Retarded Youth as Related to the Costs of Vocational Training in the Public Schools," unpublished doctoral dissertation, University of Northern Colorado, 1967.

3. Ability to resist social pressure
4. Cheerfulness
5. Ability to maintain oneself in a living situation

MOTOR SKILLS
1. Adequate strength, speed, and coordination for unskilled and semi-skilled work

VOCATIONAL SKILLS
1. Persistence or perseverance
2. Ability to work under pressure or distraction
3. Pacing
4. Evaluation of own work
5. Initiative
6. Judgment in the care of materials and property

Although the literature is much less clear regarding skills of independent living, they can be identified as those behaviors required of a person to live successfully in society. These are:

HOME MANAGEMENT
1. Budgeting and buying
2. Maintenance of property and clothes
3. Meal planning and preparation
4. Child care and family living

PERSONAL CHARACTERISTICS
1. Cleanliness and grooming
2. Interpersonal relationships
3. Management of time
4. Dependability and responsibility
5. Ability to use public transportation

The teaching of these skills and characteristics is not quite so simple as stating them. Even if we discounted the complexity of the things to be learned and assumed that retarded youngsters could learn if they were given enough time, roughly twice the usual time would be needed. That is, a program that normally takes 12 years to complete would require 24 years to accomplish. Assuming the child started school at the same age as his peers (about 6 years old), graduation from high school would take place at the age of about 30. From the standpoint of time alone, such programming is not feasible. From the standpoint of self-esteem, the program could be disastrous. Being identified as a 25-year-old high school sophomore does not hold out a promise of winning much respect from the typical 15-year-old sophomores. Furthermore, the content of the regular program is developed for youngsters who have a wide variety of adult roles open to them. The adult roles open to the retarded are much more limited. College attendance, for example, is not apt to be a viable alternative for many, if any, of them. Therefore, a program of regular high school offerings such as science, humanities, math, and foreign languages would not be appropriate either in time or in the comprehensiveness of content.

Whatever the program will be, it must be fitted in to the time frame of most other programs, namely some 12 years. The content, however, must be governed by the principle of flexibility. This simply recognizes the right of any youngster to try to benefit from any of the offerings of the school, subject only to his ability to participate successfully and his interest in the program. Thus any option open to other youngsters should also be open to the retarded. In addition, their special needs in understanding complex problems must be recognized and provided for. The opportunities to learn those intellectual, personal, social, motor, recreational, vocational, home management, and interpersonal skills must not be limited by any artificial barrier nor by any program restrictions. The skills need to be learned. Where they are learned is of much less importance.

While the problem of curricular content and presentation can be simply stated, implementation is far from simple. Fortunately, many people have attended to this problem, and substantial progress has been made.

Instructional Outcomes

Since the 1950s many professional workers have developed curriculum guides appropriate to their respective school systems. These have generally been based on the teachers' experiences of what activities were successful with their charges, what goals they wished to achieve, and what facilities were available in the community. Many of the curriculum guides have great utility locally, but not many have universal applicability. This weakness can be overcome by starting from the other end of the developmental sequence; that is, a careful listing of those skills and behaviors needed for successful living and working as adults in society provides the goals of the program. These can then be projected backward through developmental levels so each stage forms a base upon which the next higher level can be built. What needs to be taught is revealed through research on the characteristics of retarded persons who are making a satisfactory adjustment to society vocationally, personally, and socially. These characteristics are then arranged sequentially starting at the level at which educational programs begin and related to the maturity level of each stage of development.

In 1960, a group of experienced teachers working under the direction of Tony D. Vaughan at the University of Northern Colorado specified instructional outcomes in six core areas of learning and at five developmental levels.[26] The core areas were: (1) arithmetic competencies; (2) social competencies; (3) communicative skills; (4) safety; (5) health; and (6) vocational competencies. Since these did not provide for the leisure and recreational needs of the youngsters, Kolstoe in 1970 modified the outcomes by adding motor and recreation skills plus the esthetic activities of art and music.[27] In addition Wilbur Millslagle added the areas of drug and alcohol abuse. In 1974 the special education teachers of Berrien County, Michigan, under the leadership of C. Neal Henderson translated the outcomes list into behavioral objectives. These have been further modified by this writer into the current list that appears in the appendix of this book.

Stating the outcomes by core areas and developmental levels in behavioral terms makes it possible to monitor more systematically the progress of each child through the program. At each level, command or possession of certain behaviors must be attained before proceeding to the next higher level. Thus the learner can be exposed to experiences that build one upon the other until the behaviors necessary for independent living and vocational competence are achieved.

Although behaviors are specified in the areas of communication, arithmetic, social competencies, motor and recreational skills, esthetics, health, safety and vocational competencies, what is emphasized and how it is presented is dependent upon the needs, development level, and learning skills of the learner. Therefore, no single method of organization or presentation may be appropriate for each child. In addition to individual differences between learners, the needs of each learner change as a function of maturation and experience. The things to be learned can be explicitly stated, but the key to presentation is flexibility.

The developmental levels in most school systems are encom-

[26] Tony D. Vaughan, *The Colorado State College Outcomes Chart* (Greeley, Col.: Colorado State College, Department of Special Education, n.d.).

[27] Oliver Kolstoe, *Teaching Educable Mentally Retarded Children* (New York: Holt, Rinehart and Winston, 1970).

passed in a grade-level program often starting with preschool and kindergarten and proceeding through the grades of first through twelfth. Numerous writings have called attention to the inappropriateness of grade-level designations for children who are mentally retarded. Instead, levels of cognitive change have been suggested, which correspond to the developmental levels of Piaget mentioned in Chapter 1. Kephart has proposed a theoretical framework that uses Piaget's levels as a base, but transposes the levels into perceptual and conceptual growth.[28] He believes that the motor exploration of things in the world provides the basis against which all other sense images are compared. The individual experiences the world in his own unique way because everything he learns comes through his senses of touch, taste, smell, vision, and hearing. All the sense impulses are combined by the person to form his impression of the world about him, but the final arbiter of all these sensations is the sense of touch. Accurate information therefore depends upon the opportunity for motor exploration. In Kephart's scheme, all that the child sees, hears, smells, or tastes is related to touch. Hence, motor exploration dominates all other perception and is divided into two levels, gross motor and motor-perceptual stages of development. They differ only in that the gross motor stage is likely to be characterized by pretty haphazard movement, while the motor-perceptual stage employs purposeful motor activity.

The next higher level of development, the perceptual-motor stage, finds the youngster using motor activities to stabilize thousands of sense perceptions that come from widening encounters with the world. At this point, the primary strategy for learning is called the perceptual-motor match, where the child learns to explore objects with other senses, much as he explored objects by touch. The trick is for him to learn to transduce information; that is, to secure sense impulses visually, for example, which exactly match information previously communicated by touch.

Later, in the perceptual stage, the child extends the perceptual-motor match technique to other senses. Because he is able to compare one kind of sensory perception against other sensory perceptions, he is now able to demonstrate auditory discriminations, memory, and sequencing. At this stage, children can ordinarily sort things by shape simply by looking at them.

At the perceptual-conceptual stage, the child can deal with per-

[28] Newell C. Kephart, *The Slow Learners in the Classroom*, 2d. ed. (Columbus, Ohio: Charles E. Merrill Books, Inc., 1971).

ceptually similar things by combining them into a higher level of organization based on some meaningful characteristic. For instance, all chairs have a back, a base, and a seat. Even though each chair has other perceptually apparent characteristics they are not relevant to the concept of "chairness."

The conceptual stage is demonstrated when the child can generalize perceptual information and use the characteristics of things for useful purposes. This stage requires a symbol system of some kind because the child must be able to deal with objects abstractly; in other words, the child is able to manipulate things without the things actually being present.

The child has reached the conceptual-perceptual stage when he can adopt a purely hypothetical point of view or frame of reference and, based on this point of view, can project a world of what might be. This is the highest level indicated by Kephart and appears to correspond to the level of formal operations of Piaget.

Kephart's framework will play a significant role in this book, not because it has been validated, but because it closely parallels the levels discovered by the research of Piaget, but deals with them in perceptual and conceptual terms. Since teaching strategies employ perceptual and conceptual organizations, it seems more meaningful to teachers to use the terminology with which they are familiar than to employ a totally new one.

Preschool Program

Mentally retarded children below the chronological age of about six would be in the preschool level of programming. Zeaman and House[29] suggested that retarded children have difficulty in attending to relevant stimuli at this level in particular. Operating on this information, there is the clear mandate for the teacher to present unambiguous cues and carefully controlled stimuli so the retarded child will develop correct perceptions from which later concepts and associations can be derived. The preschool program, even if it starts within a few weeks after the birth of the child, should be a structured one in which the child is exposed to stimuli that are carefully controlled. It should build from a motor exploration program to a sensory training program aimed at

[29] D. Zeaman and Betty J. House, "The Role of Attention in Retardate Discrimination Learning," in Norman R. Ellis (ed.), *Handbook of Mental Deficiency* (New York: McGraw-Hill, Inc., 1963).

developing perceptual-motor matches and perceptual-perceptual comparisons, and lead to the formation of visual discrimination, memory, sequencing, association, and closure as well as auditory discrimination, memory, sequencing, association, closure, and sound blending skills, which contribute to his language development. These experiences are expected to provide the child with perceptions of the world that are relatively undistorted by irrelevant stimuli.

Primary Program

Children at the primary level would ordinarily have chronological ages between six and eight or nine. They would also need a structured program in which more precise perceptions are introduced, but in which concept formation is the dominant theme. Increased attention to the precise use of language is of paramount importance. Additionally, the child needs to be introduced to simple cause and effect relationships, an expanded experience with the surrounding world, and an opportunity to interact with his peers and adults in meaningful activities. The beginnings of academic work can be introduced if it is presented in a systematic manner. The chief purpose of the primary level work is to provide the child with an opportunity to develop adequate academic skill foundations.

Intermediate Program

The intermediate level is most characterized by academic experiences. Reading, writing, arithmetic, and spelling are presented as skills to be learned and to be used to obtain information of a more vicarious nature. Information then must be classified by conceptual characteristics and multiple dimensions. Principles of using the skills become the media for understanding the world and modifying the expectations of the child in terms of consequences of actions. At this level, some notions of the possible future for each child should be explored.

Prevocational Program

The prevocational level should be concerned with using the academic skills to explore and evaluate the vocational world which may be open to the youngster. In addition, tentative physical exploration of the world of work may be initiated through sheltered work experience of a limited and carefully supervised nature. Self-evaluation should be introduced in relationship to general work skills in a realistic yet controlled manner. Thus, developing realistic expectancies about work demands is a crucial aspect of the program at this level.

Vocational Program

The vocational level is the final stage in preparing the youngster for independent living and vocational competence. Physical exposure to increasingly demanding work experiences while continuing to stress self-maintenance at an increasingly independent level becomes the focus of the program. Specific attention to problems of living and working becomes the means through which academic skills can be brought to bear on problems to be investigated and evaluated. The concentration of the program is not on skill development as such, but rather on the use of skills already partially learned in a work or living environment.

The entire program from preschool through the vocational level is designed to prepare mentally retarded youngsters for self-management in work and living. It is designed to develop a realistic image of the world for each individual, so that incoming stimuli from the environment can be evaluated realistically for incongruity with the expectancies of the person, and plans which have adaptive validity can be developed.

Book Plan

The plan of this book is specified by the behavior and knowledge outcomes at each level and in each area. Each of the outcomes is as important as every other. The lists presented are indicative of what each youngster is expected to have mastered through the instructional procedures described at each level before he is exposed to the instructional procedures of the next level. They are to be visualized as building blocks in a total structure—the lower ones support succeeding levels in the structure.

Only those outcomes which contribute to the development of skills of independent living and work are included, and the instructional suggestions are those which are relevant to achievement of the final goals of independence in living and work. A complete listing of all the outcomes is presented in the appendix at the end of the book. In addition, outcomes expected at each level and in each area introduce the discussion of the instructional program. Outcomes in each area are grouped as follows:

COMMUNICATION
1. Oral communication
2. Listening skills
3. Written communication
4. Reading

ARITHMETIC
1. Facts and processes
2. Money
3. Time
4. Measurement

SOCIAL COMPETENCIES
1. The self
2. In the school
3. In the home, neighborhood, and community

ESTHETICS
1. Art
2. Music

HEALTH
SAFETY
MOTOR AND RECREATIONAL SKILLS
VOCATIONAL COMPETENCIES
1. Analysis of occupations
2. Occupational skills

In all, outcomes are specified at five developmental levels (preschool, primary, intermediate, prevocational, and vocational), in eight areas (communications, arithmetic, social competencies, esthetics, health, safety, motor and recreational skills, and vocational competencies), and are listed in 18 subareas. A total of 513 behavioral outcomes must be developed if the mentally retarded youngster is going to learn those skills necessary for his vocational and independent living survival as an adult in society.

Although the goals of the teaching program and the content that leads to those goals can be specified, neither is useful unless the experiences are presented in a manner and sequence appropriate to the characteristics of the learner, with adequate feedback of results to the learner. Whether learning is explained by contiguity, reinforcement, insight, or association, it seems apparent that behavior is modified by the ensuing consequences of an action. That is, without any extended discussion, it is probably safe to conclude that rewarded behavior or behavior that reduces incongruity has a high probability of being repeated. Thus teachers are generally trained to use various kinds of rewards to reinforce behaviors perceived by them as desirable. It can probably be expected that teachers will have varying degrees of sophistication in this area, but that all will have some command of the technique.

This assumption is basic to the program presented in this book. That is, teaching is defined as the management of the learning environment in such a manner that the learner is surrounded by optimum opportunity to profit from those experiences included in the curriculum. Chapter 3 will discuss this point in more detail. The fact remains, however, that the good teacher is one whose management techniques are most effective.

CHAPTER 3

The Organization

Program Delivery

From the first recorded attempts at teaching the mentally retarded, beginning with the work of Itard in the early 1800s, the historical story has been one of continuous disagreement on the best procedure. Each procedural change from the individualized tutoring practiced by Itard, Seguin, and Montessori, to the special classes of Inskeep and Ingram came from emerging understandings of the nature and needs of the retarded. Each reflected some serious questioning of the effectiveness of previous efforts, but the questioning became really serious starting in the 1960s when numerous writings from many different sources unleashed a flood of criticism on programs for the retarded, and suggested that the efforts actually hindered rather than helped their development. Although there are many criticisms, some of the most important ones need to be considered if we wish to determine the most effective ways to provide services to the mentally retarded.

Criticism 1. Mental retardation is noticeable during the school-age years but disappears when the youngsters attain adult status.

This notion seems to have been given credence from several surveys, notably the Onondago, New York survey of 1955 and Bluma

Weiner's survey of Hawaii in 1958.[1] Although the surveys are not comparable in technique, they both report the lowest rates of incidence below the age of five and above the age of fifteen. The 1929 study in England by E.O. Lewis, as reported in Farber, likewise reported that between:[2] ages 5–9, 15.5 per thousand were found; ages 10–14, 25.6 per thousand were found; ages 15–19, 10.8 per thousand were found; ages 20–29; 8.0 per thousand were found; ages 30–39, 6.0 per thousand were found; ages 50–59, 4.0 per thousand were found; ages 60+, 2.0 per thousand were found.

A conclusion drawn from these figures is that the retarded appear to be inadequate because the demands of the school are academic and somewhat unrealistic for them, but when they are grown up and faced with the demands of acceptable vocational performance and self-management, these same children no longer seem retarded because they can cope with those societal demands. In other words, they are inadequate in learning but adequate in adaptive behavior.

The validity of this conclusion depends primarily upon evidence from follow-up studies of the adult retarded. Nearly all of the follow-up studies are confounded by failure to account for the effects of social class on adult living patterns and the degree of retardation studied. Fortunately, one study that does control both severity and social class is the 1948 study by Ruby Jo Reeves Kennedy and her 1960 follow-up.[3] Kennedy compared the family background, marital adjustment, economic adjustment, anti-social behavior, and social participation of 256 morons (IQs 50 to 75) and 129 nonmorons (IQs above 75) matched on age, sex, nationality, religion, and father's occupation. In every area of comparison, the retarded were inferior in some important characteristics (for example, employer satisfaction). The crucial point, however, is that in 1960 the retarded (morons) were just as inferior as they had been in 1948 (for example, median weekly earnings $88.50 versus $102.50). Thus when the retarded are compared with peers who differed only in IQ, it seems they are no more adequate as adults than they were as students in school. Their retardation does not just appear

[1] Samuel A. Kirk and Bluma B. Weiner, "The Onondago Census—Fact or Artifact," *Exceptional Children*, 25 (January 1959), 226–228, 230–231.

[2] Farber, Bernard, *Mental Retardation: Its Social Context and Social Consequences* (Boston: Houghton Mifflin Company, 1968).

[3] Ruby J. Reeves Kennedy, "A Connecticut Community Revisited: A Study of the Social Adjustment of a Group of Mentally Deficient Adults in 1948 and 1960," in Thomas E. Jordan, *Perspectives in Mental Retardation* (Carbondale, Ill.: Southern Illinois University Press, 1965).

in response to unrealistic school demands; they are also inadequate in the adult world.

Criticism 2. Special class placement is bad for the child's self-concept.

Two studies are generally pointed to in support of this allegation. In 1962 J.H. Meyrowitz used the Illinois Index of Self Derogation (IISD) with two groups of six-year-old retarded youngsters, half of whom were in special classes, while the other half were in the regular grades.[4] The IISD consists of 22 pairs of statements, one neutral or positive and one derogatory. The child then chooses the statement that is most like him and the index is obtained from the number of derogatory statements he chooses. In the Meyrowitz study, the mean number of derogatory statements was 3.0 for the retarded in regular classes and 3.4 for the retarded in special classes. In 1967, Ann Welch Carroll replicated the study, but this time with youngsters who were slightly over eight years old in two groups, one in a totally segregated program, the other in a partially integrated one.[5] The IISD was given in the fall and repeated again eight months later in the spring. The mean scores for the segregated group in the fall and spring were 6.50 and 7.60, while the mean scores of the partially integrated were 7.53 and 6.11. The increase of 1.1 versus the decrease of 1.42 is a statistically significant difference that has been interpreted to mean that youngsters in segregated special classes develop a poorer self-concept than youngsters in partially integrated special classes.

The believability of this research really pivots on the reliability of the Illinois Index of Self Derogation. In this connection Meyrowitz indicates that the test-retest reliability of the IISD is 80 percent. That is, four out of five choices do not change from test to test but one does. In the 22 item test, 4.4 items (or 2.2 plus and 2.2 minus) could be expected to occur by chance alone. If we assume a mean score of 6.50 on a first test, then retest scores could run from 4.3 to 8.7, by chance alone, without presuming to reflect a real change in self-concept. Neither the Meyrowitz nor the Carroll study contain any evidence that special class placement has a negative effect on the self-concept of the youngsters. A recent review of research in this same area by Mac-Millan, Jones, and Aloia, approaches the problem from a different

---

[4] J. H. Meyrowitz, "Self Derogation in Young Retardates and Special Class Placement," *Child Development*, 33 (1962), 443–451.

[5] Ann Welch Carroll, "The Effect of Segregated and Partially Integrated School Programs on Self-Concept and Academic Achievement of the Educable Mentally Retarded," *Exceptional Children*, 34 (October 1967).

point of view, using different data, but arrives at the same conclusion.[6]

Criticism 3. Teachers contribute to the self-fulfilling prophesy of low academic achievement.

The credibility of this charge depends upon the validity of the research by Robert Rosenthal and Lenore Jacobson, who wrote *Pygmalion in the Classroom*, which contended that the achievement of children was significantly influenced by the expectation of teachers. The review of this research was written in 1968 by Robert L. Thorndike,[7] who pointed out that the alleged effect of the prophesy appears in only 19 children in grades 1 and 2, out of a total population of 320 students in 6 grades, and that in one of the classes the reported average IQ was 31. He goes on to say:

"They just barely appear to make the grade as imbeciles! . . . What kind of a test, or what kind of testing is it that gives a mean IQ of 58 for the total entering first grade of a rather run-of-the-mill school?"

Thorndike closes his review by saying:

"In conclusion, then, the indications are that the basic data upon which this structure has been raised are so untrustworthy that any conclusions based upon them must be suspect. The conclusion may be correct, but if so it must be considered a fortunate coincidence." Thus there does not appear to be data to support the self-fulfilling prophesy charge.

Criticism 4. Segregated special class programs are ineffective.

This question of the efficacy of special classes has been a continuing one, but it was given major publicity by Johnson in 1962, who pointed out the paradox that special classes were accomplishing their educational objectives at the same or a slower rate than regular classes.[8] Dunn, in 1968, questioned the effectiveness of a special program and then voiced a plea to stop expanding programs that he felt were undesirable for many of the children in the programs.[9] Dunn presented no data to prove his allegation of undesirability. Johnson,

---

[6] Donald L. MacMillan, Reginald L. Jones, and Gregory F. Aloia, "The Mentally Retarded Label: A Theoretical Analysis and Review of Research," *American Journal of Mental Deficiency*, 79 (November 1974).

[7] Robert L. Thorndike, "Review of 'Pygmalion in the Classroom' by Robert Rosenthal and Lenore Jacobson," in *Review of Educational Research*, 1968; also Robert Rosenthal and Lenore Jacobson, *Pygmalion in the Classroom* (New York: Holt, Rinehart & Winston, 1968).

[8] G. Orville Johnson, "Special Education for the Mentally Handicapped—A Paradox," *Exceptional Children*, 29, (October 1962), 62–69.

[9] Lloyd M. Dunn, "Special Education for the Mildly Retarded: Is Much of It Justified?" *Exceptional Children*, 35, (September 1968), 5–22.

however, cited studies by Pertch (1936), Bennett (1932), Baller (1936), Kennedy (1948), and Charles (1953). However, none of these studies followed the fundamental principle of random assignment, and therefore none had an appropriate group of youngsters who could be compared with the special class children.

One study that did have equivalent groups is the 1965 study of Goldstein, Moss and Jordan.[10] These investigators screened all entering first-grade children in schools in three communities in central Illinois. All children who had individual IQ test scores below 85 were randomly assigned to regular or special classes. After four years:

1. Both groups had raised their average IQs from 75 to 82.
2. Neither group was superior in academic achievement.
3. Neither group was superior on a test of social knowledge.

Johnson's allegation that the special classes were no better than the regular classes in fostering academic achievement was therefore confirmed. But Dunn's allegation that the classes were undesirable was unsubstantiated. True, the special classes were no better, but they were likewise no worse. The achievement of the groups was equal.

However, the major function of programs for the retarded is not simply to teach reading, writing, and arithmetic; it is to teach skills of employability and self-management. Here the research is very clear. All of the studies point to superior results from work-oriented programs. As an example, the 1967 study of Jerry Chaffin seems to be most believable.[11] Youngsters from a work–study and a non–work–study special class were carefully equated to assure that they were similar, then compared for employment success after they left school. The non–work–study group had 68 percent employed, but the work–study group had 94 percent employed (a 50 percent improvement). In 1971, when the groups were restudied, the percentages shifted from 68 to 75 percent for the non–work–study group and from 94 to 83 percent for the work–study group (still a 12 percent superiority). If this were an isolated instance, there might be room for skepticism, but similar results are reported from Michigan, Missouri, and California. In the area of preparation for employment, there exists not one

[10] Herbert Goldstein, James Moss, Laura Jordan, "A Study of the Effects of Special Class Placement on Educable Mentally Retarded Children" (Urbana, Ill.: University of Illinois, 1965).

[11] Jerry D. Chaffin, Charles R. Spellman, C. Edward Regan, and Roxanna Davison, "Two Follow-up Studies of Former Educable Mentally Retarded Students from the Kansas Work–Study Project," *Exceptional Children*, 37 (Summer 1971), 733–738.

shred of evidence to suggest that regular class placement is superior to special class placement. Indeed, all the evidence suggests that the products from the regular class are inferior.

About 1970, surveys by a number of people in different parts of the country noted a disproportionate number of minority children assigned to special education classes largely on the basis of low scores on IQ tests, which were given in the English language. They reported about three times as many blacks and twice as many Chicanos as would be expected by the percentage of blacks and Chicanos in the total population of this country. As a result, in 1971 California passed legislation that required a psychological reevaluation of all the youngsters labeled "educable mentally retarded." The new IQ cut-off was set at 70 (two standard deviations below the mean), rather than 85, and non-English-speaking youngsters were given a test in their primary language or, when this was not possible, these children were given non-language performance tests. As a consequence of this legislation, large numbers of these children were "declassified" and returned to regular classes with tutor-counselors assigned to help them make the adjustment back to the regular classroom.

This procedure was consistent with a movement toward mainstreaming (educating mildly retarded children in regular classrooms rather than in segregated special classes), which was gaining momentum in many parts of the country. The movement had received impetus from the articles of Johnson (1962) and Dunn (1968) and reflected the civil rights charge that minority children were being denied equal educational opportunity because of classification by unfair tests and segregation in programs that did not do a good job of teaching the academic skills so necessary for achieving equal opportunity in adult living. These charges were given further support from economy-minded administrators who believed that the excess cost funding of special classes could not be justified because the youngsters were not learning any more in the special classes than they could in regular classes. In addition, the inhuman treatment of the severely retarded in institutions, as exposed by Burton Blatt, and the subsequent articulation of the principle of normalization as a way of humanizing the lives of the retarded, as practiced in the Scandinavian countries, were interpreted to imply that any deviation from mainstreaming in school was not only dehumanizing but a denial of civil rights. As a result, many school systems have made a concerted effort to provide for the mildly retarded in the regular classroom.

What happens to retarded youngsters who remain in regular classes has come in for considerable study. Here the classic studies of Johnson and Kirk in 1950 are our most venerable sources of information.[12] Using a sociometric technique, these investigators found in 25 classrooms with 689 subjects:

1. Three times more stars among typical than M.R. children
2. 69 percent isolates among M.R.s versus 39 percent typical children
3. Over 10 times more rejectees among M.R.s versus typical

Johnson and Kirk point out that the retarded child in a regular class is as socially isolated as he would be if he were not physically present. Jordan (1966) further contends that special class placement does not precipitate a cleavage between the retardate and his peers, since the cleavage already exists whether the retardate is segregated or not.[13]

In an effort to end this kind of cleavage, a court suit in Washington, D.C., challenged the legality of assigning youngsters to different tracks on the basis of ability. The suit was won, and tracking was subsequently halted. Dunn expressed concern over the legality of special class programs based upon the Judge J. Skelly Wright decision in Washington, D.C., that the tracking system was in violation of the Fifth Amendment. When the tracks were abolished and all youngsters were integrated in the regular classroom, Dunn described what happened:

> Complaints followed from the regular teachers that these children were taking an inordinate amount of their time. A few parents observed that their slow learning children were frustrated by the more academic program and were rejected by other students. Thus, there are efforts afoot to develop a special education program in D.C. which cannot be labeled a track.[14]

In 1969 Hayball and Dilling reported to the Scarborough, New York, Board of Education that the mentally retarded youngsters who had been returned to regular classes were achieving below grade level in their academic subjects.[15] Such a report by itself could be quite

---

[12] G. O. Johnson and S. A. Kirk, "Are Mentally Handicapped Children Segregated in the Regular Grades?" *Exceptional Children,* 17 (1950), 65–68.

[13] Thomas E. Jordan, *The Mentally Retarded,* 2d ed. (Columbus, Ohio: Charles E. Merrill Books, Inc., 1966), p. 119.

[14] L. Dunn, "Special Education for the Mildly Retarded."

[15] H. Hayball and H. Dilling, "A Study of Students from Special Classes Who Have Been Returned to Regular Classes" (Scarborough, N.Y.: Board of Education (Ontario), 1969).

suspect, except that exactly the same finding was reported in a doctoral dissertation done by Britton at the University of Southern California in 1972.[16]

In Philadelphia, Iano et al. set up a program that provided resource rooms to help mildly retarded children be successfully integrated into regular classrooms in three different elementary schools. They reported:

> Despite the availability of supportive resource room services, the educable children in this study were apparently not any better accepted in the regular grades than were educable children in previous studies who had not received such supportive services.[17]

Finally in San Bernardino, California, Wilson studied the children in 25 different school buildings who had been declassified and returned to regular classes.[18] He reported that the youngsters were making only a marginal adjustment despite the help of tutor–counselors and that even though they were no longer classified as mentally retarded, they still showed many of the behavior characteristics associated with retardation.

It is most disturbing that catch words like normalization and mainstreaming lend themselves to being used to exploit special education programs for purposes that have little to do with what has been demonstrated to be helpful to children.

To be more specific, both normalization and mainstreaming have been used to assure nondiscriminating programs for minorities, despite clear evidence that these programs are not very successful. In addition, educators and legislators who have been opposed to spending more for the education of handicapped children than for the nonhandicapped have called for integration as a way of reducing the costs of education without lowering the quality. Some also foster the belief that either all children have equal educational potentials with all other children and therefore should be given equal educational treatment, or that individual learning problems are primarily associated with the rate at

[16] A. L. Britton, "An Evaluation of Transition Programs in Selected California School Districts," unpublished doctoral dissertation, University of Southern California, 1972.

[17] Richard P. Iano, D. Ayers, H. B. Heller, J. F. McGettigan, and V. S. Walker, "Sociometric Status of Retarded Children in an Integrative Program," *Exceptional Children*, 40 (January 1974), 267–271.

[18] R. J. Wilson, "Characteristics of Former Special Class (EMR) Children Who Have Been Integrated Into the Regular Classroom," unpublished doctoral dissertation, University of Northern Colorado, 1973.

which children learn, which is a function of age and experience, not individual differences. Individual differences, if they exist at all, involve sensory abilities such as hearing and vision. Therefore, individualization of instruction only calls for: (a) a slowing down of the program; (b) a broadening of life experiences; or (c) instruction in the child's natural or cultural language or in a medium that circumvents the visual or auditory barrier. Thus a value is attached to the kinds of services given to retarded children which is related not to the needs of youngsters, but rather to the services themselves.

The best service is presumed to be placement in a regular class with age peers and with no provision of special help. Service provided by an itinerant consultant to the regular class teacher in the form of suggestions on methods and materials to be used for the child is considered the second best approach. Next on the list is help given directly to the child by an itinerant teacher. The consultant may actually work with a child for a few minutes or hours each day to help him keep up with his peers. And the least positive technique is thought to be the resource room with its almost infinite variety of services and differences in the amount of time spent there. His resource room time may either be spent on activities designed to improve his learning skills or be devoted to tutoring in specific subjects in which the student is weak. This service is ancillary to the regular program, and does not constitute a program in and of itself. In it and the other foregoing programs the base assignment of the child is in the regular classroom. Special class placement is considered bad in any form; however, the least objectionable form is when the special class is in the regular building, especially if some integration in activities with nonhandicapped youngsters is provided. A special class in a segregated school is worst, and the worst of all possible placement is institutionalization in a state-supported school. Deno describes these options as a cascade of services, schematized in Figure 1.[19]

It should be obvious that there is nothing inherently good or bad about any administrative arrangement. Positive or negative aspects can only be judged in relation to whether the needs of the children are being met.

While special classes are far from a panacea for the problems of individual differences, some things should be said in their defense. First, although the classes vary quite widely in their approaches, even the most traditional, academically oriented classes recognize in-

---

[19] Evelyn Deno, "Special Education as Developmental Capital," *Exceptional Children*, 37 (November 1970), 229–237.

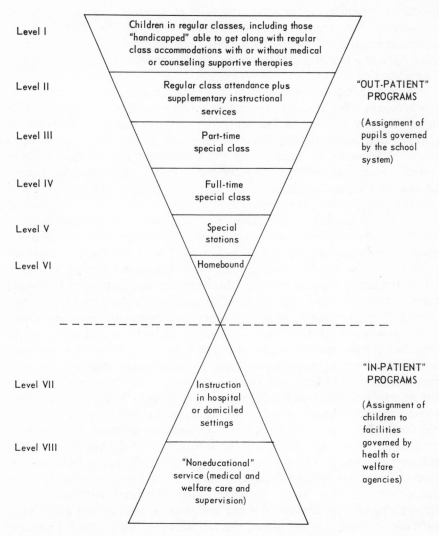

Level I — Children in regular classes, including those "handicapped" able to get along with regular class accommodations with or without medical or counseling supportive therapies

Level II — Regular class attendance plus supplementary instructional services

Level III — Part-time special class

Level IV — Full-time special class

Level V — Special stations

Level VI — Homebound

"OUT-PATIENT" PROGRAMS

(Assignment of pupils governed by the school system)

Level VII — Instruction in hospital or domiciled settings

Level VIII — "Noneducational" service (medical and welfare care and supervision)

"IN-PATIENT" PROGRAMS

(Assignment of children to facilities governed by health or welfare agencies)

Figure 1

dividual differences and do not present impossible tasks to the children. For example, reading is not expected of children until their mental ages are sufficiently high so as to assure a good probability of success (usually a mental age of about six, with a chronological age of eight or nine). Thus the classes expect achievement that is consistent with the ability level of each child. Second, the teachers use concrete materials for instruction. This allows the children to be active participants in learning rather than passive recipients. Furthermore, the lessons do not require them to deal with abstractions that they are ill-equipped to understand. Third, the large majority of programs now lead to work–training experiences with eventual job placement and counseling.

Special education services of the past have erred not so much in the services offered as in the lack of a wider option of programs. This is particularly critical as the understanding of learning problems increases and professionals increase their diagnostic skills. With each advance, it becomes clearer that the conditions surrounding what is called mental retardation form a complex of characteristics that cannot be adequately accommodated by just the traditional self-contained special classroom of the past.

Since the needs of youngsters vary so widely, it is obvious that the tendency to offer "all or nothing" services instead of recognizing the need for options for different youngsters, or even for the same person at different times in his life, has seriously underestimated their needs.

In the other service models, the basic assignment is in a special class. However, there are degrees of segregation ranging from total to very little. The historical special class was completely self-contained with a teacher responsible not only for all aspects of classroom work, but often for the establishment of a curriculum or course of study also. Sometimes the classes were even in segregated special schools, physically isolated from the regular public school campus or at least set apart from the other buildings. At a slightly less isolated level, self-contained classes have been located in buildings that house regular classes, but they have been assigned to such remote areas as remodeled basement rooms, and the interaction of the youngsters with children in regular classes has been so carefully controlled that recesses and starting and dismissal times have been scheduled when the other children were occupied with in-school activities. Thus children in special classes did not arrive at school at the same time as their nonhandicapped peers, did not share playgrounds for recess, and were not dismissed at the same time. It is difficult to picture much interpeer activity under such circumstances. Some schools have allowed integration when the activities were of a nonacademic nature, most often in classes such as physical education, music, art, and sometimes shop or homemaking. Occasionally some schools have provided opportunities for integrating the handicapped youngsters in social studies or science, but rarely have the academic skill classes of reading, arithmetic, writing, and spelling been opened to include the handicapped.

As our experience with and understanding of the conditions included in the classification of the mentally retarded have expanded, our recognition of the vast differences between the children has likewise increased. And with this understanding has come the recognition that no one method of providing services is suitable for all children. The simple fact is that all of the options need to be open, subject only to a performance test of the individual. That is, arbitrary barriers that prevent individual children from participating cannot be justified; any child should be allowed to participate in any of the service options. Exclusion is permissible only after he demonstrates that he cannot perform at a minimally satisfactory level, and this should be determined by a group of experts, such as the case conference committee, not by any single individual regardless of his title or qualifications.

Identification

As was indicated in Chapter 1, the criterion currently used to identify retardation is a score on a test of individual intelligence at least two standard deviations below the mean. The administration and interpretation of such a test ordinarily requires about two hours per child. Since there are roughly 180 school days in a year, one psychometrist would have to spend full time testing to be able to examine 300 youngsters in a given year. This is neither possible nor desirable in most school systems, so other methods of screening are usually employed.

A study by Burris and Elkema examined the percent of retarded children identified by various screening procedures.[20] They used teacher nomination, a score of below 85 IQ on a group test of intelligence, evidence of emotional problems, achievement test scores of two years below chronological age, and medical examination information. They then checked the percentage of children correctly identified using the various criteria. Teacher nominations alone identified only 12.4 percent of the actual number who were retarded. Likewise, medical examinations, a two-year retardation in achievement, and a score below 85 IQ on the group test were not very efficient in identifying the children. The most efficient system employed all of the criteria. Using this system, 100 percent of the retarded were identified and only 10

[20] W. R. Burris and C. E. Elkema, *A Study of Screening Procedures for Special Education Services to Mentally Retarded Children* (U.S. Office of Education Cooperative Research Project 139, 1960).

percent were misidentified. The 10 percent who were misidentified provided an unexpected dividend. These were children whose test performance indicated potential problems of school adjustment. The cause, however, was not mental retardation. It was sensory, as in hearing loss or visual disability, emotional maladjustment, or learning disability. In all cases, some kind of special educational attention was needed to help each child profit from his school experience, but the kind of help needed varied from child to child. Many of these youngsters might have gone undetected and unaided had they not been picked up in the screening procedures.

This kind of efficiency had led many school systems to use a combination of: (1) school failure, such as an achievement test score of at least one year below chronological age in reading, arithmetic, language, or all three; (2) teacher nomination of an individual who is markedly immature in his motor, attention, or emotional behavior; and (3) a score of below 85 IQ on any standardized group test of intelligence. It should be noted that these steps are a hierarchy of importance. School failure is considered most serious, immature behavior second, and group test performance least important. In every case, some significant problem must be identified before the child is referred for an individual psychometric and educational diagnostic evaluation. These records along with the school, social, and physical records are then referred to a case conference committee for evaluation.

Diagnosis

The purpose of the identification procedures is only to find those youngsters who are not making normal progress in school. The procedure is the same, whether this is done at a kindergarten level, after the child enters first grade, or even later; however, the instruments used to find out why he is having trouble and to give some guidance in the direction to take in order to correct the problems differ.

The most obvious reason for failing to learn in a school setting is some sensory impairment. Since nearly any defect in vision or hearing will seriously interfere with learning, it seems almost ludicrous to have to say that tests of vision and hearing administered and interpreted by trained professionals should be mandatory in any diagnosis, yet many schools fail to include this basic information. Physical and health records are often similarly ignored or omitted from the case record yet they are just as basic to understanding a child's problems as are the sensory tests. In addition, a social history that probes the emotional, physical, and values climate of the home is likely to shed considerable light on the degree to which the goals and objectives of the school are compatible with those of the home. Just knowing that the home and school are in conflict in what they are trying to accomplish sometimes goes a long way toward solving the problem.

Even though sensory acuity is basic to learning, it is not sufficient unto itself. Of equal importance is sensory efficiency. This is the skill with which sense impulses are gathered and interpreted by the child. The actual efficiency of gathering sense data is revealed by tests that sample both visual and auditory discrimination, memory, sequencing, closure, and blending. This ability or lack of ability to receive, gather, interpret, relate, and store sense data can combine to produce a wide variety of problems that seriously interfere with a child's learning effectively in school. In every case it is mandatory that in addition to sensory acuity, the sensory efficiency of the child be accurately evaluated so meaningful educational plans can be made.

Formerly, in many schools it was a common practice to use school failure and/or immature behavior combined with a score lower than 85 on an individual test that yields IQ as proof of mental retardation. This was all that was needed to qualify a child for assignment to a special class. In 1971, when the state of California passed innovative legislation concerning classification of the mentally retarded (see discussion on p. 51), it was recognized (at least partially) that mental retardation at a mild or moderate level could not be accurately identified by the subnormal IQ score and poor adaptive behavior; both of these criteria need to be weighed against the background of the child. Mercer, for example, has pointed out that the socioeconomic background of a child has a significant effect on his IQ score.[21] Using various socioeconomic indices, she obtained increasingly low scores related to the presence of subcultural index in the child's background. Five SES indices associated with the home reduce the average IQ score by 20 points and fewer reduce the scores correspondingly.

Services Assignment

It was contended in Chapter 1 that mental retardation is related to the complexity of the thought processes demonstrated by the young person, but that no standardized tests currently exist to measure these

[21] Jane R. Mercer, "Pluralistic Diagnosis in the Evaluation of Black and Chicano Children: A Procedure for Taking Sociocultural Variables into Account in Clinical Assessment," Presentation at American Psychological Association, Washington, D.C., (September 1971).

processes. Thus it appears no sure way is presently available to identify the condition of mild retardation with children who are below the age of about 16 or so. A solution to this apparent dilemma has been to combine a number of indices (lack of academic or behavioral accomplishment, an IQ of below 70 earned on a test given in the child's natural language preferably administered by an examiner of the same sex and ethnic background as the child and some consideration given to the background and motivation displayed). Then the identification of possible retardation is modified by the term *tentative.* This is by way of recognizing that the child's low IQ is a deviation from average. Whether the deviation is a handicap depends upon what an individual will be called upon to do and the environment in which he will be performing. The function of the evaluation committee is to judge whether the low IQ will be a handicap, and what might be the best educational placement for the child. It is also their responsibility to determine whether any other agencies will need to be called upon for help with either the child or the family involved.

These decisions generally are not simple ones of determining whether a deviation is a handicap and recommending special education services. They often involve other community agencies, the family, and frequently a recommended education procedure or management technique. Sometimes medical care or counseling procedures are a necessary part of the prescription. Many states recommend that the committee be made up of the regular class teacher, the special class teacher, a social worker familiar with the youngster's family history, a nurse or physician who has given the child a medical examination, the psychologist who examined the child, the building principal, who often chairs the meeting, and the director or supervisor of special education, who also may chair the meeting.

The meeting usually opens with the presentation of information about the child from each of the experts involved: educational history by the regular class teacher, psychological findings from the psychologist, medical information from the nurse or physician, and family history from the social worker. This information is then discussed by the committee to try to determine: (1) the best educational placement for the child; (2) the need for ancillary services (for example, clinical speech therapy or medical treatment); (3) whether family counseling is desirable; (4) a possible educational program for the child; and (5) a specified future time for reevaluation of the effects of the program decided upon. Such a case conference should be standard procedure for every child considered to need special services. A decision to intervene in the life experiences of a child is not a routine matter. It deserves serious consideration of the alternatives and implications. Furthermore, once a decision has been made, the assignment of a child to a special service should continue only if it continues to provide him the best of the services available. There is no reason or justification to continue a program that does not benefit the child. If it appears that return to the regular program would be best for the child, even on a part-time basis, machinery for smooth transitions should be provided and used. Every child's program plans should be reevaluated at least every three years. Should the need for reevaluation appear sooner, the reevaluation should not be delayed. In any such reevaluation, a change in IQ is an irrelevant matter. The test of the effectiveness of the program is based on the achievement of the child and his behavior patterns, not IQ.

Should it be judged that special class placement will probably be of most benefit to the child, then placement should be made without delay. Both the child and his parents should be told that the child is being transferred into the special class because the class is special. It will provide him with opportunities not available in the regular class, and the small class will allow the teacher to provide individual instruction of a type he cannot get in a regular classroom. Teaching will be based on a careful study of his learning characteristics, and the materials and programs are especially designed or selected to fit the characteristics. The entire program should be explained so the parents will understand what lies ahead for the child and so they can support the efforts of the teachers with the child. The special class should be described as an opportunity, not a punishment for poor accomplishment or bad behavior.

Criteria for assigning children to any of the levels represented by the cascade of services are more likely to be related to the circumstances of the particular school a child is in than to any absolute rules that could be set up. There are, however, some considerations that should be attended to in any kind of assignment. First, the mental age of the child is still the best index of the level of work at which he will probably be able to succeed. It is not a very precise indicator, but within a six-month range, it can be used to provide a good starting point. Second, the nature of the child's learning problem should be the focus for beginning the intervention. This can only be determined by a very careful educational diagnosis that describes exactly what the child can and cannot do in the academic area. If, for instance, a child cannot carry from one column of numbers to another, but can add single digit numbers, it is apparent that place value is the specific weakness in his number skills and will need to be learned by the child before he can progress in his skills. Special materials may very well correct this deficiency and his special assignment can be arranged to provide that help. Third, the probable length of time needed to correct the problem generally determines whether the child's basic assignment should be in the regular classroom with ancillary services provided or in a special classroom with a provision for partial integration. Fourth, the willingness of a regular classroom teacher to try to help a handicapped child may be a much more crucial factor than the kind of problem the child has. Fifth, the attitude of the child and his parents toward the kinds of services suggested by the case conference team may be more important than all the rest of the considerations combined. Without that support and voluntary participation, none of the other efforts may be very meaningful. Sixth, because of the trend to lower the IQ ranges of the children eligible for services from 85 to 70, the ability levels of children served are apt to be less on the average than in years past. Thus the number of children who will need long-term developmental programs may be expected either to increase or remain the same rather than decrease. That is, even though the actual number of children in need of services may decline, the seriousness of their problems may be greater than those seen in the past. Thus the need for intensive services would not be expected to drop appreciably.

Grouping for Services

To be able to offer a special opportunity to retarded children, the service must be organized in a special manner. The training of the teacher, the materials used, the techniques of instruction, the diagnosis of learning needs, the supporting personnel and services, and the facilities provided should reflect a special concern for providing the best available services to children with learning problems that seriously hamper their ability to cope with life. Many states offer extra financial help to support a special opportunity for these children, and the school program should reflect this support.

The key to a special program is real attention to individualizing instruction. Basic to individual learning is the presentation of learning tasks at a level and in a manner appropriate to the characteristics of the child. Perhaps the most useful index to the level of learning appropriate to each child is his mental age. Such an index, however, is only suggestive and, unless it is carefully supported by information about the learning skills of the child, it may be a serious detriment to an effective teaching approach. Nevertheless, grouping children by mental age and chronological age within about three to four years is a useful way to approach the task of providing for individual instruction. Adjustments for individual learning differences are then the responsibility of the teacher working with each child.

For children whose basic assignment is the regular classroom, the actual program will be determined by the considerations enumerated in the preceding section on diagnosis. Some flexibility in class assignment relative to mental age and chronological age can still be made. Furthermore, the behavioral outcomes for each developmental level are fully applicable to this group also. This simply means that a child may be chronologically a year or so older than his classmates and mentally a year or so younger and still be in a proper group. This will depend to a large extent on his social maturity, but it is quite likely that the social maturity will more nearly approximate his mental age than his chronological age. As in other aspects of providing services for these children, good judgment mandates flexibility. Any assignment should be considered tentative and subject to change when the needs of the child warrant the change.

Preschool Level

For those children whose basic assignment is in a special class with or without integration into regular program activities, grouping by chronological and mental ages can be somewhat more broad. For all these children up to the chronological age of about eight, grouping should not exceed a span of about three to four years. Typically children below the age of five would be served either at home or in day-care centers where a heavy emphasis on sensory stimulation, motor development, language, problem solving, and self-care activities would predominate. For those children between chronological ages of five or six and eight, since their IQs would be between about 50 and 70, the mental ages would range from about three to five and a half. The actual grouping of the children for instruction would be dependent more on social and physical maturity than upon mental age because all would probably be in need of readiness experiences.

Using the combined chronological age and mental age grouping, the preschool level should include children up to about seven. The older group would have mental ages ranging to about six. In a given class of 15 students, probably the lowest group would have mental ages of below four, the middle group, about 5, and the most mature group, about 6. Grouping into three levels would have one group below three, one at about three to four, and one group at about four to six.

The program at the preschool level should be concerned with the perceptual and language development of those skills that will be called for in the academic program of the primary level. In addition, the behavior training that is basic to social competence must be provided. While many different approaches could be used, it seems most important to provide a framework to guarantee that none of the essential learnings will be neglected.

One organizational plan that has the capacity to attend to each of the tasks involves a skill-training program in the morning with a unit-experience studies approach in the afternoon. Specific periods for sense training should be in the morning. The skills to be developed would be visual discrimination, visual memory, visual closure, sequential orientation, auditory discrimination, memory, sequencing and closure, motor coordination, and language. Unit experiences in the afternoon should be based on an expanding experience concept. The morning should be designed to teach specific skills, while the afternoon should be planned to provide for the use of those skills in meaningful activities. Behavior management skills should be emphasized throughout the entire program. A sample day would be:

9:00– 9:10	Opening, planning
9:10– 9:40	Visual discrimination, memory, and closure training
9:40–10:10	Auditory discrimination, memory, and closure training
10:10–10:40	Physical education
10:40–11:10	Language (listening and sequential activity training)
11:10–11:30	Music and art (alternate days)
11:30–12:30	Lunch
12:30– 2:00	*Unit on home*
2:00– 2:15	Evaluation, cleanup, and planning for next day

Since the purpose of the preschool program is to develop skills required in the primary program, the sense training should begin with gross activities which become more precise and eventually phase into an academic readiness program for the children whose chronological ages approach 8 and whose mental ages are about 6. For the lowest group, an extra year may be needed, but preacademic skills should be developed before the youngsters are promoted to a primary program.

Primary Level

The primary level includes children whose chronological ages are between eight and ten and whose mental ages are no less than about six. The group will have mental ages from about five and a half to eight and a half, necessitating groupings of those youngsters whose mental ages are about six for the low group, seven for the middle group, and eight for the highest group. The primary program would use the same format as the preschool (skill training in the morning with unit work in the afternoon), but the sensory and readiness activities should be gradually replaced by academic training. A typical day would be:

9:00– 9:10	Opening exercises and planning
9:10– 9:40	Arithmetic
9:40–10:10	Reading
10:10–10:40	Physical education
10:40–11:10	Writing or language on alternate days
11:10–11:30	Music or art on alternate days
11:30–12:30	Lunch
12:30– 2:30	Unit on neighborhood, borough, community, city, or region
2:30– 2:45	Cleanup, evaluation, and planning

The purpose of the primary program is to develop a more precise image of the world and to use more complex thought processes in adapting to the demands of the world. The academic skills are taught during this period as skills. However, the unit work in the afternoon should make use of student-dictated experience charts to allow the students, first, to get experiences of wider scope about the world which surrounds them and, second, to use their developing academic skills in learning situations. It is the purpose of this program to teach the academic skills and to provide some practice in using the skills for learning.

Intermediate Level

The primary program should articulate with the intermediate program in a sequential manner. Again, the format is the same as the preschool and primary program, with academics in the morning and unit work in the afternoon. The intermediate program will have youngsters whose chronological ages are between ten and twelve. Mental ages would range between seven or eight to ten. Grouping would include those whose mental ages are about eight, nine, and ten, respectively. The program would emphasize developing concepts, cause and effect, precision in grouping, and multidimensional classifying. The afternoon would be devoted to unit experiences involving the city or region, state, nation, and the world. A typical day would be:

9:00– 9:10	Opening exercises and planning
9:10– 9:40	Reading

9:40–10:10   Arithmetic
10:10–10:30   Physical education
10:30–11:00   Music and art
11:00–11:30   Writing
11:30–12:30   Lunch
12:30– 3:00   Units on the city or region, state, nation, and world
3:00– 3:15   Cleanup, evaluation, and planning

The intermediate program is the last format program of skill instruction, so special attention needs to be paid those students who have any problems or academic skills that are amenable to remediation. The intermediate level essentially is the last emphasis on formal developmental academic skills. Beginning with the prevocational level, the major commitment is preparation for vocational and independent living competence. To fulfill this emphasis, a different kind of program needs to be provided.

Prevocational Program

It is expected that the prevocational program will be housed in a junior high school building. The special education program should be considered a part of the junior high school program just as other programs in music, homemaking, shop, and so forth, are parts of the program. The prevocational program focuses on preparation for employment, however, rather than on academic skills. Instead, the academic skills are used to help the students prepare for the world of work. To achieve these goals, the program combines an introduction to work with specific units of study designed to aid in preparing the student for success in work and in independent living. A typical schedule would be:

9:00–10:00   Occupational information
10:00–11:00   Physical education and recreation
11:00–12:00   Occupational exploration
12:00– 1:00   Lunch
1:00– 2:00   Shop and home economics
2:00– 3:00   Social studies

Youngsters in the prevocational program will be chronologically between twelve and fourteen or fifteen years, with mental ages ranging from eight or 9 to twelve. No special grouping is recommended except for specific attention to specific remedial problems. The program format may be identical except that a period or two each day may need to be devoted to the further development of academic skills for some youngsters, but the program is not an academic one—it is prevocational.

Vocational Program

The vocational program is designed to allow for the systematic development of skills of independent living and vocational competence (Chapter 11 contains a suggested schedule for more traditional programs). Youngsters will be chronologically 15, or 16 to 20 or 21, with maximal mental ages of approximately 12. The chief difference between the lower aged groups and the higher aged groups may be the slightly lower achievement levels of the first group, and a prediction of more training time needed to prepare them for the world of work and self-management. The format for the program is similar to the prevocational program with up to one-half day of work and one-half day or more of study during their work exploration and training. However, the last year of the program should be devoted to full-time supervised work with weekly counseling sessions designed to deal with problems of work or living. Graduation from high school should be provided upon successful completion of the requirements of the program. Participation in the extracurricular aspects of the high school program should be open to the special education students, provided their work is satisfactory in the special program.

While the level of presentation has been discussed along with the sequence of experiences, the manner of presenting the experiences has been only peripherally indicated. In each area, subsequent chapters will deal with content, methods, and materials. Some general considerations that derive from the nature of mental retardation as conceptualized in this work need further amplification.

Instructional Methods

Learning Characteristics

It is assumed that all organisms modify behavior as a result of their perceptions of the consequences of their actions. It is here contended that behavior is learned or modified when the individual reduces the incongruity between incoming stimuli and his standards or expectancies. Mental retardation is conceptualized as a reduced ability to form stable perceptions and concepts, plus restricted thought processes available to develop plans of adaptive validity. The behavior unit TOTE (test, operate, test, exit) would be expected to be both less efficient and less effective among retardates than among normal peers. By comparison, the retarded would appear to learn more slowly, less perfectly, more concretely, and less generally than their peers. Such descriptions abound in the literature. Acting on these observations, it seems apparent that the manner of presentation should be most effective if it is understandable and concrete, if overlearning is stressed, learning stimuli are controlled, and if immediate feedback of results is followed closely by reinforcement or reward.

There are three generally recognized major models of instruction for handicapped children. One is the use of operant conditioning procedures where desired behavior is accelerated by systematically rewarding the behavior or decelerated by withholding rewards. A second major instructional model is the use of test information on the learning style or strengths and weaknesses of a psycholinguistic nature to provide a clinical-educational diagnosis from which to develop an individual program of instruction (IPI) based on the learning strengths and weaknesses of the child. A third model involves the use of instructional units in which problems that extend throughout the life span of an individual provide the framework within which the instructional program is couched. Every teacher of retarded children should be thoroughly familiar with all three models, since the characteristics and needs of the children vary so widely that at any one time any of the models may be the most appropriate one for instruction. Even more convincing is the fact that all three can complement each other for specific purposes and together may make for a more effective approach than to ignore the possible contribution any one might make. The needs of the children are much too pervading to neglect any source of possible amelioration.

Reward reinforcement or operant techniques have been effectively used by many people in the area.[22] The technique is based on the theory of learning, advanced by B. F. Skinner, that an organism is constantly interacting with its environment and that those behaviors which are rewarded tend to be repeated.[23] By controlling the rewards, the orga-

[22] Fredrick L. Girardeau and Joseph E. Spradlin, "Token Rewards in a Cottage Program," *Mental Retardation*, II (December 1964), 345–351; and Norris Haring and Richard Schiefelbusch, *Methods in Special Education* (New York: McGraw-Hill, Inc., 1967).

[23] B. F. Skinner, *Science and Human Behavior* (New York: Crowell Collier and Macmillan, Inc., 1953).

nism can receive a pleasurable consequence for performing acts which an experimenter or teacher wishes the organism to perform. Acts which are not rewarded tend to disappear. This is known as extinction.

Under laboratory conditions, a count or record of the frequency of a behavior is established by counting or time sampling. The desired behavior is carefully identified, and approximate behaviors are specified. Rewards are then decided upon and proffered to the child on performance of approximate behaviors. The rewards are generally scheduled so they are offered on a systematic basis: 100 percent, 50 percent, 33⅓ percent, 25 percent, 10 percent, or on some timed basis. Each reward schedule tends to generate a different learning rate. Behavior standards are then raised until the approximate behaviors are no longer rewarded (they extinguish), and the exact desired behavior is elicited. Reward conditions are then varied until the child performs the desired act in a stable manner.

In the classroom, the technique may not be quite so precise, but it is nonetheless effective. There are three essential principles that must be followed: (1) the child must be given a suitable task to perform; (2) the child must be presented meaningful rewards for successful performance; and (3) the teacher must decide upon the appropriate degree of structure that will be imposed.[24]

The operant process has been called "precision teaching" by Lindsley because it is concerned with the development or diminishing of specific behaviors or specific rates of behaviors.[25] To accomplish this behavior control, it is necessary to follow a three-step procedure: (1) pinpointing the behavior; (2) recording the rate at which the behavior occurs; and (3) consequating the behavior.

"Pinpointing" refers to identifying the elements in the behavior chain in order to decide the precise behavior that is to be increased or decreased. This may be any act in the chain, but the process is usually more effective if the behavior at the beginning of the habit chain is controlled. In the elimination of cigarette smoking for instance, the chain starts with reaching for a cigarette, removing one from the pack, putting it in the mouth, searching for a light, lighting the light, igniting the cigarette, breathing in, removing the cigarette from the mouth, inhaling, exhaling, and so forth. The elimination of any crucial act in the chain breaks the sequence. However, residual acts

[24] F. Hewett, "Teaching Reading to an Autistic Boy through Operant Conditioning," *The Reading Teacher*, XVII (1964), 613–618.

[25] O. R. Lindsley, "Direct Measurement and Prosthesis of Retarded Behavior," *Journal of Education*, CXLVII (1964), 62–81.

in the chain may persist even after the habit of smoking has been stopped (for example, searching the pockets for cigarettes). Eliminating the "reaching" part of the chain effectively stops the sequence, and tends to eliminate other acts in the chain because they do not act as stimuli for the next act. This seems to be more effective than simply not smoking by not carrying cigarettes. Stopping smoking is certainly no easier than teaching retarded children. Elimination of the smoking habit requires concentrated and systematic efforts clearly consistent with the desired goal. This is inherent in behavior modification techniques. Haphazard effort is not effective and must be so recognized.

Recording behavior may take many forms, but the most reliable system appears to be counting the rate at which the behavior occurs. Establishing the rate makes it possible to evaluate the progress being made in increasing or decreasing behavior by making a count and comparing the rate with the original rate. No elaborate statistics are necessary—just counting and comparing.

Consequating is the procedure of providing an appropriate reward or punishment (consequence) immediately contiguous to the act. This must be done in a consistent manner or according to a prearranged schedule, or else the pinpointing and recording are for naught. Rewards (consequences) should be tangible and of importance to the child. A smile, nod, or appropriate comment may be sufficient; or candy, tokens, money, prizes, free time, desired activity or something else may be used. Rewards are highly individual and should reflect the standards of the child rather than the good intentions of the teacher. It is important to vary the reward conditions so that the child will progress from concrete reinforcers, to symbolic reinforcers, to intermittent reinforcers, to delayed gratification. Consistency, however, is the key to successful behavior control. Suppose, for example, the teacher is blessed with a child who does not attend to the task of reading. In this example, the immediately desired behavior is that of paying attention. The reward conditions may be in the form of giving such items as candy, money, tokens, or prizes, or allowing the child free time to pursue activities he enjoys (high probability behavior reward).[26] The teacher could record the time during which the child sits still at his desk. A candy reward might then be proffered to the child for five seconds of sitting still. This may then be increased to ten

---

[26] Lloyd E. Homme, "Human Motivation and Environment," University of Kansas Symposium, "The Learning Environment: Relationship to Behavior Modification and Implications for Special Education," *Kansas Studies in Education*, University of Kansas Publications, School of Education, 16, (June 1966).

seconds, then sixty seconds, five minutes, ten minutes, through thirty minutes. Generally about two weeks of this kind of instruction, given daily, will be sufficient to stabilize the behavior of paying attention. The technique is uncomplicated, but it is highly specific and does not provide for generalization of behavior, unless this is also systematically programmed.

Contingency management is a derivative of the operant conditioning procedure in behavior modification. On the surface contingency management resembles the operant procedure, but with a very important difference. In operant conditioning the kind, magnitude, and frequency of the reward is decided by the teacher or behavior modifier. In contingency management, the person whose behavior is being changed participates in those decisions. He must agree to the performance that will qualify him for the reward and also to the suitability of the rewards. It is perhaps because of this participatory aspect that the technique has received such widespread acceptance, because from an efficiency point of view the two techniques appear to be equally effective. Also, the rewards can be accumulated and awarded all at once because the person whose behavior is being changed is aware of what they are and when they will be awarded. This, of course, considerably reduces the clerical duties that attend the usual operant conditioning procedures.

Individual Programs of Instruction

The development of a program of instruction based on the learning style of an individual borrows from the pinpointing part of the technique of operant conditioning, but goes considerably beyond that in describing the conditions involved. While observation of behavior is fundamental to the technique, some of the observations are made through the medium of standardized or criterion tests.

The technique starts with a determination of the level of skill of the child. This can be determined by an achievement test of some kind that not only identifies what the child is able to do, but compares his performance with other children. If, for example, the child can recognize some words, but is unable to use phonics to sound out unfamiliar words in order to read them, it can safely be inferred that his level of skill is at least first-grade level, but below typical second graders. The evaluation of this fact is generally first related to age and experience. If the child is six years old and attending first grade, his achievement level is consistent with both age and experience. However, if the child is quite bright, he could still be an under-achiever relative to his mental age level. That is, a child of six with an IQ of 150 would have a mental age of about nine (6 × 150/100 = 9.0) or the equivalent of a beginning fourth grader in school. Since his achievement is equal to that of a first-grade child, he would not be doing as well as might be expected. The alerting symptoms of problems are nearly always tied to achievement skills significantly lower than the age, experience, and mental age would indicate to be reasonable for this child. The determination of the mental level is necessary to a judgment of whether the child is intellectually mature enough to have been able to understand the concepts or relationships involved in the achievement test.

If the child has the age, ability, and opportunity to have learned, but did not, then the search may turn to other variables that block learning. Sensory acuity is one area in need of assessment, for problems in either hearing or vision can seriously interfere with learning. Likewise, lack of sensory perceptual skill can have the same effect as sensory acuity problems, for in either case, inaccurate, impaired or distorted sensory cues are provided to guide the child in his learning. Finally, a determination of his experience background to determine whether he has the prerequisite language, manipulation, or familiarity skills to be able to function at the level consistent with his age and ability.

Tests used to help make these observations are those which assess achievement, capacity, sensory acuity, perception, psycholinguistics, and language. Representative ones are listed below. The information furnished by the observations and test results can then be put to use in developing the individual program of instruction (IPI). These are set in behavioral terms and are similar to the outcomes provided in this book, but may be even more specific than those listed.

I. GENERAL ABILITY
   A. Peabody Picture Vocabulary Test—Range: 2.5 to 18 years; approximately 15 minutes to administer; consists of a word pronounced by the examiner that the child identifies by pointing to a picture that illustrates the word; requires only a pointing response; especially good for nonverbal children.
   B. Raven (Coloured Progressive Matrices)—Range: 5 to 11 years; approximately 30 minutes to administer; individual or group administration; this is a nonverbal, perceptual test of observation and clear thinking. It consists of colored designs in which a part is missing; 6 possible missing parts are presented from which the child picks the correct one.
   C. Slosson Intelligence Test—Range: 2 weeks to adult; individual

test. Based primarily on both the Stanford-Binet and the Gesell Developmental Schedules, it uses mostly observation, verbal problems, and vocabulary.

D. Stanford-Binet Intelligence Scale—Range: 2 years to superior adult; administration time depends on person tested, because only portions of the test are given to each person. Since the items are arranged by chronological age, the difficulty of the item answered reflects the mental maturity of the child.

E. Wechsler tests—Probe information, comprehension, vocabulary, similarities arithmetic, design interpretations, picture sequences, picture completion, object assembly, coding, and mazes.

   1. Wechsler Preschool and Primary Scale of Intelligence— Range: 4 to 6.5 years; individual; approximately 50 minutes to administer; verbal and performance subtests.

   2. Wechsler Intelligence Scale for Children—Range: 5 years to 15 years 11 months; individual; 40 to 60 minutes to administer; verbal and performance subtests similar to the other Wechsler tests.

   3. Wechsler Adult Intelligence Scales—Range: 16 years and over; test length varies considerably; verbal and performance subtests similar to other Wechsler tests.

II. ACHIEVEMENT TESTS

A. Gates Mc Ginity—Range: grades 1 to 12 in 6 levels measuring vocabulary, comprehension, speed, and accuracy. Time for administration is from 15 to 60 minutes depending on level.

B. Grays Oral—Range: grades 1 through 16 and adults; individual; designed to assess oral reading skills and aid in diagnosing reading difficulties.

C. Key Math Diagnostic Test—Range: preschool to junior high school. Consists of arithmetic problems in a hierarchy of difficulty so process and application difficulties can be accurately diagnosed; about 15 to 20 minutes to administer.

D. Peabody Individual Achievement Test—Range: kindergarten through grade 12; individual; approximately 30 to 40 minutes to administer; scores in math, reading recognition, reading comprehension, spelling, general information, and total.

E. Wide Range Achievement Test—Range: Level I—5 to 11 years; Level II—12 years to adult; approximately 20 to 30 minutes to administer; diagnosis of reading, spelling, and arithmetic abilities.

III. PSYCHOLINGUISTICS TEST

A. Illinois Test of Psycholinguistic Abilities—Range: 2 to 10 years; purpose—to test the receiving, processing, and relating of information from the environment through the auditory, visual, and motor and vocal channels; useful for identifying areas in need of further examination; approximately 45 to 60 minutes to administer.

IV. VISUAL EFFICIENCY TESTS
 A. Keystone Telebinocular—Range: 5 years and over; individual; tests of simultaneous perception, vertical posture, lateral posture, fusion, usable vision, depth perception, and color perception.
 B. Spache (Binocular Reading Test)—Ranges: nonreaders and grade 1, grades 1.5 to 2, and grades 3 and over; individual; test of eye preference in reading and ability to use the eyes together.

V. AUDITORY EFFICIENCY TESTS
 A. Wepman (Language Modalities Test for Aphasia)—Range: 5 years to adult; individual; approximately 10 to 15 minutes in 1 session; purpose—to test the ability to comprehend verbal symbols to detect likeness and differences in word structure.

VI. MOTOR TESTS
 A. Lincoln-Oseretsky Motor Development Scale—Range: 6 to 14 years; individual; approximately 30 to 60 minutes to administer; purpose—to test motor ability in activities from gross to fine coordination.
 B. Purdue Perceptual Motor Survey—Range: 6 to 10 years; individual; approximately 20 minutes to administer; purpose—to identify those children lacking the perceptual-motor abilities related to directionality, laterality, coordination, ocular pursuit, and spacial orientation.

VII. LANGUAGE TESTS
 A. Berry-Talbot Language Tests (Comprehension of Grammar)—Range: 5 to 8 years; exploratory test of linguistic structure; assesses: (a) the plural and the two possessives of the noun; (b) the third person singular of the verb; (c) the progressive and the past tense; and (d) the comparative and superlative of the adjective; teacher administered; can be included as a daily exercise.
 B. Myklebust (Picture-Story Language Test)—Range: primary grades through high school; purpose—a diagnostic tool for the appraisal of language development; assesses vocabulary, sentence length, paragraph length, and abstract level of context of story.
 C. Englemann (Basic Concept Inventory)—Range: children beginning academic tasks with upper limit 10 years; purpose—to evaluate

the instruction given in certain beginning academically related concepts, exclusive and inclusive words, polar opposites, and reasoning.

In developing an IPI, it is important to distinguish between goals and objectives. A goal is a general statement of the purpose of instruction, which encompasses at least three behavioral objectives or specific statements of behavior. For example, the goal may be to teach the child to use phonics for word attack. The behavioral objectives that lead to the goal start at the point identified by the achievement test as the top performance level of the child. Each objective proceeds sequentially from that point until the last objective is reached and the goal achieved.

Behavioral objectives specify: (1) the outcome; (2) the content or conditions; and (3) the criteria used to determine when the outcome has been reached. Usually the outcome is specified in verb form and deals with identifying, naming, describing, constructing, sequencing, or something similar, which specifies that the learner is doing something as a result of instruction. The content or conditions specify what is used or how it is to be done, and the criteria describe the level of performance that signifies when success has been achieved. What is required to put all this together can be demonstrated in an analysis of what is involved when a child is asked to draw a geometric square. It seems a simple task, so much so that any four-year-old child is usually expected to be able to draw one without much difficulty.

To be successful, however, a great many things must be done. First of all . . .

There are several basic *physical* requirements. He should be able to sit and hold his head up, move the muscles of his arms and hands, and hold a pencil or crayon. He must be able to see and move his eyes.

Second, in the *perceptual* area, he must accurately perceive and interpret the form he is to copy. He must perceive the way that the parts—two vertical and two horizontal lines—are related into a single meaningful whole figure. He must then be able to translate the whole figure he sees into a motor response that is created, piece by piece, in a series over time.

Third, to make an adequate *motor* response, he must be able to coordinate the movements of fingers, hand, and arm with accuracy. He must be able to control his left and right arms and hands in independent operations; he must be able to cross the midline of his body in making the horizontal stroke without rotating his body or the paper; he must be able to start, stop, and change direction of movement appropriately at the corners of the square.

Fourth, as he performs, visual information must be integrated with and guide motor response so that eye and hand are *coordinated*. As his hand moves, he must make visual comparisons between his own *partial* performance and the complete model in terms of the relationship of parts-to-the-whole, relative size, shape, and orientation on the page. This visual comparison must be a continuous process. He must then be able to *modify* his response, based on the feedback he gets from this updating of information as he performs. For instance, if one angle of his square is too sharp, he must compensate in the length of one side or in some other angle.

Finally, and probably first rather than last, throughout the performance he must be able to maintain focus on the task at hand, not being distracted by sounds, movements, stray marks, or other inappropriate stimuli surrounding him.[27]

In this particular example, the goal is to have the child draw a square. The observation of the child's performance takes place when the child is instructed to draw a square. The IPI will depend upon the point at which the child fails in his drawing effort. If, for instance, the child is unable to draw 90-degree corners, then the IPI would start at that point. The specific objectives might state that "given paper, pencil, and a flat square, the child will draw one-directional 90-degree angles that do not deviate from the model by more than 15 degrees in any direction." The method for achieving this objective would then need to specify just how the instruction would proceed. This could assume almost an infinite variety of methods and materials, but would most likely employ tracing concrete materials, then progressing to free-hand drawing of the angles. The next objective might specify that "given paper, pencil, and a flat square, the child will draw 90-degree angles in any of the orientations in space; left, right, and upside down." Again this may involve any number of instructional techniques but more than likely would start with concrete and then move to semi-abstract or abstract materials. Finally, the child might be asked to put together all the lines and angles involved in drawing a square and the goal would be achieved. Typically enroute objectives must be mastered in sequence to reach the terminal objective or instructional goal.

It should be apparent that operant conditioning and individual programs of instruction are far from mutually exclusive. Indeed some people seem to treat them as synonymous. The chief difference be-

[27] From *Approaches to Learning* (Boston: Teaching Resources Corporation, 1972).

tween them, however, is the broader instructional options open to IPI prescriptions. Operant conditioning has many more limiting features, but used together they can become powerful aids to individualizing instruction. Both become indispensable techniques for teacher-consultants and/or resource room teachers.

Units of instruction are a series of learning experiences organized around a central theme or problem area. The subject to be studied generally comes from some aspect of the life experience of the child, such as those mentioned in Part III of this book. Once the theme has been identified, learning experiences that will integrate oral, listening, reading and writing skills, arithmetic facts and processes, time, money and measurement, social skills, health and safety skills, esthetics, motor and recreational skills, and vocational competencies are included in the unit. The technique is described in detail in Part III. To be used effectively, however, the classroom teacher must be in control of the curriculum. This does not necessarily imply that the technique can only be used in a self-contained classroom. On the contrary, no more than an hour or two per day is required, but the program must be seen as a developmental one. It in no way lends itself to tutorial or remedial emphasis.

Classroom Management

The psychological phenomenon of identification is also an effective method for effecting behavior change. Identification refers to the process that leads a child to think, feel, and behave as though the characteristics of another person or group (model) belong to him. Although identification with a model seems to imply that it must be a conscious one, it is often quite unconscious. That is, the child may be quite unaware that he identifies at all. However, two conditions must obtain for identification to occur: first, the child must want to possess some of the attributes of the model; and second, the child must have some basis for believing that he and the model are alike in some way.

Although identification has been studied mostly with children, it seems to be a universal phenomenon that persists throughout life, even though the models change.[28] While the initial models are probably parents, models for more mature persons may be groups, peers, celebrities, institutions, or representatives of institutions, such as football teams.

Classroom use of identification may take a variety of forms. Gen-

[28] See Paul H. Mussen, John J. Conger, and Jerome Kagan, *Child Development and Personality*, 2d ed. (New York: Harper & Row, Publishers, 1963).

erally, however, the child must wish to possess some characteristic of the model—power, reward, nurturance, or privilege—before he will accept the model for identification purposes. The teacher may call attention to these characteristics by simply recognizing them. Second, the child must feel that he is like the model in some way. This also can be accomplished by verbal comment on similarities. Since identification often may be an unconscious process, frequent reiteration of the characteristics desired and the similarities observed between the child and the model may often be enough to initiate imitative behavior of the desired type.

It is possible that identification is a much more powerful factor than is usually recognized. If behavior is the result of plans developed from incongruity between incoming stimuli and the expectations of an organism, then it seems entirely possible that identification actually provides a plan of behavior for the child perceived as a way of reducing his discomfort, resulting from inappropriate behavior in the classroom. The teacher therefore is an available model with whom a child can identify. Similarly, stabilized behavior developing from operant techniques requires self-regard on the part of the child. His expectancies for feeling good (reward) must be internalized so that behavior which is desired in the classroom is the kind of behavior for which he rewards himself. His standards or expectancies become consistent with his behavior. Since no incongruity exists between his expectancies and his behavior, the behavior is appropriately adaptive. Since the goals of the special program involve competent self-management both in his living and working, the establishment of appropriate values for self-reward become paramount issues for attention by the special class teacher.

There is a clear implication in the foregoing that such techniques cannot operate effectively in a classroom environment that is too permissive. The theoretical base of this book is subjective behaviorism. Behavior, therefore, depends upon realistic perceptions and concepts, and well-developed thought processes. These cannot be developed in an atmosphere of disorder and confusion. The knowledges and behaviors to be learned must be ordered, precise, and sequential, and the child must be controlled in his responses until such time as he can exercise the required self-management activities for appropriate adaptive behavior. A punitive environment is not conducive to learning, nor is a chaotic one. But a controlled, regulated, and rewarding environment is required, and it is the responsibility of the teacher to provide this. One learns who he is and what he can do by interaction with his environment. It is the task of a teacher to provide the media for this interaction through task accomplishment with materials and experiences that are meaningful, goal-oriented, and at a level and in a manner consistent with the maturity level and the learning characteristics of the developing child. This requires both system and control.

A work-oriented classroom lends itself to orderliness much better than a play-oriented classroom does, for several reasons.[29] First, it is easy for the children to understand that there is a purpose for being in school—to learn. This is a much easier concept to grasp than for them to figure out that all the games they play are really designed to teach them something in a subtle and painless fashion. Second, rules can be simple and direct. Many children have difficulty in distinguishing between appropriate and inappropriate behavior when they do not know the purpose of the activity. Enthusiasm for the game may be appropriate in playing the game, but the things to be learned may be interfered with, just by enthusiasm. The conflicting goals can be most confusing if the teacher rewards the children for enthusiasm in one instance and punishes them for not learning in the same activity. Third, feedback on performance standards is more meaningful when the criterion is unambiguous. If the child knows what he is supposed to do, a "no" response from the teacher clearly indicates he has not performed in a satisfactory manner. Without a clear notion of what is expected, "no" may either refer to his unsatisfactory performance, his personal inadequacy, or his teacher's displeasure. Such confusion is often the basis for extensive dependency or failure-avoiding behavior observed among many retarded children.[30] Fourth, rewarding and punishing can be kept objective. If the child is expected to accomplish something and is rewarded for succeeding, or if the reward is withheld when he does not succeed, the teacher is only the administrator. She is not judging him personally, only the adequacy of his performance. In no sense does the teacher "buy" his cooperation. The child by his own effort earns a reward, or does not. Fifth, one of the goals of the total program is to establish an accomplishment motive in each child. Systematic rewards for behavior that meet established standards are possible only when the children know what is expected. Sixth, because of the general inefficiency of the learning of retarded youngsters, there is time only to concentrate on those elements which are judged to be most relevant to their well-being. It does not seem reasonable to be selective of content because of time pressures and then waste that precious time in meaningless activity.

[29] Carl Bereiter and Siegfried Englemann, *Teaching Disadvantaged Children in the Preschool* (Englewood Cliffs, N.J.: Prentice-Hall, Inc., 1966).

[30] See Rue Cromwell, "A Social Learning Approach to Mental Retardation," in Norman R. Ellis (ed.), *Handbook of Mental Deficiency* (New York: McGraw-Hill, Inc., 1963).

Given a work-oriented classroom, the climate is maintained through both punishment and reward. Put differently, the consequences of the child's behavior give him information as to whether the behavior has adaptive validity. Providing this feedback information in an unmistakable manner is the responsibility of the teacher. To be effective, the communication must be direct, immediate, and understandable to the child. In short, rewards must give visceral pleasure and punishment must hurt. In all instances, positive rewards are to be preferred to punishment, but there are instances where punishment can and should be used. Bereiter and Engelmann have detailed the place of punishment in a preschool program.[31] In a briefer version:

1. Physical punishment should be used only to enforce clearly stated instructional rules.
2. Physical punishment should be used when a child's behavior is unthinking and automatic. Quick response to this kind of behavior in the form of a slap or a good shaking serves to arrest the unthinking behavior of the child as well as to demonstrate that the teacher will do whatever is necessary to preserve order.
3. Isolation from the group, activity, and room seems to be a better control for more "calculated" behavior. Clowning, pouting, and refusing to participate call for a punishment that provides no reinforcement. A single warning followed by isolation serves this purpose very well. One further caution, the isolation should be unpleasant: sitting in a bare closet—not too well lighted and with a hard chair— for a few minutes often works well.
4. Behavior rules should be enforced in a matter-of-fact way. Do not coax. Coaxing appeals to whether or not a child wants to participate. The children should learn that they are expected to take part or obey the rules. Whether they want to or not is irrelevant.
5. To make the work-oriented classroom functional, rewards must follow the efforts of the children. The children should be rewarded for trying. Edible rewards such as cookies are excellent reinforcers. Again, the cookie is given for trying and is accompanied by smiles, nods, patting on the back, hand shaking, and any other demonstrations of approval. These accompanying demonstrations are calculated to become secondary reinforcers. In time, they are expected to replace the edibles. The time sequence starts with immediate rewards for trying. After a month or so, the rewards may be delayed for a short time. For example, "John, that was fine. You will get a cookie at juice time." Delayed gratification can be eliminated except for intermittent reinforcement when it is clear that the secondary reinforcers are working. Ultimately

[31] Bereiter and Englemann, *Teaching Disadvantaged Children in the Preschool*, pp. 78–91.

the children must provide their own reinforcement, but this is apt to be many years away from the cookie reinforcers. It seems the better part of prudence to have an adequate budget to provide a lot of edibles for a long period of time, but the teacher should move from immediate to delayed gratification as soon as possible.

6. Generally, the troublesome child will respond to isolation, and the indifferent child, to punishment, or withheld rewards if he does not try. The withdrawn child, however, needs protection and consistent reinforcement. Often the teacher will have to depend upon peer support and single out his contribution to the group effort for rewarding. His emergence as an individual may take a long time. Patience is a virtue in this situation. A single disastrous attempt at emergence may send the child back into his nonparticipating cocoon. Quiet praise and obvious pleasure with his tentative attempts at participation seem the best strategies.

Learning Paradigm

Throughout the entire program the teacher is seen as the manager. What should be accomplished in the program is identified by the twin goals of independent living and work competence and detailed as instructional outcomes in each area, through five developmental levels. The following chapters suggest methods and materials appropriate to achieving the outcomes. Teaching, however, is the key to accomplishment.

Stimulus Presentation

Many discussions of good teaching have centered upon what the teacher does to facilitate learning. It is properly contended that a teacher does not "teach" anybody anything. A teacher arranges conditions that allow people to learn. To explain this process, a learning paradigm of the S-R variety has been used. Classical behaviorists have tended to explain teaching as the management of the stimuli presented to the child. This has been extensively studied and discussed in terms of frequency, intensity, relevance, and a host of other variables.

Mediation

Phenomenologists have generally interjected a mediational system between the stimuli and the response which plays a selective or screening role with both the stimuli and response. Motives, feelings, and self-concepts, which are all highly personal, have been assigned mediational values that account for both style and performance differences between different people and groups of people.

Response Control

Those theorists who have studied operant conditioning techniques have essentially concentrated on manipulating responses through reinforcement as a means of effecting behavior modification.

Subjective Behaviorism as a Teaching Model

In essence, attending to different parts of the S-R paradigm defines different roles for the teacher to play and may have contributed to the present state of confusion over what a good teacher does and should do. In the behaviorist framework, a good teacher concentrates on controlling the stimuli presented. In the phenomenological scheme, a good teacher is concerned with the feelings and understandings of the child. In operant conditioning, the good teacher is an expert at consequating responses. It is the thesis of this writing that good teaching can be explained somewhat more understandably through the subjective behaviorism theory of Miller, Galanter, and Pribram. If behavior depends upon the evaluation by the organism of the incoming stimuli for congruity with his standards—and this includes an evaluation of the effect of his behavior—then a good teacher must pay attention to the stimuli presented, the manner in which the child mediates the stimuli, and the effective reinforcing of relevant responses. This means that a good teacher must select material that is consistent with the level of understanding of the students and then arrange the material in a sequential manner for presentation. The learning environment must be such that the proper stimulus cues are readily identified by the child, and the reinforcing of correct responses must be meaningful and consistent.[32]

The following chapters which deal with instruction in the various areas will treat all of the aspects of the learning paradigm: stimuli presentation, mediational processes, and response reinforcement. Whenever possible, materials that fit this total S-R paradigm are recommended.

[32] See Leon Charney and Edward LaCrosse, *The Teacher of the Mentally Retarded* (New York: John Day Company, Inc., 1965), pp. 1–70, for an excellent description of good teaching.

Part II

METHODS AND MATERIALS

CHAPTER *4*

Communication Skills

Perhaps no single area of skills is of greater importance to the process of adapting than that of communication. Nearly all civilized living depends upon our degree of success in this area. Indeed, interpersonal disruptions are often explained as a breakdown in communication.

Included in this area are skills of oral communication, written communication, listening, and reading. Each is a vital skill and thus requires specific instructional attention. Yet all are interrelated and so may be treated together. More fundamentally, the skills have both mechanical and dynamic aspects. That is, not only must the skills be taught as skills, but the use of the skills in adaptive behavior must also be practiced by the retarded learner. Each of the subareas has a developmental sequence and each level of development is related to the others. Although the subareas are treated separately, this is only for convenience in discussion.

Oral Communication

The function of oral communication in our culture has been described by Jordan as: (1) communication; (2) behavior control; and

(3) the medium for thought.[1] Adequate communication between people requires a common set of verbal symbols, a common set of referents for the symbols, and a common set of sounds to represent the symbols and referents. The task of the teacher is to help each child to learn the words, grammar, meanings, and correct speech sounds appropriate for each developmental level and to provide practice in using these skills for communication, behavior control, and thinking. To expedite this task, the outcomes for each level are that:

PRESCHOOL LEVEL
1. Given a verbal question, the child can say first and last name.
2. Given a verbal question, the child can say his/her age.
3. Given a verbal question, the child can say his house number and street name.
4. Given a verbal question, the child can say his home city and state.
5. Upon request, the child can formulate a verbal affirmative statement, e.g. this is a ball.
6. Upon request, the child can formulate a verbal negative statement, e.g. this is not a book.
7. Given a one-word cue, the child can identify polar opposites; e.g. big–little.
8. Given one end of a verbal proposition, the child can make simple deductions, e.g. if this is big, then it is not little.
9. Given a cue of one part of a statement, the child can formulate alternative statements, e.g. you may go or you may stay.

PRIMARY LEVEL
1. Returning from a field trip, the child can state five things he has seen.
2. Given a set of objects or pictures of five fruits, vegetables, people, or animals, the child will be able to name them correctly.
3. Given a call on the telephone, the child can answer correctly and sustain a simple conversation.
4. Upon request, the child can formulate a meaningful four-word sentence.

INTERMEDIATE LEVEL
1. When asked to relate specific incidents, the child can reply in clear and understandable speech.
2. The student uses complete sentences of five words or more in informal conversation with his peers.
3. When asked to make a formal introduction of a student to another student, or a student to an adult, the child makes a correct presentation.

[1] Thomas E. Jordan, *The Exceptional Child* (Columbus, Ohio: Charles E. Merrill Books, Inc., 1962), Chap. 5.

4. When asked to make an announcement to the class, the student can make the announcement in clear and precise speech.
5. When presented with a task, the student will ask for help on the details he does not understand.
6. When asked by the teacher, the student can give simple directions to the: fire exit; principal's office; rest room; library; cafeteria; gymnasium; nurse's office.
7. Given a telephone or pay telephone, the student can: call home; call the operator; call the fire station; call the police; call an ambulance.

PREVOCATIONAL LEVEL
1. When presented with the task of criticizing another student's oral expression, the student will be able to state at least one strength and one weakness.
2. When called upon to make a report to the class, the student can demonstrate his ability to organize his thoughts and present them in an understandable manner.
3. In a group meeting, the student demonstrates a knowledge of simple parliamentary procedure as a participant.
4. In a group meeting, the student demonstrates a knowledge of simple parliamentary procedure by properly conducting the meeting.
5. Given a telephone, the student can demonstrate proper etiquette in answering, taking messages, leaving messages, and making long distance calls.

VOCATIONAL LEVEL
1. Given a list of items, the student can place an order for the items.
2. Given an interview, the student can correctly respond to questions of identification, experience, and qualifications for a job.
3. When questioned about a job with which he is familiar, the student uses vocabulary appropriate to the equipment and the job.
4. Given a social situation, the student participates in the conversation using the appropriate vocabulary and responses to other participants' comments.
5. Given a real or simulated need for household repairs, student can demonstrate the ability to contact the proper artisan, clearly explain the nature of the problem, and negotiate the proper time, place, and responsibilities of the repair.

The language development of mentally retarded children has been extensively studied. Jordan[2] and Spradlin[3] have provided excellent

[2] Thomas E. Jordan, *The Mentally Retarded*, 2d ed. (Columbus, Ohio: Charles E. Merrill Books, Inc., 1966), Chap. 5.

[3] Joseph E. Spradlin, "Language and Communication of Mental Defectives," in Norman R. Ellis (ed.), *Handbook of Mental Deficiency* (New York: McGraw-Hill, Inc.), 1963.

reviews. The research is consistent in indicating that language develops slowly, that grammar and syntax are poorly used, that improper speech sounds are common, and that meaning is poverty stricken.

Bereiter and Englemann have suggested that undifferentiated auditory perceptions lead to the "giant word syndrome." They describe the giant word syndrome as combined oral sounds which are used to express affectional needs and wants, but which do not lend themselves to cognitive thought processes. "I want to go home," for example, is expressed as a single, oral, giant word, "Iwantagohome." The lack of differentiation between words is unimportant when the message is affectional, but seriously interferes with the precision function of language so necessary for cognitive thought. To detect this lack of precision in the use of language, Englemann has developed a Cognitive Maturity Test. The following is an abridged version of the Englemann Cognitive Maturity Test:

A. Have the child repeat the statement, then ask the question.
  1. Puppies are baby dogs.
     What are puppies?
  2. A big truck is not a little truck.
     Is a big truck a little truck?
  3. Babies eat and cry.
     Do they eat? Do they cry?
  4. She ate the pie because she was hungry.
     Why did she eat the pie?
  5. He got the wood so he could build a fire.
     What did he get?
  6. There were many cars going to the city.
     Where were many cars going?
  7. It is in the box.
     Is it in the box?
B. Present the following:
  1. (Examiner shakes his head, "No.")
     This means "no."
     (Examiner nods his head, "Yes.")
     What does this mean?
  2. (Examiner claps.)
     What am I doing?
     (Examiner walks.)
     What am I doing?
  3. Do what I say:
     Hold up your hands.
     Touch your ear.
     Hold up your hand.
     Touch your ears.

Scoring the test is a simple matter of counting the number of correct responses made by each child. The children may then be grouped with other children who make a similar number and the same kind of incorrect responses. As was indicated in Chapter 3, the program at the preschool level provided a specific language-training period for 30 minutes each day. In this period it is recommended that the Peabody Language Development Kit be the central materials used.

The Peabody Language Development Kits consist of four levels of work, each designed for one year of instruction. The materials were developed by Lloyd M. Dunn and James O. Smith, in cooperation with a large number of teachers who tried the lessons and materials in experimental classes, prior to inclusion in the kits. The program represented is compatible with the learning paradigm presented in Chapter 3. The stimulus materials have been carefully selected for intensity, contrast, and sequence. The lessons are designed to teach the thought processes of memory, cognition, convergence, divergence, and evaluation. The responses are reinforced both by tokens and by praise. Thus the lessons are designed to attend to stimulus presentation, mediation, and response reinforcement in a sequential and systematic manner. This is in keeping with the thesis that effective teaching must be grounded on a sound theoretical bedrock. The materials and lessons are practical in that they teach language skills in a sequential manner consistent with the learning levels of the youngsters and in harmony with the desired outcomes specified in the outcomes list presented in this chapter.

Each kit contains a detailed teacher's manual with 180 daily lessons—one for each day in the school year. In Kit 1, for example, are 430, 7 by 9-inch stimulus cards arranged in categories of activity, animals, clothing, colors, fruit and vegetables, food, household items, numbers, people, toys, transportation, "I Wonder," and miscellaneous cards of common things and shapes. These cards are numbered to provide for easy selection for the daily sessions. Six large story cards designed to elicit stories, and four large "I Wonder" cards designed to stimulate creative imagination, complete the stimulus materials. In addition, 350 interlocking plastic chips (35 each of 10 different colors) to teach colors, motor skills, sequencing, and memory and which can be used for reinforcement are also used. Two soft hand puppets, "Peabo" (Peabody), and "Telsie" (Tell and See), provide for motivation and are especially effective for withdrawn and distractable youngsters. The authors recommend the use of a tape recorder for use in the lessons and include a tape that contains six favorite fairy tales suitable for developing listening skills.

Each lesson in the manual lists the materials needed and then describes the activities covered—for example, listening, brainstorming, vocabulary building, following directions, and listening again—with a paragraph of detailed instruction for both the teacher and the children for each activity. Kit 1 teaches 23 different language areas: activity, brainstorming, classification, conversation, critical thinking, describing, dramatization, following directions, guessing, identification, listening, looking, memory, pantomime, patterning, rhyming, speech, speed-up, story, touching, and vocabulary building, repeating them many times, ranging from a minimum of seven times to a maximum of 63. Thus virtually all of the language development skills are presented with adequate opportunity for overlearning, without the usual attendant boredom of drill.

The other three kits follow the same format as Kit 1: Kit P (Preschool) precedes Kit 1, and Kits 2 and 3 follow.[4] Although many teachers may wish to develop their own materials for language skills, the completeness, soundness, and practicality of the Peabody Kits recommend them for use even by highly skilled teachers for the pre-primary language program. Furthermore, with the sound basis provided by the Peabody materials, the formal language development program may be partially discontinued above the primary level to allow more time for reading and writing activities. Unit work with experience charts serves as adequate media for reinforcing and extending the language training began at the preschool level and has the advantage of providing for language development in the context of social utility.

At the primary level, it is important that the language foundations be directed to the enlargement of the vocabulary of the youngsters, the use of meaningful sounds such as prefixes, suffixes, and word endings, and the ordering of words to determine meaning. These are referred to respectively, as lexical, morphological, and syntactical uses of language, and they constitute the basic skills necessary for successful later academic work.

Lexical practice, for example, becomes meaningless unless the words being learned have some experience association for the child. No amount of practice in repeating, spelling, or recognizing the letter configurations will help in vocabulary enlargement if the word itself has no experience referent (meaning) to the child. Thus, talking about experiences, things, plans, and the like with new words being added as they occur in the ordinary discussion have this meaning relationship

---

[4] The Peabody Language Development Kits are available from the American Guidance Service, Publishers Building, Circle Pines, Minn. 55014.

so necessary to learning. Likewise, morphemes related to word tense, such as prefix beginnings of words or suffix endings of words, are meaningful because they are used in context. Syntax can be emphasized by word games and puns in which word meaning is determined by where the word occurs in a sentence. Having the child supply missing words to complete a meaningful statement when one letter at a time is furnished as a clue, is one way of teaching syntax. For example, "always behind" could be completed by the word "caboose." While the example may be a little far out, the principle and procedure illustrated are practical and vital.

At the prevocational and vocational levels, group discussions, projects, field trips, movies, and TV shows can provide the stimulus for the oral activities. Of particular worth are formal word study periods where the new words introduced have not only vocational but social relevance as well. There seems to be no reason why some history, cultural enrichment, or moral teaching cannot be surreptitiously tied to the study of words themselves. It is a rather painless way to broaden the knowledge base of the youngster.

Listening Skills

Auditory perceptions not only are the means through which people constantly monitor the state of the world, but they also are the building blocks upon which written symbols take on the meaning that makes reading a reality. To many retarded children, sounds do not become well differentiated because the child is flooded with auditory noises so he learns *not* to hear those which have no immediate relevance to him. Listening skills involve auditory discrimination, auditory memory, auditory sequencing, and auditory closure in the beginning instructional program. At later stages of development, the child must learn to identify selectively those sounds which are important, and to interpret the message intended by the speaker. This involves much more than just paying attention. It involves reorganizing and synthesizing those sounds into a related group of meanings that have relevance for the child himself. The outcomes of good listening skills to be developed at each level are:

PRESCHOOL LEVEL
1. After having heard a story or song, the child can tell the name, gist, or theme.
2. Given the following verbal commands to: close, open, hands-up, put

on, take off, put away, take out, in reference to a particular object, the child will complete the command.
3. After the teacher presents two rhythm patterns, the child will identify whether they are similar or different.
4. Given a rhythm pattern of tapping, the child will be able to reproduce it by tapping on his desk.
5. The child responds correctly to words like "stop," "go," and "look out."

PRIMARY LEVEL
1. Given four words, the student will be able to repeat them.
2. Given two directions, the student will be able to follow them.
3. Given a short message, the student will be able to restate the main points correctly.

INTERMEDIATE LEVEL
1. Given one line of a two-line rhyme, the student will be able to finish the next line with a rhyming word.
2. Given the short vowel sounds, the student will accurately associate each with the correct letter.
3. Given three words, the student will correctly identify two that start with the same sound.
4. Given the individual sounds of a four-sound word, the student will correctly identify the whole word.

PREVOCATIONAL LEVEL
1. After listening to a story, the student will be able to retell the story in his own words.
2. Given a record to listen to, the student can accurately identify the type of music played.
3. Given descriptions of three tasks to perform, the student will perform the tasks in the correct sequence.
4. Given a three-point lecture to listen to, the student will be able to recall the points correctly.

VOCATIONAL LEVEL
1. Given a verbal work plan, the student will be able to follow the plan correctly.
2. Given a group discussion, the student will be able to relate his comments to those of the other participants.

The relationship between speaking, reading, and listening is close and vital. While the purpose of developing listening skills is to provide an aid to interpersonal relations, it is nonetheless true that there are specific skills which need developing and that these skills need to be practiced in meaningful activities. This involves both formal training and practice in using the skills. Because of the comprehensiveness of the Peabody Language Development program, it is assumed that these listening skills will be taught concomitantly with the other skills of language development. In those schools which use the Peabody Kits, probably no other formal instruction will be necessary. Nevertheless, the outcomes list should be used as an evaluation of the effectiveness of instruction in this vital area. Any deficiencies detected can then be attended to by instructional exercises specific to the deficiency. The auditory exercises developed by the staff at Laradon Hall, Denver, Colorado, can be most helpful in teaching auditory discrimination and memory.[5]

The use of a Language Master has been found to be very helpful in training auditory skills. The Language Master is a machine that provides auditory feedback to the child. A card that has a word or sound written on it and a piece of magnetic tape at the bottom on which the sounds are recorded is fed into the machine from the side. As the card moves across, a recorded voice pronounces the word or sounds. In addition, the child can pronounce the word and the machine will play back his pronunciation as well as the correct sound of the word. Some 36 card programs ranging from kindergarten through twelfth grade are available in addition to blank cards, which can be used by the teacher to make her own program. The interactive element and the immediate feedback to the response of the child makes this a popular and useful device. The Language Master was initially developed by Bell and Howell, but other companies now have similar devices on the market.

Written Communication

Both the mechanics of writing and the expression of ideas are involved in this skill. First things come first, so the teacher first must concentrate on mechanics and then the communicative aspects of the skills. Outcomes to be expected at each level are:

PRESCHOOL LEVEL
1. Given paper and crayons, or pencils, the child can use them correctly.

---

[5] Ladoca Projects and Publishing Foundation, Denver, Colorado; also, there is a good description of the use of the materials in *Mental Retardation*, "Teaching Aids for the Mentally Retarded Child," V (August 1967), 33–35.

2. Given paper, scissors, and paste, the child will be able to cut out simple shapes and paste them on the paper.
3. Given a picture outline of dots, the child can connect the dots to complete the picture.
4. Given a picture of an animal missing a significant part, the child can draw in the missing part.
5. Given a paper containing four letters of the alphabet, two of which are the same, the child can draw a line connecting the two identical letters.
6. Given elementary manuscript paper, with one label word written in manuscript, the child can correctly copy the word.
7. Given a strip of paper on a child's desk on which his first and last name have been printed, the child can correctly print his name on a piece of manuscript paper.

PRIMARY LEVEL

1. Given four label words such as, water, desk, door, and crayons, printed in manuscript on the chalkboard, the child can correctly copy each word on manuscript paper.
2. Given instructions to write his name, the child can accomplish the task.
3. Given headings, dates, and time, the child can copy them correctly.
4. Given a sentence to copy, the child will begin the sentence with a correctly made capital letter.
5. Given a sentence to copy, the child will end the sentence with the proper punctuation.

INTERMEDIATE LEVEL

1. When presented with material written in manuscript, the student will be able to rewrite it in cursive writing.
2. Given an envelope, the student will properly place the address, the return address, and a stamp.
3. Given a reason for writing, the student will be able to write a friendly, coherent note.
4. Upon request, the student can define orally the abbreviations of: Mr., Mrs., Ms., Miss, Dr., St., Blvd., Rd., and Ct.

PREVOCATIONAL LEVEL

1. Given a job application blank, the student can correctly fill in his name, date, address, telephone number, age, parents' names, etc.
2. Given a job application form, the student will be able to write the date two ways (January 1, 1978 or 1-1-78).
3. Given a topic to discuss or describe, the student will be able to write a paragraph using complete sentences.

4. Given a reason for writing, the student will be able to write a correct business or friendly letter.
5. Given a mail order form, the student will fill it out correctly.

VOCATIONAL LEVEL
1. Given a job application, the student can fill in the blanks including the education and experience sections accurately and legibly.
2. Given a situation, the student will be able to formulate and write an invitation or a note of condolence, congratulations, or regrets.
3. Given a need for shopping, the student will be able to formulate a meaningful shopping list.
4. Given banking forms, the student will be able to fill out the forms correctly.
5. Given an inventory record, the student will be able to fill it out correctly.

Teaching Writing

While many of these skills will be learned as concomitants of unit instruction, especially at the preschool and primary levels, definite instructional attention of a formal nature must also be provided. It is the task of the teacher to introduce the motor movement involved in writing as specific skills as early as possible in the educational career of the youngsters, and to provide practice in these skills with concrete but meaningful activities so the children will experience the rewarding consequences associated with having use for the skills. In addition, materials written by the child should be those things for which he has some reason for writing. Learning the skills is greatly facilitated if the child has a need to use the skills he is learning. This need should be provided by the units of instruction pursued in the afternoon sessions.

Preschool Level At the preschool level, emphasis should be placed on providing the children with practice in the eye-hand coordination prerequisite to the learning of manuscript and cursive writing. For this purpose, the visual-perceptual materials developed by Marianne Frostig are recommended because of their consistency.[6] The materials are developed in five areas of visual perception. Poor eye-hand coordination is purported to be evident among children who have difficulty in writing. Children who could not recognize words were reported to have difficulty in figure-ground perception. Poor form constancy was associated with difficulty in recognizing letters or words written in different

[6] Marianne Frostig, and others, *Manual for the Marianne Frostig Developmental Tests of Visual Perception* (Palo Alto, Calif.: Consulting Psychologists Press, 1966).

sizes or colors. Mirror writing was associated with difficulty in perceiving position in space. Spatial-relation difficulty was demonstrated by children who interchanged letters. These five visual perceptual skills (eye-hand coordination, figure-ground perception, form constancy, position in space, and spatial relations) are presumed by Frostig to be relatively independent of one another.

The materials consist of five tests designed to identify the achievement level of a youngster in each of the areas examined. The eye-hand coordination test requires drawing continuous lines from left to right between boundaries of various widths. The boundaries are straight, curved, and angled. Remedial exercises derived from the test items are provided so they may be begun at the point at which a child fails and are continued until mastery of the skill is demonstrated.

The figure-ground test involves shifts in perception of figures against grounds that increase in complexity until intersecting and hidden geometric forms must be found. Again, remedial exercises compatible with the test items are provided.

The constancy-of-shape test requires the discrimination of circles, squares, rectangles, ellipses, and parallelograms presented with similar figures in a variety of sizes, shadings, textures, and positions. Remedial exercises that parallel the test items are available.

The position-in-space test presents schematic drawings of common objects in reversals and rotations for identification. Remedial exercises that stem from the whole series are provided.

The spatial-relations test requires the child to copy lines of varying length and angles, and it is designed to have the child analyze form and pattern. Remedial exercises are provided similar in format to those of the other tests.

Factor analysis of the Frostig tests by Hueffle indicates that two major skills are required: eye-hand coordination and understanding of the tasks.[7] Because these two elements are requisite to successful writing skills, the Frostig materials can be endorsed as helpful in this area. Perhaps the most sanguine characteristic is the simplicity with which individual differences can be accommodated. On each test, the child's point of failure is precisely identified. Remedial materials that coincide with each failure point are provided. Because of the continuity of the materials, the child has a ready-made program to take him through the entire sequence of each skill. Grouping children by related

[7] Keene M. Hueffle, "A Factor Analytic Study of the Frostig Developmental Tests of Visual Perception, the Illinois Test of Psycholinguistic Abilities, and the Wechsler Intelligence Scale for Children," unpublished doctoral dissertation, University of Northern Colorado, Greeley, Colorado, 1967.

weakness is thus facilitated so the teacher is freed to work with individuals whose problems require special attention or additional materials.

Primary Level Actual writing should probably be begun through the use of manuscript letters. Arguments, pro and con, generally revolve around the problem of transfer versus continuity. Some teachers prefer to use cursive writing because it is presumed to provide continuity of line and perceptual whole-word closure. Manuscript is preferred by others because it is simple and because it is similar to the type found in books. Since transfer is necessary to read books effectively, manuscript writing is stressed in this program.

To teach manuscript writing, the children need only to learn to draw lines and circles which they then combine to form letters and words. To help them, each child should be furnished with paper that has one-inch squares, a round disc which fits just within the square, a short (perhaps six-inch) ruler, and a large, soft-lead pencil.

The teacher should demonstrate the forming of letters on a chalkboard, using a disc and ruler just as the children will do. A music liner can be used to draw the lines on the chalkboard since this insures uniform spacing for the letters. The chalkboard should be squared just as the paper is squared.

Start with the letter *o.* The teacher should now explain to the children what they are going to do. Next place the disc in a square on the chalkboard. Start tracing at the top of the disc and trace to the left (counterclockwise) down and around and up. Often the children may wish to make *o*'s on the chalkboard, but this is not a necessary learning step. Let the children make *o*'s on their papers while you check their work. After the children have mastered the tracing of *o*'s, then consonants like *p, d,* and *b,* can be demonstrated. These should be followed by *a, u, n, m,* and *w.* The letters *t* and *i* should be taught together along with *h.* The letter *c* should be introduced before the letter *e.* After that, the other letters should be introduced, each with its peculiar characteristic.

The teacher would be well advised to purchase a manuscript letter strip from any school supply company, to post above the chalkboard, or in any conspicuous place for reference purposes. In introducing new letters, a short discussion can be held which is devoted to analyzing the circles and lines which make up a new letter. The directions—*left, right, top, bottom, down, up, across,* and *around*—should be introduced in the context of the specific letters which make use of the directions, so there will be no confusion about what the direction words mean.

Experience charts for unit work should be made by the teacher demonstrating the formation of the letters while the chart is being written. It is often a good idea for the teacher to use the disc and ruler in preparing the chart so the children can see that the lessons from the writing period have utility in making words that carry a message.

Short words, such as those in the first few lessons of the Hegge, Kirk, and Kirk *Remedial Reading Drills*, can be combined to make meaningful sentences for the children to copy.[8] The squared paper makes it possible to leave proper spaces between words so the children will learn visual closure. Gradually the squared paper should be replaced by double-lined paper, and finally by single-lined paper. All writing by both teacher and pupils should be consistently manuscript during the primary level of work.

Intermediate Level   At the intermediate level cursive writing should be introduced. It seems to be somewhat less confusing to introduce cursive writing with words rather than letters. Short words such as "boy," in manuscript and in cursive should be presented and compared. The children can analyze the differences and then copy from the chalkboard illustrations. A cursive letter strip can be purchased and posted alongside the manuscript letter strip to illustrate the similarities as well as the differences. During unit work, the teacher should start using cursive writing on the experience charts so the children can understand the transition in a meaningful context. If any confusion is detected, the teacher should use both manuscript and cursive writing for individual words to demonstrate similarities. In teaching writing, all of the letters should be presented in the context of words and practiced individually until the children make an unerring transition. It is especially helpful to use the writing period for writing messages or informal letters that have relevance to what the children are studying in their other classes.

Prevocational and Vocational Levels   Except in rare cases with individual children, the teaching of writing can be dropped at the prevocational and vocational levels. At these levels, the skills themselves should have been mastered to the degree that the youngsters can now use writing skills to record and write messages, letters, descriptions, and experiences. Emphasis should be on the use of writing, not the mechanics.

To aid the teacher and the child in both manuscript and cursive

---

[8] Thorlief G. Hegge, Samuel A. Kirk, and Winifred D. Kirk, *Remedial Reading Drills* (Ann Arbor, Mich.: George Wahr Publishing Company, 1965).

writing, extensive materials have been developed by the Zaner-Bloser Company.[9] Paper, pencils, charts, transparencies, and many other devices are available. Probably each teacher may wish to select materials suitable for particular classes. However, the teachers' manuals and the letter analysis charts are a must for all but the most experienced teacher.

Teaching Grammar

Teaching grammar is largely a matter of providing some system for learning the conventions of language structure so the written communications of the youngsters will be consistent with those of the rest of society. It is not necessary that grammatical rules be explicit so long as the children learn the style represented by grammatical standards. One system that has been used successfully with deaf children is the Fitzgerald Key,[10] developed at the Clark School for the Deaf to teach language structure. This chart makes use of a system for classifying parts of sentences according to function. It is a semiconcrete method for demonstrating what part each word or phrase plays in carrying the sentence meaning. The subject, verb, modifiers, and objects are separated and classified on the chart, so it is clear that each part of the sentence has a unique yet vitally related role to play in conveying a clear message. Since the system begins with very simple sentences and extends to the most complex sentence analysis, a teacher of retarded children can carry them along on sentence structure to whatever depth they are able to understand. It is an excellent teaching device because it is easy to use, clear, sequential, and consistent.

In addition to language structure, simple rules of punctuation can probably be taught best in the context of experience charts developed for units of instruction. Here the demonstration of capitals, commas, question marks, colons, periods, and so forth, take on meaning because they establish the points of emphasis in a meaningful context. Drill may or may not be necessary. If so, numerous workbooks can be purchased which are advertised to make punctuation easy. Few do, but they may be worth trying anyway.

If one does not choose to use the Fitzgerald Key, the same goals can be accomplished by classifying words according to function. *What*

---

[9] Zaner-Bloser Company, 612 N. Park St., Columbus, Ohio 43215.

[10] Bessie L. Pugh, *Steps in Language Development for the Deaf Illustrated in the Fitzgerald Key* (Washington, D.C.: Volta Bureau, 1955).

or *who* words serve as subjects for a sentence. Action words are the verbs. These are followed by the modifiers, which indicate *how*. Finally words that indicate what or where complete the simple sentence. Grammatical organization is determined by what words do in a sentence. Concentrating on how words function in sentences rather than what words that function in given ways are called, i.e., subjects, verbs, adverbs, adjectives, prepositions, conjunctions, objects, etc., is an effective way to make grammar vital.

Reading

It is perhaps not unreasonable to state rather categorically that of the skills that differentiate man from lower animals, none is more important nor has received more investigation than reading. So much has been the concern that one finds historians, artists, educators, psychologists, lawyers, engineers, and housewives publishing plaintives and panaceas concerning this vital skill.

General agreement exists regarding some aspects of reading. Few would argue, for example, that reading is not a process of interpretation very like, and perhaps identical to, the understanding of cartoons, tracking, Morse code, or African drums. The essence of reading involves a reaction of a person not to the signs, but to the meaning the inscriber wishes the signs to convey. This is no mystery and certainly there is ample evidence of the psychological nature of this perceptual phenomenon. As Stroud aptly states, "The perceiver reacts not to what is seen but to what the seen things signify."[11] Yet agreement on the precise nature of the stages one must pass through in learning to make consistent, meaningful responses (either ideational or motor) to printed symbols, despite voluminous research, remains highly debatable and obscure, if not invisible.

Not that efforts have not and are not still being extended. However, since methods of teaching reading have closely paralleled progress in learning theory, and since attempts at explaining learning continue to reside at a theoretical level, not much light has been shed on what occurs in the reading process. Here we get our clues mostly from chronological events.

Perhaps historically, the most important of the "first" methods of teaching reading were those exemplified by the McGuffey reader. This

[11] J. B. Stroud, *Psychology and Education* (New York: David McKay Company, Inc., 1946), p. 180.

historical educational material seems to have been presented in ele-
mental steps. That is, the child first learned the alphabet by a purely
rote method. He then combined these letters to form words like *cat*
and *rat*. He then combined these words into easy (although often un-
common) phrases and sentences. This was rote memorization of essentially a spelling method of learning to read—repetitive, uninspirational,
and, one might suspect, dreadfully dull.

During the early 1900s, the influence of Gordon and Beacon brought
about a modification of the spelling methods, and phonics was chiefly
employed.[12] This was hailed as a modern innovation, psychologically
as well as logically much more defensible than spelling methods. Here
the *sounds* of the letters rather than the *names* of the letters were
emphasized. Thus a child was in less danger of being confused since,
when he sounded a word, he really was pronouncing it in a manner
that allowed him to identify it from his vast store of already-familiar
auditory sounds. Seemingly, this phonics approach was the "new"
method of teaching reading through the 1900s up until the early 1920s.

Schools of psychological thought were undergoing periods of rapid
change (and bitter controversies) during this period. Educators were
beginning to look for help to this basic science of human behavior for
guidance in methodology and materials to use in the staggering tasks
of teaching America's children to read. New facts were coming from
the laboratories of James,[13] Watson,[14] and Thorndike,[15] and the more
progressive educators were trying almost desperately to cope with
these facts in the complex environment of the nation's classrooms.

The teaching of reading (always a bothersome problem) was being
subjected to new scrutiny and isolated concomitants were laid bare for
examination. Dearborn published new facts on the movement of the
eyes in reading.[16] Buswell,[17] and others refined, reanalyzed, and ex-

---

[12] *McGuffey Readers* in Gerald A. Yoakum, *Basal Reading Instruction* (New York:
McGraw-Hill, Inc., 1955), p. 1; and Gordon and Beacon *Phonics* in Yoakum, *Basal
Reading Instruction*, p. 3.

[13] William James, *Psychology* (New York: Holt, Rinehart and Winston, 1890).

[14] John B. Watson, *Psychology from the Standpoint of a Behaviorist* (Philadelphia:
J. B. Lippincott Company, 1919).

[15] E. L. Thorndike, *Educational Psychology* (New York: Bureau of Publications,
Teachers College, Columbia University, 1913).

[16] W. F. Dearborn, "Teaching Reading to Non-Readers," *Elementary School Journal*,
XXX (1929), 266–269.

[17] Guy T. Buswell, "Fundamental Reading Habits: A Study of Their Development,"
Supplementary Education Monographs, No. 21 (Chicago: Department of Education,
University of Chicago, 1922).

tended this research. Tinker,[18] Bond,[19] and Gray[20] studied problems of comprehension. Traxler[21] became interested in association time rates. Axline[22] and Fernald[23] investigated emotional factors. Monroe[24] and Orton[25] had much to say about reversals and laterality. But although these aspects of reading were well examined, no consistent theory emerged from the work until the Gestalt school of psychology investigated problems of perceptual closure, which grew out of Wertheimer's observation on apparent movement.[26] This doctrine which sought to impress that the "whole was greater than the sum of its parts" was ready-made for educators who still found reading failures among its spelling and phonics-taught clients. Here was a modern theory of psychology that "explained" the process of reading. Just who was responsible for embracing this theory and applying it to reading is not quite clear. Yet the logic of the presentation is beautiful. "Since," one reasons, "adult reading involves the instantaneous interpretation of symbolic wholes, and since children react perceptually in a similar manner, albeit imperfectly, then words should be presented as wholes." This logic was presumably based on the observed phenomenon that discrete elements tend to be unified by the human organism, and that disorganized perceptual patterns tend to be reproduced in an orderly manner. Thus the scientifically fine work of Wertheimer was applied uncritically to reading, with the effect that both the spelling method and the phonics method fell into disrepute.

During the 1920s, 1930s, and 1940s the most respectable method of teaching was that of the presentation to the child (for memorization purposes) of whole words for his initial contact. To be sure, some ex-

[18] Miles A. Tinker, "The Study of Eye Movements in Reading," *Psychological Bulletin,* XLIII (1946), 93–120.

[19] Guy L. Bond, *The Auditory and Speech Characteristics of Poor Readers* (New York: Bureau of Publications, Teachers College, Columbia University, 1935).

[20] W. S. Gray, *On Their Own in Reading* (Glenview, Ill.: Scott, Foresman and Company, 1948).

[21] See Yoakum, *Basal Reading Instruction.*

[22] Virginia M. Axline, "Non-Directive Therapy for Poor Readers," *Journal of Consulting Psychology,* XI (1947), 61–79.

[23] G. M. Fernald, *Remedial Techniques in Basic School Subjects* (New York: McGraw-Hill, Inc., 1943).

[24] Marion Monroe, *Children Who Cannot Read* (Chicago: University of Chicago Press, 1932).

[25] S. T. Orton, *Reading, Writing, and Speech Problems in Children* (New York: W. W. Norton & Company, Inc., 1937).

[26] See Stroud, *Psychology and Education.*

tremists extended this to initial presentation of whole phrases, sentences, and even paragraphs, but for the most part the introduction of words was the method most modern.

It is interesting that no well-accepted theory of the nature of the reading process has been advanced to replace the now highly suspect Gestalt-based theory. Debates flourish, methods and materials come and go, but throughout, there is a noticeable lack of theory which tends to explain the nature of the reading process itself. Thus one finds that so-called modern reading methods embrace an eclectic approach, and that a variety of techniques are employed by good teachers, each of which seems to be necessary for efficient learning of the reading art.[27]

Reading Theory

In his 1929 book, Coghill, working with *Ambystomae* (salamanders) in the tadpole stage of development, observed that skills learned by an organism were first learned as massed action.[28] This, after practice, was replaced by differentiated action in which elements of the task were retained or discarded, relative to their usefulness. Somewhat later, the specific, identifiable elements were integrated into a well-organized, efficient pattern. Thus the learning sequence started with massed action, progressed to differentiated behavior, and culminated in integrated action.

In 1940, Kirk postulated that the massed-differentiated-integrated theory might aptly describe the process of learning to read.[29] He suggested that the reactions or perceptions of a child, when he is being introduced to reading, are mass action, or learning words by the total outline or configuration of the word. In this perception, the child probably is unaware of the elements of the words he learns to recognize, and perhaps has no real need for knowing them at this time. This perception of the mass or total outline gradually is replaced by a recognition of the elements involved in the words. It is at this stage in his development that the child can learn to distinguish between "there" and "three" and "their." This stage leads to an integration of mass action and differentiated action. That is, the child learns to recognize words instantaneously by the total configuration of the word.

[27] Jeanne Chall, *Learning to Read* (New York: McGraw-Hill, Inc., 1968).

[28] G. C. Coghill, *Anatomy and the Problems of Behavior* (New York: Crowell Collier and Macmillan, Inc., 1929).

[29] Samuel A. Kirk, *Teaching Reading to Slow-Learning Children* (Boston: Houghton Mifflin Company, 1940).

When he encounters a new or an unfamiliar word, he then uses numerous skills to aid him in the differentiation of the word into elements that are understandable to him. He may resort to spelling the word, use some phonic system, employ some method of structural analysis, guess by use of context clues, or use some combination of all of these which will enable him to identify and discover the meaning of the word.

It is at the integration stage that speed and comprehension become the primary criteria for judging the excellence of an individual's reading skill. Superficially, the massed and the integrative stages appear to be the same. That is, in each case the individual reads the words instantaneously upon seeing them. However, the chief difference between these two stages is that a child who reads at the mass stage must simply stop or guess wildly when he encounters a word that is unfamiliar to him and that he cannot recognize by its over-all outline, while a child who is in the integrative stage in reading has the skills of word analysis, which he learned at the differentiation stage, to help him unlock the meaning of a new word.

Another aspect of the difference between reading at a massed or at an integrative level is that of comprehension. Practically all the reading done at a massed level is at "word-calling" stage. That is, the individual is able to make almost what amounts to a specific response to a specific stimulus without any interpretation of meaning being involved. The fact that a child can read a sentence like, "Run, Flip, run," does not imply at all that there is very much meaning to this sequence of words. At the integrative level, however, the child reads in order to get the meaning behind the printed symbols. Here he reads for a sequence of ideas, to get a central message, or to gain some information. This is a higher level of intellectual process, and results from inferences made by the child from the words that are presented as stimuli. The understandings are not in a one-to-one relationship of the words presented, but rather take the form of a subclosure, in that a sequence of words may be short circuited into a single idea or a series of ideas. This kind of reading involves not just the ability to recognize the words, but the ability to relate those words to the experience background of the child, and to the series of other ideas that were presented by the author. Thus integration involves not mere recognition of words, but depends on specific "sets" such as reading for ideas, reading for central thought, reading to solve a problem, or reading to get information.

Massed skills may be seen as those in which children may have quantitative differences. That is, one child may have a large number of sight words while another may have a smaller number. The differentiating skills, however, have an aspect of qualitativeness to them, as do the integrative skills. That is, a child may have many or few skills of differentiating, and these skills may be more or less effective, depending upon the degree to which they have been perfected by each individual child. At the integrative level, this becomes even more apparent in that not only may a child have a greater number or fewer number of specific integrative skills, but there is a degree of experience that differs with each child and with the skills involved.

This application of the massed-differentiated-integrated theory to the process of learning to read points up several aspects of earlier used methods in a new light. As regards the spelling method, it is easily recognized as a differentiating skill. One might guess that those youngsters who learned to read by this method probably learned to recognize words as wholes first. Phonics fits into the same general category of differentiating skills. The whole-word presentation method obviously is a massed approach. If it is the only method of instruction, it leaves out the skill of differentiation and integration. Probably most children learn to make differentiations on a phonics basis, by visual analysis, structural analysis, use of context clues, or some other method or combination that occurs to them, whether these skills are taught or not. That is to say, the human organism is such a wonderfully adaptable thing that perhaps almost regardless of the method used to teach reading, most children are able to supply the missing steps by themselves and thus learn to read. Within the framework of the massed-differential-integrated theory of reading, certain outcomes can be identified for each level:

PRESCHOOL LEVEL
1. Given the letters of the alphabet, the child can tell the names and the sounds of the letters.
2. Given the letters of the alphabet, the child can identify the similar and dissimilar letters.
3. Given a list of meaningful words like "stop," "men," "women," "caution," the child recognizes the words.

PRIMARY LEVEL
1. Given initial consonant blends, the child can read the correct sounds for each blend.
2. Given words with common endings, the child can say the correct ending sound.
3. Given word families, such as, et, at, etc., the child can read the correct family sounds.
4. Given simple stories that the child has helped develop, the child can "read" the story on request.

INTERMEDIATE LEVEL
1. Given the first 100 words of Dolch or a similar word list, the student is able to read the words.
2. Given simple labels on drugs, household goods, groceries, and tools, the child is able to read them correctly.
3. Given a consonant letter, the student can associate it with the correct sound of a key word.
4. Given a compound word, the student will be able to read both little words in a big word.
5. Given a prefix or suffix, the student will be able to explain what it does to change a word.
6. Given a work sheet with missing words, the student will be able to fill in the missing word.
7. Given a newspaper, the student can identify on request, the different sections of the paper.

PREVOCATIONAL LEVEL
1. Given a familiar book, the student will be able to demonstrate: the use of the table of contents; the use of the index; the use of the glossary; how to use bold print; how to scan for information.
2. Given a newspaper, the student will demonstrate that he can find specific information in the paper when requested to do so.
3. Given a dictionary, the student can demonstrate how to use it.
4. Given free time in school, the student will voluntarily choose material to read that is of interest to him.

VOCATIONAL LEVEL
1. Given a bill and/or statement, the student will be able to interpret the information needed and respond with an action to fulfill his obligation to the bill.
2. Given a sales contract, the student will be able to identify the sales conditions, cost, interest, time, and penalties.
3. Given the need to look up information, the student will demonstrate the application of the alphabet system to the dictionary, telephone book, and catalogue index.
4. Given an uncomplicated set of directions for a work task, the student will demonstrate his understanding by following the directions.
5. Given free time and a selection of popular magazines to choose from, the student will select a magazine appropriate to his/her interest and skill.

Teaching Reading

Reading, listening, speaking, and writing should be integrated as much as possible because they are all skills of communication. To the degree that unit experiences involve all of these skills, so are the units more valuable. Reading, however, like the other communication skills, has both mechanical and dynamic aspects. The child must learn to read first. He then may use reading to learn. This development must be provided in the instructional program.

Preschool At the preschool level, the reading program should emphasize the development of the readiness skills and introduce the children to a whole-word sight vocabulary of words that they will encounter in their first contact with books.

The sensory skills should be systematically taught as a part of each daily lesson, and the sight words should also be taught in a systematic method reinforced by incidental instruction.

Auditory skills to be taught are memory, discrimination, sequencing, and closure. A variety of reading-readiness workbooks are available to teach these skills, but the teacher must supplement the workbooks to provide sufficient repetition for the retarded youngsters. In addition, the Peabody Language Development Kits provide practice in auditory discrimination, memory, and sequencing, but not much attention is paid to closure. This will be further discussed in the section on phonics.

Auditory memory can be trained through a variety of exercises. The teacher may use boxes that contain different materials that emit characteristic sounds when rattled. Laradon Hall in Denver has developed a series of boxes that can be used to play guessing games. Instruments such as those in a rhythm band are also very good for training both auditory memory and discrimination. Guessing the directions from which a sound comes is another effective game. Perhaps one of the most neglected aspects of auditory training is that of sequencing. Clapping patterns, tapping patterns, or striking different materials or objects in a pattern sequence and having the children imitate the pattern is an excellent training device. The teacher should provide for about 10 minutes of auditory training each day with games that involve memory, discrimination, and sequencing. Whether these occur at the beginning, in the middle, or at the end of the period is irrelevant, but they should be presented each day.

In addition to the visual-perceptual training provided by the Frostig materials and the many workbooks that provide for visual training in memory, discrimination, sequencing, and closure, the teacher must provide supplementary training. This area also should be scheduled for at least ten minutes each day in the program. Laradon Hall has developed a series of materials that aid this training.

Visual discrimination may be trained by many games in which the children match pictures, name things that look alike or are different, collect match books, leaves, rocks, flowers, or any other class of objects in order to find likenesses and differences. An essential aspect of visual training is to use words to describe accurately what is seen. This seems to be necessary in helping youngsters to remember and order their observations and is a critical aspect of the training.

Visual memory training is aided by games in which the children must recall what has been seen. Some games that have been useful involved showing a series of articles, removing one, and having the children tell what is missing. Copying bead or color chip chains from memory is another good exercise for both memory and sequencing. Naming objects in pictures, finding hidden objects in picture puzzles, completing a sequence of designs, and drawing designs from memory are also good training. Since these are supplements to workbooks, seat work of the readiness-workbook variety allows the teacher time to attend to the individual differences of the children.

Sight words should be taught in the context of meaningful activities. Labeling things in the room and writing the names of the children on their personal possessions is standard procedure, but is excellent. Yoakum reports a system developed by Emma Watkins in 1926 which has great utility today.[30] Using cards on which words were written, she played games with the children in which they were required to act out or pantomime the word. As a reward, the child was allowed to keep the word he correctly identified. Yoakum has listed the words by categories:

ACTION WORDS

stand	come	bend	whisper	laugh
draw	kneel	sit	go	hop
wave	touch	clap	run	jump
skip	fly	walk	nod	scratch
cry	write			

OBJECTS

chair	wagon	plate	cow	pencil
telephone	table	truck	knife	horse
book	kettle	basket	block	fork
dog	crayon			

PREPOSITIONS

These were taught by pantomime.

up	out	behind	right	bottom
from	down	across	before	left
beside	beneath	in	around	on
top	under	between		

[30] See Yoakum, *Basal Reading Instruction.*

OPPOSITES

In this game, the teacher flashed a word and the child gave its opposite.

rude	polite	up	down	friend	enemy
fine	coarse	fat	thin	false	true
quiet	noisy	hard	soft	far	near
long	short	in	out	over	under
north	south	slow	fast	like	dislike
east	west	old	young	ugly	beautiful
good	bad	high	low		

According to Yoakum, Watkins used these and a large number of quite complex words that had relevance to the children and even printed directions on cards, such as "close the door," and "go to your seats," as part of the prereading work. Other categories of word games were: personal history, salutation, animal characteristics, numbers, colors, calendar, morning duties, things in the room, parts of the body, signs, conduct, telling time, and many others. The key to her success apparently was the relevance of the words and the challenge of the games. Again, at least 10 minutes per day can well be spent in this activity.

Primary Level When the children demonstrate good sensory skills of auditory memory, discrimination, and sequencing, and visual memory, discrimination, sequencing, and closure, and have a sight vocabulary of at least 75 words, phonics instruction may be begun. By this time, the children have demonstrated they can "read" at the massed or whole-word stage, so skills of differentiation should be introduced. Generally, this is at the beginning of the primary level.

Many different systems of phonics are available to teachers. With retarded children, however, it seems better to use a method that introduces individual letter sounds uncomplicated by rules and exceptions. The *Remedial Reading Drills*, by Hegge, Kirk, and Kirk,[31] with some modification, is an excellent system.

Phonics is just a tool for attacking new words. It is an essential tool, but its effectiveness depends upon the ability of a youngster to sound accurately the letter elements of a word and to blend those sounds into a meaningful word. This sound blending or auditory closure is essential to the use of phonics as a word-attack skill, and so must be taught to the children prior to the introduction of the sounds of the

[31] It is published by the George Wahr Publishing Company of Ann Arbor, Michigan, and can be purchased for about $2.00.

letters. A game in which the teacher sounds two-sound words (such as me, go, shoe) and has the children identify them is a good beginning. The sounds should be separated by a quarter second pause. When two-sound blends have been mastered, the teacher should introduce three-, four-, and five-sound words, and help the children practice blending the sounds into words.

Letters should be introduced next. Not only do letters have a variety of sounds as they are used in different words, but they also may be continuous, as in the letter *m*, or stop sounds, as in the consonant *t*. For these reasons, the sound of the letters introduced should be only one sound, and the continuous sounds should be taught first, with the stop sounds introduced later. The Hegge, Kirk, and Kirk *Remedial Reading Drills* introduces the short sounds of the vowels first. These are all continuous sounds, and so lend themselves to initial phonics instruction. First the *"th"* sound of *the* should be introduced. Then the consonants that have continuous sounds can be taught. These are: *s, h, f, w, v, m, n, l, r*. Nonsense words can then be sounded such as *san, lan, vam, val*. Consonant stop sounds such as *p, t, k, b, d*, and *g* can then be introduced to be used at the end of the word. *Fat, hap, map*, and the like can be introduced so the children will learn to blend the continuous sounds into stop sounds. The stop sounds should then be used to begin the words as in *cat, pat, pad*, and *bat*. Then the Hegge, Kirk, and Kirk drills should be begun. The drills introduce the short vowels; *a, e, i, o, u*, and the long sounds as configurations. In each lesson are a number of words that can be sounded by the children. The first line of words has the same final consonants. Each succeeding line in the first group has a different ending consonant for each line. The next group of words features identical beginning consonants, and the last two groups present different patterns. Thus sufficient repetition is presented to insure mastery, yet provision to inhibit a tendency for perseveration is also provided.

Although the drills should be used until the children have gone through the entire series, books can be introduced after the first seven drills have been learned, if the books are carefully chosen, or after the first 18 drills, if all the vowels are found in the books.

For beginning book reading, the M. W. Sullivan Series[32] complements the phonics instruction of the Hegge, Kirk, and Kirk drills. Each book is preceded by a correlated workbook which is written in pro-

---

[32] It is published by the Behavioral Research Laboratories, Box 577, Palo Alto, California.

grammed form and which requires the student to make a response to each workbook item. When the student has completed the workbook, he is then given a book that contains the words taught by the workbook. The accompanying teacher's manual explains in step-by-step fashion the use of the workbook and the book in such a fashion that the students quickly learn to use the material.

Because the Sullivan materials are programmed, both success and reinforcement of responses are provided. This is consistent with the procedure of the Peabody Language Kits, and so is also consistent with the learning paradigm suggested throughout this book. Since there are four workbooks and books on Level I, and four workbooks and books on Level II, the series is suitable for reading instruction at least through the primary level. Perhaps most important, the series is designed for the pupils to proceed at each one's individual pace. This facilitates grouping, and also individual work, so the teacher has more time to attend to individual problems of learning.

Intermediate Level   Although phonics is probably the most basic work-attack skill, it is only one and, because of the irregularity of the English language, it is not sufficient unto itself. Other word-attack skills need to be introduced as soon as possible, probably at the beginning of the intermediate level of work. These skills include using context, dictionaries, various forms of structural analysis, compound words, prefixes, suffixes, and rules for multisyllable word division.

Guessing the meaning of words from the context of the sentence can be encouraged by the teacher from the very beginning of the reading instruction. Such a technique is very useful, but it severely limits the independence of the reader if it is the major technique available. It is therefore well to introduce fairly formal word study skills early in the reading program. Common word endings such as *-s, -ed, -ing, -er, -est, -y*, and *-ly* are among the most often encountered. Prefixes such as *re-, un-, dis-, de-, ex-, en-, in-, im-*, and so forth, are equally as common. Lists of "like" words can be made by using any standard word lists. However. the Dolch list is probably as basic as any. There are also a series of games developed by Edward Dolch, available from the Garrard Press, Champaign, Illinois. The games are generally fun for the children to play and take some of the sting out of the word drill.

The Webster Publishing Division, McGraw-Hill, Inc., St. Louis, Missouri, has developed a series of word wheels and charts which have standard words changed by prefixes and suffixes. These are especially useful for teaching word-attack skills.

Rules for syllabication can get extremely complicated, but there are three standard rules that apply to most of the multisyllabic words:

1. When the letter pattern is vowel, consonant, consonant, vowel (vccv), the syllables break between the two consonants (for example, bet/ter).
2. When the letter pattern is vowel, consonant, vowel (vcv), the syllables break before the consonant (for example, pre/fix).
3. The sounding vowels in a word determine the number of syllables (for example, ab/so/lute).

Obviously a great deal of practice will be needed to fix these rules firmly, but they are invaluable rules and need to be mastered.

A large group of multisyllabic words are "put-together" words, since much of our language is made up of compound words. Most children see the total configuration of the words and need help in searching for little words in the big words. Word lists that are compound words—bookcase, cowboy, downstairs, playground, stoplight, fireman—can be presented either on joining flash cards or tagboard cards to demonstrate that each word can stand alone, but can also be combined for another word. Drill in game form using the word list from books used by the children can help to reinforce this vital analysis skill.

At the intermediate level, the children should make use of some of the excellent books that have low vocabulary demands. Science Research Associates of Chicago, Illinois, has developed a series of books that cover a variety of subjects.[33] The *Readers Digest* series also has a large number of books that lend themselves to both group and individual study.[34] In addition, the Winston Company,[35] the Beckley-Cardy Company,[36] and most other major publishers have lists of books suitable for retarded children.

Prevocational and Vocational Level   Reading in the prevocational and vocational levels should be devoted to reading for information rather than developing skills. With some youngsters, it will be necessary to be concerned with remedial instruction. It should be remembered that a child whose reading skills are roughly two years or more

---

[33] Science Research Associates, 57 Grand Avenue, Chicago, Ill.
[34] Readers Digest Educational Service, Inc., Pleasantville, N.Y.
[35] Holt, Rinehart and Winston, 383 Madison Avenue, N.Y.
[36] Beckley-Cardy Company, 1632 Indiana Avenue, Chicago, Ill.

below his mental age is a remedial reading case. A youngster who is a legitimate remedial prospect is one who has failed to master some one or more of the developmental reading tasks. For that reason, remedial instruction starts with a search for the point of failure and then concentrates on detecting the possible reason or reasons for failure. How one proceeds in this search depends upon how perceptual and conceptual development is viewed. There are many different approaches, each with its own school of advocates. Allegedly new developmental and remedial reading approaches seem to appear almost daily. Most of them are designed for nonhandicapped children, but that fact is never mentioned since their authors make no distinction between their suitability for children with differing abilities. Gillespie and Johnson (1974) and Aukerman (1971) have quite comprehensive descriptions of various systems.[37]

Developmental Approaches

Most of the programs are based either on some specific materials or on a procedure that has been developed by the author to accomplish a particular purpose. They typically reflect a child-centered approach and depend upon some unusually interesting or simple materials and procedures. Aukerman comments on the new linguistic phonemics approaches in the following words:

> The two characteristics that all promoters of linguistic-phonemic approaches have in common is their belief that they have discovered something new and their zeal in promoting it as *the linguistic approach* to beginning reading. An historical survey of the development of materials and methods of teaching beginning reading in the United States reveals that the linguistics-phonemics approach is little, if any, different from a number of structured phonics approaches suggested during the past century. Word patterns, word families, phonograms, initial consonant substitution practice, controlled phonics reading, phonics consistencies, and numerous other labels have "had their day" in reading.
>
> The recent arrival of *linguistics*, surrounded by an aura of scientific-sounding terms, renewed hope and brought promise to the distraught world of reading. . . .

[37] Patricia H. Gillespie and Lowell Johnson, *Teaching Reading to the Mildly Retarded Child* (Columbus, Ohio: Charles E. Merrill Publishing Company, 1974); Robert C. Aukerman, *Approaches to Beginning Reading* (New York: John Wiley and Sons, Inc., 1971).

In spite of the fact that many "outsiders" have developed linguistics-phonemics approaches to reading and naively think that they have discovered something new; in spite of the fact that some of the approaches were marketed with no definitive research to verify their claims; and in spite of the fact that some of the linguistics-phonemics reading materials are outrageous nonsense, there is one positive feature that outweighs these negative aspects. It is the fact that the phonemic elements of reading are structured in a developmental step-by-step sequence.

This structure which the linguistics scientist provides assures the teacher and learner that the sequence of learning will proceed in regular patterns.[38]

One phonics approach that is unique is the Initial Teaching Alphabet or i/t/a. Actually it is not a method, it is just that it uses a 44-character alphabet rather than the conventional 26-character alphabet. Each character has its own unique sound and therefore double vowels, silent e's, and other irregularities are nonexistent. The system is far from new, having antecedents that date back to the work of Sir Isaac Pitman in the early 1900s and perhaps even further to the efforts of Southwork schoolmaster Richard Hodges who sought to teach the true spelling of English in the 1640s and 1650s. A revival of interest in the approach occurred in the 1960s when Sir James Pitman introduced it into 75 schools in Great Britain. Subsequently the alphabet was used in the development of a large variety of materials of very high interest level and became immediately popular in the United States, particularly in the east. The materials are organized into three Phases, with books of six levels of difficulty that move the child from strictly i/t/a/ characters to the traditional orthographic 26 characters and our time-honored confusing conventional spelling.

Research on the effectiveness of the i/t/a with mentally retarded youngsters is neither plentiful nor convincing, but the use of the system does have one logical argument in its favor, which is that it allows children to record their life experiences in written language without the usual restrictions imposed on beginning readers and writers by the necessity of using words that have regular rather than irregular spelling peculiarities. Any word the child knows, he can read or write without fear of orthographic conventions. This broadens the linguistic horizons of retarded youngsters quite substantially. At a minimum the alphabet deserves critical examination under good re-

---

[38] c.f. Aukerman, *Approaches to Beginning Reading.*

search conditions to evaluate its effectiveness with retarded youngsters.

A second unique approach is Distar. Developed by Carl Bereiter and Siegfried Engelmann at the University of Illinois, it is an acronym for Direct Instruction System for Teaching Arithmetic and Reading. It was developed by the authors from an analysis of the skills and knowledge required for a child to be successful in the primary grades in school including beginning reading and arithmetic. Consequently, it takes the position that "the teacher must be a highly trained technician, not a combination of educational philosopher and social worker." As a result the program attends to teaching as a technique for developing certain specific responses from the child that he will need to make if he is to learn to read. Such a teacher-dominated approach may not seem humane, but it need not be. Among the techniques for reinforcing correct responses are hugging, applauding, back slapping, smiling and cheering. It is hard to imagine that kind of atmosphere as anything other than emotionally very warm.

It should be obvious that any program that specifies exactly what teachers are to say and do, and exactly what children are to say and do in response is going to draw fire from critics, particularly those from child-centered orientations. Yet the Distar program has gained popularity precisely because it does attend to those behaviors crucial to successful academic performance and is designed to be used with children of impoverished cultural backgrounds and verbal skills. As such it shows promise for helping retarded children survive in the usually academically demoralizing primary grades to a greater extent than so many other approaches. Certainly it deserves evaluation to determine whether its performance is consistent with its promise.

Remedial Approaches Delacato[39] starts with the premise that the neurological organization suggested by Hebb[40] follows the pattern that ontogeny recapitulates phylogeny. He maintains that an individual's development follows the same pattern believed to have been the evolutionary path followed by man in his rise from forms of lower life to his present complex organization. Neurological organization is presumed

---

[39] C. H. Delacato, *The Diagnosis and Treatment of Speech and Reading Problems* (Springfield, Ill.: Charles C Thomas, Publisher, 1963).

[40] D. O. Hebb, *The Organization of Behavior* (New York: John Wiley & Sons, Inc., 1949).

to be determined by motor movements, and intact neurological organization is fostered by repeated motor movements that are sequenced through the range from fish, through reptiles, and on to anthropoids and to man himself. The remedial program of Delacato concentrates on diagnosing inadequate or incomplete motor acts and then practicing motor patterns that are appropriate to the sequence. The remediation program has been referred to as "patterning," but many people fail to appreciate the care devoted to diagnosis before remediation is begun. So far, the few controlled investigations designed to test the validity of the techniques have been disappointingly negative.[41] Clinical reports published by practitioners, however, have been generally salutary.[42] Perhaps the effectiveness of the system may depend upon some specific developmental defect not yet clearly identified.

Kephart also accepts the Hebb theory of neurological organization, but proposes a quite different theory of perceptual and conceptual development.[43] It is the thesis of Kephart that motor exploration starts with the discovery of the body members—what they do, what happens when they do something, and what must be done to make them function. This is extended to the motor exploration of things in the immediate environment and is the basis for perceptual consistency. That is, the final arbiter of the nature of reality is provided by motor kinesthetic exploration of things—all kinds of things. Extended exploration is motor, followed by perceptual, but the medium of perceptual examination remains the sense of touch. As the child develops more mobility, he discovers that thousands of perceptual stimulations can be handled by his other senses, but motor kinethesis is used to check the perceptions for system or congruity. In later stages of development, like perceptual elements can be matched for congruity with other perceptual elements to form stable perceptions. Since all perceptions are distorted and assume perspective only when they are mediated by a person's knowledge of reality, motor exploration is the final arbiter. Concepts develop from like perceptual elements and principles from like conceptual elements. The final organization stage is conceptual-perceptual, in which perceptions are deliberately distorted to fit an individual's conception of the nature of reality.

[41] Melvyn P. Robbins, "A Study of the Validity of Delacato's Theory of Neurological Organization," *Exceptional Children*, XXXII (April 1966), 517–523.

[42] Delacato, *The Diagnosis and Treatment of Speech and Reading Problems.*

[43] N. C. Kephart, *The Slow Learner in the Classroom* (Columbus, Ohio: Charles E. Merrill Books, Inc., 1960).

Remediation as practiced by Kephart involves a careful diagnosis of form or perceptual inconsistencies and remediation designed to enhance motor-exploration-information consistency. Controlled investigations of the validity of this approach are quite encouraging, but they have been largely confined to children with demonstrated perceptual distortion problems.

A different approach has been prepared by Kirk, McCarthy, and Kirk.[44] Using the S-R model of behaviorist psychology, this approach starts with the premise that children with learning problems have uneven cognitive growth patterns, which accounts for the individual learning styles. They have adopted a psycholinguistic model proposed by Osgood to schematically represent the communication and learning processes.[45] It is the contention of these authors that messages are received by the individual primarily through the senses of vision and hearing (decoding), that these messages are mediated by automatic or associational thought processes, and that the individual communicates with others (encodes) through speech or gestures. They have developed the Illinois Test of Psycholinguistic Abilities (ITPA), which identifies the sensory avenue most efficient for receiving, mediating, and giving information (vocal or motor). Profiles developed from the test scores indicate the remedial presentation for sensory avenues from which the child can most profit, and the sensory avenues most proficiently used by the child to give information to the others. If a child learns best through auditory means, for example, it would probably be best to teach him through a phonetic approach.

While Delacato and Kephart focus their remedial methods on strengthening the detected weaknesses of the children with learning problems, Kirk, McCarthy, and Kirk advocate teaching by stimuli presentation to the strong sensory areas, with supplemental exercises designed to strengthen the weak areas. This makes psychological sense, since every youngster in need of remedial help will have had a history of failure, and all seem badly in need of success experiences. However, the precise failure point is not detected by the ITPA. The remedial instructor still must identify which skills are deficient (sensory, word recognition, word attack, or integrational) and select materials commensurate with the failure point for each student. The ITPA profile can be of great aid in selecting the most appropriate

[44] S. A. Kirk, J. J. McCarthy, and W. D. Kirk, *The Illinois Test of Psycholinguistic Abilities*, rev. ed. (Urbana, Ill.: University of Illinois Press, 1968).

[45] Charles E. Osgood, *Contemporary Approaches to Cognition: A Behavioristic Analysis* (Cambridge, Mass.: Harvard University Press, 1957).

sensory avenue for presentation when used with the series of lessons designed for the ITPA by Wilma Jo Bush and Marion Giles and published by the Merrill Book Co.

For teachers who may wish to give extended attention to remedial instruction, William Kottmeyer in 1959 wrote a book called, *Teachers' Guide for Remedial Reading*. It is available from the Webster Publishing Division, McGraw-Hill, Inc. It is a clear, concise description of some causes of reading failure and some appropriate remedial methods. As such, it is a highly useful resource.

CHAPTER 5

Arithmetic Skills

Adaptive behavior appropriate to the demands of living and working in our society depends to a considerable extent upon the ability of the individual to order and arrange things in their relation to each other. The language that has been invented to facilitate this arranging and to express the relationships is arithmetic. In a society that increasingly makes use of machines to do the computation, the need for arithmetic seems to be increasing rather than decreasing. This seeming paradox has come about partly because machines are not human and therefore do not correct themselves if they malfunction, and partly because they are so rapid that many more uses are made of machines today than in the past, so many more phenomena are presented in arithmetic terms than formerly. For example, weather forecasts are currently presented in terms of a 10 percent, 50 percent, or 80 percent chance of rain; or some other probability statement is made. The need for understanding mathematical relationships becomes greater than formerly, rather than less. However, the need for arithmetic skills of a routine type is largely confined to elementary rather than complex operations.

In the world of the retarded, arithmetic demands do not appear to be very substantial, but relational understandings are. In an analysis of 1240 jobs in 62 different occupations done in Cheyenne, Wyoming, in 1967, the highest functioning arithmetical skills were those of multiplying, making change, and measuring by fractions.[1] The vast majority of jobs required little more than counting.

The objectives of an arithmetic program involve not only teaching the skills of computation but also the use of these skills in solving problems and forming relational concepts. The areas to be developed include those of arithmetic facts and processes, money, time, and measurement. While all are interrelated, unless specific attention is paid to each area, the mechanical aspects are easily neglected. The use of the skills in relational and problem-solving tasks becomes meaningful when they are included in unit work.

Arithmetic Facts and Processes

Specific attention to the development of these skills is the essential focus of instructional periods in the daily schedule. The outcomes expected at each level are:

PRESCHOOL LEVEL
1. Upon request, the child will be able to respond with the proper meaning of such quantitative terms as all, more, less, big, little, and some.
2. Upon request, the child will count up to ten.
3. Upon request, the child will count ten things.

PRIMARY LEVEL
1. Upon request, the child will group objects according to color, size, and shape.
2. Upon request, the child will count up to 100.
3. Upon request, the student will tell how many objects are represented by any given number up to 20.
4. Upon request, the child can state what number comes before or after a given number less than 100.
5. Given single digit numbers, the child will be able to add them correctly.
6. Given single digit numbers, the child will be able to subtract them correctly.
7. Upon request, the student will be able to point to objects in the correct ordinal position from first to tenth.

[1] Wilma Hirst, *Occupational Needs of the Socioeconomic, Disadvantaged, and Other Handicapped Youth of Laramie County School District Number One, Phase One,* June 1, 1967.

INTERMEDIATE LEVEL
1. Upon request, the student will be able to count by twos, fives, and tens to 100.
2. Given a picture or object, the student will be able to divide it in half, thirds, or quarters.
3. When the student is given the symbols +, −, ×, or ÷, he will be able to name them correctly.
4. Given a number with a zero, the student will be able to explain its value in the number.

PREVOCATIONAL LEVEL
1. Given a number up to 1 million, the student will be able to read it on request.
2. Given numbers in which a carrying function is required, the student will carry to the second and third columns.
3. Given columns of numbers in which borrowing is necessary for subtracting, the student will be able to perform the operations correctly.
4. Given problems in which rate, ratio, interest, and percent are used, the student will be able to demonstrate the meaning of each.

VOCATIONAL LEVEL
1. Given an example of an income, the student will be able to prepare an uncomplicated budget.
2. Given an example of a paying job, the student will be able to determine the income earned.
3. Given an example of withholding tax, the student will be able to fill out simple tax forms.
4. Given a work task that uses numbers, the student will demonstrate his competence in using them.

The development of skills seems more amenable to instruction through a formally set-aside period for instruction each day. The use of these skills, however, becomes meaningful when tied to unit instruction of a purposeful nature. The discussion following is therefore devoted to the skill and knowledge development through the intermediate level. Units become the vehicle for using arithmetic at the prevocational and vocational levels.

Money

Money is a medium of exchange. It is also symbolic of values. Thus instruction in this area not only involves skill in the mechanics of manipulating money, but also the use of money as a medium of exchange and an understanding of the symbolic significance of money —that is, its relative value. Outcomes expected to be achieved at each level are:

PRESCHOOL LEVEL
1. Child can verbally state that money buys things.
2. Child can verbally state that people are paid for work.
3. Upon request, the child can identify a penny, nickle, dime, quarter, half-dollar, and dollar.

PRIMARY LEVEL
1. Upon request, the child can verbally identify @, ¢, and $.
2. Child can verbally state that: 5 pennies equal 1 nickle; 2 nickles equal 1 dime; 2 dimes and 1 nickle equal 1 quarter; 4 quarters equal 1 dollar.

INTERMEDIATE LEVEL
1. When asked to select a coin or bill through $5.00, the child can select the appropriate one.
2. Given a list of money numbers, the child will read them correctly.
3. Given a series of items of differing prices, the child will be able to compute the correct total cost.
4. When asked to describe verbally the function of a bank, the child will respond appropriately.
5. When requested to make change for $1.00, the child can correctly use any combination of coins available.

PREVOCATIONAL LEVEL
1. Given an item of purchase, the student can make change up to $100.00.
2. Upon request, the student can offer two reasons why social security taxes are withheld from pay.
3. Given a signature card to open a checking account, the student will be able to: print full name; print address; print the name of the place of employment; sign his full name.
4. Given a deposit slip, the student will correctly fill it out.
5. Given a check, the student will correctly fill it out.
6. Given a check stub, the student will record the check number, date, payee, amount, purpose, and effect a balance.

VOCATIONAL LEVEL
1. Given a menu, the student will be able to list the items desired and compute the cost for a meal.
2. Given a newspaper, the student will be able to identify ads of homes and apartments and compute the yearly costs.

3. Given a newspaper, the student can discriminate the difference between two brands of food on "special" to determine the best buy.
4. The student can explain verbally the cheapest way to get to work and compute the daily and weekly costs.
5. Given a problem of maintaining an appliance, the student can compute the difference between maintenance and repair.
6. Given a problem of buying an appliance, the student can compute the cost including interest and carrying charges.

At the lower levels the mechanics of manipulation are the primary concern of the instructional program. Through successive learnings at the upper levels, the youngsters should come to understand the place of money as a medium of exchange and a symbol of values through practice in the use of money and experience with those activities in which money plays a central role. Units on banking, borrowing, budgeting, and related activities form the core of these experiences.

Time

Of all the accoutrements of civilization none is more central than time. The regulation of nearly all of an individual's activities is so intimately controlled by the clock that the role of time in our daily activities is often overlooked. As with other quantitative activities, time has both mechanical and utility aspects. One must learn to measure time, but one must also learn to coordinate his activities with the measurement. There is no casual or incidental method of teaching time that seems very effective. Time consciousness deserves frequent and systematic instructional attention. Outcomes expected from this attention are:

PRESCHOOL LEVEL
1. Upon request, the child can state verbally whether the present time is morning, afternoon, or night.
2. Given the name of a scheduled activity, the child can state whether it takes place in the morning, afternoon, or night.
3. Upon request, the student can verbally name the days of the week.
4. Given a clock, the child can verbally describe its function.

PRIMARY LEVEL
1. Upon request, the child can verbally state what day of the week it is and tell which days come before and after.
2. Given a calendar, the student will be able to use it to count, to tell how many days and how many weeks are in the month.

3. Given a calendar, the child will be able to locate the present day and date.
4. Upon request, the child will be able to name the months of the year.
5. Upon request, the student can verbally state what the letters AM and PM represent.
6. Given a clock or clock face, the child will be able to state the time by the hour and half hour.

INTERMEDIATE LEVEL

1. Upon request, the child will be able to name the seasons of the year.
2. Given the name of a month, the child will be able to associate it with a season of the year.
3. Upon request, the child will be able to state the correct month, day, and year.
4. Given the room schedule, the child can tell when it is time for school to begin, to go to the library, physical education, or lunch.
5. Given the room schedule, the child will be able to tell when to begin certain blocks of academics or go to other rooms without being reminded by the teacher.
6. Given a clock or clock face, the child will be able to tell time in relation to past, before, after, noon, midnight, by the quarter hour.

PREVOCATIONAL LEVEL

1. Upon request, the student can state three reasons why punctuality is important on a job.
2. Given a job situation, the student will be able to use the time of work and rate of pay to compute the weekly pay.
3. Given a situation, the student will be able to develop a daily schedule of activities around the job demands.
4. Given a situation, the student will be able to develop a daily, weekly, and monthly schedule around household chores.
5. Given a recipe, the student will be able to compute the total cooking and preparation time required.
6. Given a projected travel destination, the student will be able to compute the trip time using time tables, schedules, and maps.

VOCATIONAL LEVEL

1. Given a series of time cards for a week, the student will be able to determine the number of hours worked per day and for the total week.
2. Given a projected task, the student will be able to determine the amount of time necessary to complete each part of the task and the total task.
3. Given a pay check statement, the student will be able to identify gross and net pay and verbally explain the difference.

Measurement

Measuring is the method most common for making quantitative judgments in all areas of living. As in any other comparison, judgments are made with varying degrees of precision. To judge someone as "a good guy" implies some standard of behavior against which the behavior of the guy judged is compared. Teaching this skill then involves attention to developing standards of both a precise and crude type, and also teaching the mechanics of measuring and the use of the measuring skills. Since this is an area that permeates social judgments as well as arithmetic, the skills need to be *learned* first and then *used* in a variety of social contexts. However, the key concept is learning that standards are developed from which all comparisons are made. The establishing of standards therefore becomes integral to all measuring. Outcomes expected at the various levels are:

PRESCHOOL LEVEL
1. Upon request, the child will be able to respond correctly to elements that are long or short, big and little, near and far, heavy and light, few and many, and all and none.
2. Given a yardstick, the student can identify an inch, a foot, and a yard.

PRIMARY LEVEL
1. Given a measuring container, the child will be able to fill it with the appropriate amount of liquid for a half cup, 1 cup, 1 pint, 1 quart, or 1 gallon.
2. Given a weight scale, the child will demonstrate the use of the scale.
3. Given a weather thermometer, the child will be able to read the temperature correctly.
4. Upon request, the student can select from a large number of objects the correct number to equal a dozen.
5. Given a large number of geometric forms, the child will be able to sort by shape the circles, squares, rectangles, and triangles.

INTERMEDIATE LEVEL
1. Given a 12-inch ruler, the student can correctly measure the length and width of a room and convert them to yards.
2. Given a ruler, the student will correctly measure to one-eighth of an inch.
3. Given an identified building, the student will determine the distance in blocks, miles, and time.
4. Given a standard recipe, the student will correctly use the measure called for.

5. Upon request, the student will identify the directions of left, right, up, down, north, south, east, and west.
6. Given a thermometer, the student can take his own temperature.
7. Given a large number of three-dimensional objects, the student will be able to sort by sphere, cylinder, cone, cube, and pyramid.

PREVOCATIONAL LEVEL
1. Given the symbols of feet ('), inches ("), and degrees (°), the student will correctly identify each.
2. Given a yardstick or tape measure, the student will be able to find the numbers of specific feet and inches.
3. Given a tape measure, the student will be able to measure the height of a classmate and convert it into feet and inches.
4. Given a road map, the student can identify specific symbols and verbally state their meaning.
5. Given a road map, the student can demonstrate the route to be taken from one point to another.
6. Given the route on a road map, the student can determine the mileage between points.

VOCATIONAL LEVEL
1. Given clothing sizes, the student can identify his own sizes correctly.
2. Given a statement of miles traveled and gallons of fuel used, the student will compute the ratio.
3. Given a three-dimensional item, the student will correctly determine the height, weight, and width.
4. Given a statement of comparison, the student will be able to state verbally what kind of standard was used for the measurement.
5. Upon request, the student can verbally describe the kinds of measurements involved in his job.

Teaching Arithmetic

Research studies on methods of teaching arithmetic to the mentally retarded have been few and not very enlightening. Cruickshank's 1946 investigation was primarily concerned with arithmetic performance differences of retarded children.[2] His findings that the retarded have more difficulty with abstract than concrete operations and that they are not well-schooled in processes have apparently resulted in present

[2] William M. Cruickshank, "A Comparative Study of Psychological Factors Involved in the Responses of Mentally Retarded and Normal Boys to Problems in Arithmetic," unpublished doctoral dissertation (Ann Arbor: University of Michigan, 1946).

teaching practices of concentrating on concrete materials and providing considerable drill, usually in game form. A study by Blackman and Capobianco on the effectiveness of programmed versus traditional instruction failed to find any superiority accruing to either method of instruction.[3]

Conclusions from the research tend only to support the notion that teaching arithmetic is not a troublesome problem if the curriculum stops short of abstractions of some complexity, and if the materials used are not confounded by reading requirements. The nature of arithmetic is such that it lends itself to being learned by youngsters who have the learning characteristics associated with mental retardation.

Facts and Processes

Fundamentally, arithmetic consists of a man-invented system of statements having to do with "how many." The only contact numbers have with the the world of reality is in the one-to-one correspondence of one thing to one symbol. Subsequent numbers depend upon this fundamental relationship, and subsequent processes are tight rules for combining groups, sequences, and relations that do not violate the one-to-one correspondence upon which quantitative statements ultimately rest. Arithmetic is concretely based and systematically ordered. This is in keeping with the learning needs associated with retarded children. It should be cautioned that the foregoing should not be interpreted to mean that teaching arithmetic to retarded children is a cinch. It does imply that arithmetic lends itself better to systematic instruction than other academic skills, but problems do exist. The youngsters must learn a set of ordered symbols and a series of rules for combining the symbols and this in itself looms as a formidable task. However, the arithmetic curriculum is sequential and this simplifies the decision about what should be taught. How the facts and processes should be taught is another unsettled question.

Preschool and Primary Levels

Our knowledge of the world about us comes through our senses, but the sensory impulses are reconstructed as we interpret the in-

[3] L. S. Blackman and R. P. Capobianco, "An Evaluation of Programmed Instruction with the Mentally Retarded Utilizing Teaching Machines," *American Journal of Mental Deficiency*, LXX (1965), 262–269.

formation in the light of our experiences. Pre-arithmetic activities have to be carried on by children as they develop some understanding of space, ordering, subdividing and constructing lines, and changing perspectives. Techniques for developing these skills are very well described by Richard Copeland. From a study of the archives at The University of Geneva in Switzerland, he selected ideas for developing pre-arithmetic skills, which are contained in his 1974 booklet, *Diagnostic and Learning Activities in Mathematics for Children*, published in New York by the Macmillan Publishing Company.

Fundamentally, Copeland suggests activities that start by having children learn to identify forms by touch but without being able to see the forms. Youngsters proceed through stages of development from being able to identify common objects up to identifying complex forms. Of primary importance, is that the youngsters learn to change perceptual information into representation of the objects examined. This translation of one kind of sensory information into other kinds requires the mental representation of space which is a pre-arithmetic skill necessary before the actual arithmetic learnings can occur. Other similar tasks require putting objects in various orders—first in straight lines (such as stringing beads) and later in patterns of different space relationships (such as circles or squares), but in which the order or sequence of bead shapes is retained. Finally, picturing objects seen from different perspectives such as up, behind, in front, on end, and so on, requires the same kind of spatial manipulations. These activities and others are well described by Copeland and can become an important part of the pre-arithmetic activities.

To learn arithmetic the children must first learn the names of the symbols and their sequence (1 2 3 4 5 . . .). Next they must learn one-to-one correspondence: one thing, one mark. Then they need to learn one-to-one comparison (for example, two is more than one) and that the quantity of "how many" is represented by a particular number. From this they need to learn grouping or sets, and then the rules for putting groups together and taking them apart. This is arithmetic at the level apparently needed by the retarded for independent living and working.

Learning the number names and symbols can be taught in many different ways, but they all boil down to a great deal of practice in counting. Simple rhymes such as:

1, 2
Buckle your shoe
3, 4
Close the door

5, 6
Pick up sticks
7, 8
Lay them straight
9, 10
Do it again

or,

1, 2, 3, 4, 5
I caught a bird alive
6, 7, 8, 9, 10
I let it go again

or,

1, 2, 3, 4
Someone clean the floor
5, 6, 7, 8
I wonder what he ate

or any number of other improvised rhymes that can be found or made up are helpful. Writing the number on a number line and pointing to each number as it is said is an excellent way of helping the children associate the number with its name and place in the sequences. Throughout the primary level, counting of any kind should be done by the teacher so the children will find out this is the language of "how many" and that it is relevant to things that are meaningful to them. If rhymes are used, having the children act them out helps to give some meaning to the words.

One of the very effective ways or systems for counting at a concrete level has recently been given attention by the Humanities Brotherhood of Green Valley School, Orange City, Florida, under the authorship of George von Hilsheimer. This is the finger abacus. If each finger is used as a one-to-one counter, an individual is restricted in counting to the number of fingers he possesses. By use of the finger abacus system, a person can count up to 99. Furthermore, the finger abacus lends itself to teaching adding and substracting in a concrete and readily understandable manner. Perhaps most significant is that once the system is learned, the youngster has a calculating device which he carries with him always and which allows him to count quantities up to 99. He literally is his own abacus.

The system starts simply by using one finger on the right hand for each sequential number until 5 is reached. At this point, the thumb represents 5 and the fingers are reused one at a time to represent 6, 7, 8, and 9. Zero is a closed fist which stands as a place holder. The fingers on the left hand represent the tens with the closed fist of the right hand being the place holder or zero. The symbols are represented as:

Adding is a simple process of more fingers being used:

$$1 + 1 = 2 \qquad\qquad 5 + 4 = 9$$

Subtracting involves only taking away fingers:

$$4 - 2 = 2$$

Even double-digit subtraction where no carrying is involved is a simple process of folding the fingers in:

$$99 - 44 = 55$$

Of the many advantages of using the finger abacus for initial number work, one that seems most important is the ease with which transition to an Oriental abacus can be made. The Oriental abacus differs from the conventional Western abacus in that it uses only 4 beads for the ones with 1 bead for five. In this way it is more similar to the hands (except for the thumb) than the Western abacus. It requires a transition of fives rather than tens and is therefore much easier to use. The numbers 9 and 10 are shown below on the finger abacus and on the Oriental abacus.

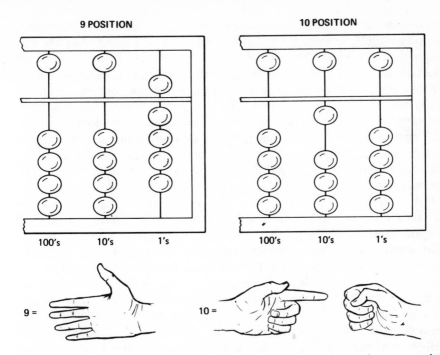

Since the grouping of five is a more natural grouping than ten, this is an easier concept to teach. However, the use of the thumb as a symbol or representative of 5 is the key to the successful use of the finger and Oriental abacus and will need a great deal of reinforcing.

If place value then is taught by conventional counting blocks such as the Stern or Cuisinaire or by counting racks, a possible confusion can be the fact that one more 1 is used before the grouping equals the next place value. This does not seem a major problem if one notices that the conventional number counters are fundamentally incorrect anyway. True, they do present the concept of "equal" in a meaningful manner, but they err in counting since 9 is the highest single digit number we use with 10 being the lowest double-digit number we use. The finger abacus and the Oriental abacus correct this error and suggest the tens' groupings of double-digit numbers.

Unfortunately the tens' group starts with 11 and 12 which are irregular cases of the tens' groupings and probably need to be taught that way. Hollister and Gunderson[4] point out that both *eleven* and *twelve* are corruptions of words whose original forms indicated the

[4] George E. Hollister and Agnes G. Gunderson, *Teaching Arithmetic in Grades I and II* (D. C. Heath and Co., 1954), p. 9.

process involved. The German words *ein und lif* (literally, one and ten) were apparently corrupted to *einlif* and then to eleven. Twelve was originally *zwa und lif*, then *zwalif*, and finally twelve. This may not help retarded children much, but it is comforting to those who need orderly reasons for things. All other tens words are "-teens" or "-tys" and are easily taught. Thirteen, fourteen, fifteen, sixteen, seventeen, eighteen, and nineteen are *three* and *teen*, *four* and *teen*, and so forth. This relationship of ones and teens is quite different from a collection of tens as in twenty, thirty, forty. . . . Yet each group is a consistent notation of "how many" and can be taught as meaningful suffixes. Furthermore, numbers are read from left to right as in 40, but from right to left as in 16. This can be very confusing unless the youngsters learn that *only* double-digit numbers which start with a 1 are read in their irregular right-to-left sequence. All others are read in a regular left-to-right manner. Confusion exists in interpreting a number like 1,111,111 not because of the numbers but because reading the number "one million, one hundred eleven thousand, one hundred eleven" involves both left-to-right and right-to-left reading in different groupings. Teaching the reading of large numbers is complicated and confusing unless the reading of the tens' grouping in the "-teens" and "-tys" is not only well-learned but thoroughly understood. It is well worth the time and effort required.

Intermediate Level   Two devices that allow for concrete teaching of arithmetic were developed by Dr. Lola May.[5] The "Count-A-Line" is a double wooden bar that uses 20 different number lines and red and black interlocking pegs to teach whole numbers including place value, addition, subtraction, multiplication, and division, fractions, multiplication and division of fractions; equivalent fractions; decimal fractions; integers and percent. This unusual device is an improvement over the usual number line because of the comparisons that can be made between different lines of numbers. It is concrete and allows for manipulation by the children. Both the "Count-A-Ladder" and "Count-A-Line" lend themselves to a transition from concrete to abstract representation of number statements. These devices are suited to the learning characteristics of retarded children at the primary and intermediate levels.

Multiplication can also be aided by a finger system described by Gary Collins.[6] As in the finger abacus, the system works for single

[5] Sold by EduKaid of Ridgewood, N.J., for about $10.

[6] Collins, Gary, "Finger Multiplication," *Teaching Exceptional Children*; Summer, 1969, p. 119.

digit numbers above 5. To multiply, each hand is balled into a fist which represents 5. Numbers to be multiplied are represented by extending the number of fingers more than five to make the numbers being multiplied. For example, if the numbers to be multiplied are 6 times 8 then one finger would be extended on one hand and 3 on the other $(5 + 1 = 6, 5 + 3 = 8)$. Each extended finger represents 10. These cumulate. Added to them are the fingers left unextended including the thumbs multiplied times each other. In this example, $(1 + 3)10 = 40 + (4 \times 2) = 48$. So 6 times 8 equals 48. Multiplying 5 times 9 would be represented by $(0 + 4)10 + (5 \times 1) = 40 + 5 = 45$.

The Metric System

All the processes discussed in the foregoing section are applicable to whatever number system is used. With the adoption of the metric system in the United States, it is incumbent upon the teacher of retarded children to make the system functional. Educationally, the techniques for teaching facts and processes employing the metric system are little different from teaching arithmetic employing the standard British system. In time, it may actually be seen as easier because the metric system has an internal integrity absent in many other systems.

The metric system (the name refers to measuring) was developed by a commission of French scientists and adopted by France as its legal system of weights and measures in 1799.[7] The basic unit of measure, the meter, was derived from the distance between the North pole and the equator. Ten million of these meters are needed to cover that distance. (In 1960 the International Bureau of Weights and Measures defined the meter as 1,650,763.73 wave lengths of the orange-red light from the isotope krypton 86.) The important thing is that although the meter is a measure of distance (a little longer than a yard) it lends itself to weight, area, volume, and even force and temperature.

The meter is made up of 1000 millimeters, 100 centimeters, or 10 decimeters. Each reduction is a multiple of 10. Increasing in length a decameter is 10 meters, 1000 meters make a kilometer, and 10,000 meters make a myriameter.

Surface measure or area is also based on the meter. A square measuring 10 meters on each side is called an are and a square measuring 100 meters on each side is a hectare. The hectare is the

[7] Metric System in World Book Encyclopedia, Field Enterprises Educational Corporation, 1964.

basic unit of land measurement and corresponds to the British acre. In size it is somewhat larger than a square football field.

Weight also is based on the meter. The basic unit of weight is called a gram, and is the weight of a cube of water (at its greatest density) measuring 1 centimeter on each side. One liter (about a quart) is equal to a cube measuring 10 centimeters on each side. Obviously a liter contains 1000 cubic centimeters (10 $\times$ 10 $\times$ 10) and since each cubic centimeter weighs one gram, the liter would weigh one kilogram. A metric ton is 1000 kilograms. At the opposite end of weight, a carat weighs 200 milligrams or one fifth of a gram. This would be the equivalent of one fifth of a cubic centimeter of water. Since the centimeter measures less than half an inch, it is apparent that a carat is not very large.

The amount of force needed to move a gram one centimeter in one second is called a dyne. This measure of force in various forms is used to calculate electricity, light waves, and solar distances.

The integrity of the metric system is further revealed in the fact that any increase or reduction in any area can be accomplished by just moving a decimal place. Likewise, the reading of numbers is identified by the proximity of the number to the decimal. For example, a number like 0.456 would be read as four hundred fifty-six millimeters. Translated that would be four decimeters, five centimeters, and six millimeters.

The use of the meter as the basic unit of measure, the gram as the basic unit of weight, and the liter as the basic unit of quantity, makes it possible to retain the root word and simply change the prefix to fit the numbers. The Latin prefixes are used throughout. Milli means thousandths; cent, hundredths; deci, tenths; deca, tens; hecto, hundred; kilo, thousand; and myria, ten thousand.

Calculations in the metric system are simplified because they operate on the decimal system. One denomination can be changed to the next higher one by moving the decimal to the left.

Conversely, multiplying the same quantity by ten (1.5m $\times$ 10 = 15.0m) reads, "one point five meters (or 1 meter 5 decimeters) times ten equals fifteen meters." Since each denomination is a multiple of ten, conversion follows an orderly sequence: 10 millimeters equal 1 centimeter; 10 centimeters equal 1 decimeter; 10 decimeters equal 1 meter; 10 meters equal 1 decameter; 10 decameters equal 1 hectometer; 10 hectometers equal 1 kilometer; 10 kilometers equal 1 myriameter.

Substituting grams for example, as the unit in the above sequence, does not alter it at all, nor does the substitution of liter.

Since both the metric and the British systems will probably be used for some time teachers may wish to use materials that teach both systems. A system that contains both is the Metric Center by Ada Booth, marketed by the Enrich Company of Palo Alto, California.

One additional area in which a derivation from the metric system is used is that of measuring temperature. As in the original determination of the meter, natural phenomena are used as reference points. The Celcius scale uses the freezing point of water (at sea level) as zero and the boiling point as 100. The points in between are equally divided. Comparison with the Fahrenheit scale requires a subtraction of 32 degrees to begin with and then about 1 degree Celcius for each 2 degrees Fahrenheit (actually $5/9 \times 2$). For example 40 degrees Fahrenheit is about equal to 4 degrees Celcius ($40-32 \times 5/9 = 4$). The temperature measurement is not directly comparable to the metric measures, but it is based on the same principle and does simplify the system. An exception is normal body temperature, which is 98.6° Fahrenheit, but turns out to be 37 degrees Celcius, a very much neater number to handle.

Prevocational and Vocational Levels At the prevocational and vocational levels the use of arithmetic should be deliberately planned for inclusion in the units that are studied. Units suggested in Chapter 10 place great stress on figuring pay rates, comparative costs in buying, figuring interest, determining the cost of excursions, planning and budgeting for parties, and a host of other uses of quantitive concepts. The teacher should be alert to the possible inclusion of arithmetic in any of the units.

Quite a few number games that are both fun and useful can be played by the children. The Garrard Press of Champaign, Illinois, has a large number of games developed by Edward Dolch that can be used. In addition, parlor games such as Monopoly, dominos, and racing games make use of number combinations. Card games like cribbage, smear (also called hi-low jack) and rummy are also excellent reinforcers. Counting points for bidding in bridge may be mastered by some of the more advanced children. Bridge, especially, lends itself to being played at a very primitive level—and often is.

Schools that have adopted the "new math" as a curricular innovation need not exclude the retarded. Although the new approach may not be as immediately applicable as a more traditional system, sets and notations are taught by an inductive method—an approach admirably suited to the capabilities of the retarded children. Von Hilsheimer of the Humanities group has developed a workbook called *How Many*, which is a new math primer that is usable with retarded children. With this as a beginning the teacher may wish to explore the programmed books of the Singer Series.[8] The systematic programs of the workbooks lend themselves to individual progress or small group activity.

Teaching Money

At the preschool level coins should be introduced and examined so the youngsters can learn the names of the coins and be able to differentiate among the coins by size, color, design, and sound. A display of coins may be used, but it is better if the children can examine the coins closely in order to see clearly the differences. Using money to buy things helps fix the notion that money is used as a medium of exchange—that is, money has meaning.

At the primary level, a part of the arithmetic period should be used to teach the value of each common coin. The hand abacus approach to teaching numbers is especially useful because a finger can be used to represent pennies while the thumb represents a nickel. Dimes are directly represented by the fingers of the left hand and half dollars by the thumb of the left hand. A quarter broken down into two dimes and a nickel is easy to represent, and 75 cents represented by the thumb, and two fingers on the left hand with the thumb on the right hand corresponds to a half dollar, two dimes, and a nickel. The quarter is not directly represented, but should be taught as a separate coin. The four quarters in a dollar can probably be better explained by a number line but still may be the most difficult concept to teach.

Frequent opportunities to use money should be provided. The use of a play store is an especially good device. Items for sale can be empty cans and boxes which have meaning to the youngsters so they can pretend they are purchasing something they want or need. Although many play stores are exclusively grocery stores, there is no reason why clothes, hardware, and even pictures of furniture or other items could not be used.

At the intermediate level the play store can be expanded in both scope and cost of merchandise. A cafeteria, or even a used car lot, could be made with pictures or models. The Fearon Publishers of San Francisco have a workbook called *Using Dollars and Sense* written by Charles H. Kahn and J. Bradley Hanna, which presents a simplified

---

[8] Developed by Patrick Suppes and available from L. W. Singer Company, Inc., a division of Random House.

introduction to money and is especially designed for retarded children. This kind of supplementary material can be used with confidence.

Units at the prevocational and vocational levels that treat installment buying, credit, withholding, budgeting, and buying make use of money as a standard of value. The use of mail-order catalogues helps to reinforce money as a criterion for judging value as well as a medium of exchange. The teacher should be alert to any possible ways in which the concept of a standard of value can be illustrated and repeatedly presented. The theme to be repeated is that money is only representational of values and worth. Money, of itself, is useless.

Teaching Time

Most children come to school with an already well-developed sense of time in a very gross sense. They are aware of a time to eat, a time to go to bed, a time to go to school, and the time sequences of TV shows. Generally they will know morning, afternoon, and night, different days of the week and seasons or even months. Their time understandings are kaleidoscopic, however, and lack the precision and relational meanings that they will need to be able to manage their living activities realistically.

At the preschool and primary levels the emphasis should be on the use of time in activities. The planning session in the opening exercises provides a good opportunity to teach time as a necessary aspect of scheduling. Days of the week can be indicated on a large calendar that has room to write in the date and the duty assignments of the children for each day. Broad references such as "after reading," "before lunch," "after music," and the like should be liberally used by the teacher in these planning sessions.

If a particular event of interest to the children is scheduled for a particular time, a cardboard clock with movable hands can be set for the time of the event. The children can then compare the hand positions of the regular classroom clock with the time setting of the cardboard clock. When they coincide, the time for the activity has arrived. Frequent use of this technique may be practiced throughout the preprimary level with great profit.

Later, when the children have learned to recognize numbers, more formal instruction should be introduced. The hour, half-hour, and quarter-hour should be systematically introduced with a real clock, a clock mockup with movable hands and worksheet problems. The concepts of *after* and *before*, *of*, *to*, and *past* should be illustrated and practiced. Many workbooks devoted to "reading" the clock are available and should be used. As the children develop some skill in telling time they should have a chance to learn about other kinds of time pieces: candles, sundials, egg timers, clock-radios, and pendulum clocks. This practice should continue through the intermediate level and the children should be introduced to making their own time schedules. For example, they should learn to estimate how long a given activity will probably take and then use time as a means of governing their efforts. "Saving" time and using time efficiently are integral aspects of good time sense and should be provided for in the unit work. The children need to learn to tell time and to have time tell them how to act. This is a difficult skill to learn unless a great deal of practice is provided.

At the prevocational and vocational levels, the use of time for scheduling and carrying out activities should be constantly reinforced. This can be meaningfully applied to *in*-school as well as *out-of* school activities if special attention is given to time by the teacher. No formal units seem called for—just frequent reference to time.

Teaching Measurement

Measurement always involves comparison and is always approximate. Any measurement requires some sequential scale that extends in equal units from a base or zero to a hypothetical infinity. Because of these requirements it is advised that only the grossest comparisons be made at the preschool and primary levels.

Formal instruction in measurement should be introduced at the intermediate level after the children have some facility in the use of numbers. Such a procedure will insure that no confusion exists between learning numbers and processes and learning to use the numbers and processes for comparison purposes.

Linear measurement should be introduced first with the introduction of a ruler and a yardstick as examples of a number line. Inches, feet, and yards can then be demonstrated as examples on a number line. Frequent practice in reading the instruments and using the units for identifying size must be provided. Any excuse for measuring during the unit work in the afternoon should be capitalized upon. Seat work involving measuring is provided in nearly all workbooks published by major companies. While these are good, they are not as effective as using actual and meaningful objects that have some purpose for being measured.

Weight measures using scales can be introduced first, as pounds and then as ounces and tons. Making a comparison chart of the weights of the children and of objects in the room is a more meaningful activity than just using unrelated objects. Relating weight to price is nicely accomplished by meat and produce examples from grocery stores or supermarkets. Comparative buying becomes meaningful in the context of food, particularly for teen-agers.

Liquid measure, such as teaspoon, tablespoon, cup, pint, quart, and gallon can be demonstrated through a collection of common containers. Pouring water or sand from one to another provides a tangible demonstration of quantity. The importance of these measures does not assume much drama until they are connected with meaningful activities. Any cooking adventure that utilizes liquid measuring is generally greeted with enthusiasm by both boys and girls.

At the prevocational and vocational levels, the excellence of the product involved in homemaking and shop studies depends upon accurate measuring. Teaching specific measuring relative to the need for the skill should be any activity pursued because of its demonstrated relevance. This becomes even more understandable when units on work, budgeting, and buying include frequent references to arithmetic functions and concepts.

Arithmetic Diagnosis

Just as communication skills may be deficient among retarded children, so may their arithmetic skills. Until 1971, no really well-constructed test that could provide both normative and diagnostic information in arithmetic was available. In that year the Key Math diagnostic arithmetic test was developed.[9]

The test is divided into three parts. Area I is content. Subtest A, Numeration, deals with the recognition of numerals—cardinal, ordinal, and Roman, the effect of decimals on place value, rounding numbers, supplying missing numbers and integers.

Subtest B, Fractions, deals with combining parts or groups, reading fractions, finding parts of numbers, improper fractions, and mixed numbers.

Subtest C, Geometry and Symbols, treats the operations, ordering, abbreviations and relationships of lines of arithmetic symbols and geometric shapes.

[9] Austin J. Connolly, William Nachtman, and E. Milo Pritchett, *Key Math* (Circle Pines, Minn.: American Guidance Service, Inc., 1971).

Area II is Operations. Subtest D, Addition, requires the combination of sets, one-digit numbers, two-digit numbers without and with regrouping, decimals, fractions and mixed numbers.

Subtest E, Subtraction, involves taking objects from a set, subtracting single-digit numbers, multi-digit numbers both without and with regrouping, and decimal, fractions, and mixed numbers.

Subtest F, Multiplication, presents low difficulty items orally, but quickly gets on one- and two-digit multipliers and multiplicands containing several digits, decimals, or fractions.

Subtest G, Division, uses one- and two-digit divisors and dividends with two or more digits, decimals, and fractions.

Subtest H, Mental Computation, is a unique test in which the child is asked to solve problems presented verbally. The computations increase in complexity from simple addition to four different computations performed in sequence.

Subtest I, Numerical Reasoning, requires the child to find and add an additional fact necessary to the solution of a problem.

Area III is Applications. Subtest J. Word Problems, has story problems read to the child by the examiner. The problems require one-step operations, multiple computations, and identifying relevant from irrelevant information.

Subtest K, Missing Elements, requires the child to identify the missing element that makes the problem solution impossible.

Subtest L, Money, requires the child to recognize money, count and make change, make value judgments in buying, interpret a budget, checks, and a checking account.

Subtest M, Measurement, requires the child to recognize common units of measure, and apply them to distance, heat, and weight in various forms.

Subtest N, Time, deals with clocks, holidays, seasons, and calendars.

One of the unique features of the test is the statement of diagnostic features in behavioral terms. For example, if the child were to miss in Area I, Content, Subtest B, Fractions, Item B-8, reference to the appendix of the Manual would indicate that the behavioral objective measured by that item would be that "Given a set of equal parts, (the child) indicates the number of parts that represent a specific fraction." Such a diagnostic statement is designed to provide the teacher with a specific instructional objective to guide the math program for the child. This unusual feature goes a long way toward helping children who have unusual problems in math. Perhaps someday similar analysis will be developed for other academic areas.

In the meantime attention to the specific problems of individual children can be guided by the diagnostic profile and the behavioral objectives appropriate to each problem failed by the child. Material specific to the identified problem is available from a wide variety of sources, but some of the more comprehensive may be those of Scott, Foresman and Company[10] or for more structured materials, Distar.[11]

---

[10] *Seeing through Arithmetic Program* K-6 (Scott, Foresman and Company, 1900 East Lake Avenue, Glenview, Ill. 60025).

[11] *Distar Arithmetic I and II* (Science Research Associates, 259 East Erie Street, Chicago, Ill. 60611).

CHAPTER 6

Social Competencies

One of the major requirements for a person's acceptance in society is appropriate social behavior. Because socially inadequate behavior is additive to the condition of mental retardation, developing acceptable social skills becomes a paramount issue in the educational program.

It is a common assumption that individuals behave in a unique manner as a function of their environmental experiences. It is assumed, for example, that a queen behaves like a queen because she always has been treated like a queen. This seems far from correct. It is more likely that a queen behaves like a queen because she has been carefully schooled in behaviors deemed necessary for functioning as a queen. Her standards of expectancy become those appropriate to a queen.

As a parallel, it seems likely that some mentally retarded children behave like mentally retarded persons because the behavioral outcomes set for them by their parents and teachers are those of substandard social behavior. If retarded youngsters are not to be further penalized by socially inadequate behavior patterns, it is vital that the educational program attend to social development in a systematic manner and that specific social outcomes be programmed.

Research on the social competencies necessary for effective work behaviors and independent living is limited, but quite suggestive. Reports from employers of what characteristics they desire in their employees are often suggestive of the Boy Scout laws: trustworthy, loyal, helpful, friendly, courteous, kind, obedient, thrifty, brave, clean, and reverent. Such an apparently cynical recitation is not as facetious as may appear on first glance. Employers *do* need employees who don't steal or lie, who can get along with the supervisor and fellow employees, and who are loyal and dependable.

Such skills are sum and substance of how one feels about himself, what kinds of social values he holds, and how he values other people. These may also be influenced by his spiritual commitments. The area of social competencies, therefore, involves instruction and experiences designed to develop the self-concept, social values, and social interaction skills. Admittedly, this is a nebulous area of instruction, but, unless teachers try to provide experiences that have relevance to the development of self-concepts, social values, and social interaction, these may never develop, and social incompetence will emerge as a product of the educational program largely by default. Such a tragic consequence certainly should not be tolerated if some positive actions show any promise at all that they may be effective in preventing socially maladaptive behavior. This chapter, therefore, has the temerity to suggest that the subjects included have relevance to social competence and are important enough to be attended to. Areas to be discussed are those related to the self, the school, the home, the neighborhood, and the community. Implicit in these areas is the reflected concern for developing adequate self-concepts, social values, and social interactions.

One difficulty of making much prescriptive sense in this area is that all social behaviors can be represented by a continuum ranging from absolutely nothing at one end to complete or constant behavior at the other. Within the social context in which one behaves, only a fairly restricted range of behavior is tolerated, and these behaviors or the range of toleration changes relative to the circumstances. Should one be insulted, for example, alternative behaviors range from walking away to attacking the insulter. However, should one choose to attack, he is expected to abide by the Marquis of Queensberry rules, and to try not to inflict permanent injury on the insulter (should the virtuous triumph). The selecting of an appropriate response to being insulted and the controlling of that response to achieve a limited goal are both the result of judgment. They are governed by the behavior repertoire and the goal-setting abilities of the insulted. To expect fine discriminations or judgments from retarded children is difficult. Yet providing some understanding and practice in this area seems mandatory. Attention in a variety of learning and experience situations should be focused on the development of social competencies—in the self, the school, the home, the neighborhood, and the community.

The Self

How one feels about himself is probably the pervading factor in all social behaviors. Since the world is evaluated through one's own eyes, the development of a self-image that is essentially optimistic yet realistic is worth considerable instructional attention. To achieve this self-concept, the child needs a great many rewarding experiences in the accomplishment of meaningful tasks and personal interactions. He also needs an opportunity to fail under conditions in which failure does not destroy his self-confidence. That is, realistic reactions to failure are part of the arsenal of appropriate adaptive behaviors. For this reason, the child should have an opportunity to learn from the failures. Therefore, the teacher must provide failure experiences under conditions that can be used to extend the child's behavior repertoire to include alternatives that turn failure into success. Most of the social development of the child occurs as a by-product of school experiences. It is not taught directly. Yet the good teacher is constantly aware of specific behaviors that need concentrated attention through unit work. In the area of the self, outcomes which should be developed at various levels are:

PRESCHOOL LEVEL
1. On request, the child can say his full name and age.
2. On request, the child can identify objects that belong to him and those that belong to others.
3. On request, the child can identify children who are taller, shorter, heavier, or lighter than he is.
4. When greeted by another person, the child will respond to the greeter either verbally, by gesture, or by facial expression harmoniously to the greeting.

PRIMARY LEVEL
1. Upon request, the child can say his home address and telephone number.
2. In a verbal discussion, the child can name each member of his family and tell two facts about each.
3. Given a self-help task such as putting on boots, brushing teeth, work-

ing zippers, buckling, buttoning, or tying, the child will respond correctly.
4. Upon request, the child will be able to wash his face, neck, ears, hands, arms, feet, and legs.
5. Upon request, the child will participate in the selection of games, food, clothing, and friends.
6. Given a task to perform, the child can determine when the task has been completed.

INTERMEDIATE LEVEL
1. Given a youngster with whom he is unfamiliar, the child will be able to make at least one acceptable gesture to become acquainted, such as: being able to name the child, play a game with him, or engage in conversation.
2. Given five pictures labeled as showing the emotions of anger, sadness, happiness, hostility, or fear, the student can identify the pictures.
3. When discussing abilities, the child will be able to choose from a list of descriptive words, those which describe his feelings when he performs well and those which describe his feelings when he performs poorly.
4. Given a law at his level of experience, the child will be able to state why it is important to obey it.
5. In a role-playing situation, the student can verbally state the difference between satisfactory and unsatisfactory behavior of the antagonists.
6. The child can participate in group discussions without arguing.

PREVOCATIONAL LEVEL
1. When verbally given the sentence started "I can," the student can tell five things he is able to do.
2. When verbally given the started sentence "I like" or "I do not like," the student can name five things for either sentence.
3. Given a situation involving the belongings of others, the student returns the property intact after every use.
4. When given a compliment, the student will respond positively with "Thank you" or a smile.
5. Given a situation in which the student is involved in a fight or becomes angry, the student will be able to verbalize what alternative actions might have been possible.
6. Given a situation involving a disagreement with another person, the child will be able to accept the situation as evidenced by his willingness to talk to or work with the other person.
7. Given a situation in which he is confronted with constructive criticism

the student will be able to respond without arguing or denying the criticism.

VOCATIONAL LEVEL
1. When someone offers to assist him, the student accepts the offer in an appropriate manner.
2. When shown pictures of interaction among people, the student will be able to identify those who exhibit cooperative behavior.
3. Given a task in which he has previously made errors, the student will be able to identify the errors and the reasons for the errors.
4. When in a social dance situation, the student can demonstrate the proper behavior for the situation.

The development of an adequate self-concept involves broadening the child's radius of concern from himself to the people with whom he comes in contact. This difficult task is dependent upon his learning to be self-directing, self-disciplining, and self-rewarding. Appropriate behavior in this area seems difficult for nonretarded individuals and apparently is even more difficult for the retarded. The teacher should be alert to the fact that social development is the constant by-product of all the interpersonal relations experienced by the child. Every effort should be made to use formal instructional periods to reinforce the lessons presented through formal instruction to develop an adequate self-concept.

In the School

Since each child must learn to generalize appropriate social behavior from the school to community living, the school becomes the place that must compensate for the fact that incidental learning is not a strength of retarded children, and that many youngsters will come from homes that represent a poor model for behavior. The school faces the difficult task of providing an atmosphere that teaches acceptable behavior both through example and planned activity. The teacher must make clear what is acceptable, and consistently reward behavior that is acceptable. Outcomes to be developed at the various levels include:

PRESCHOOL LEVEL
1. After demonstration, when asked by teacher, the child can pour liquid into a glass or cup and drink when asked.
2. After demonstration, the child can put food into a bowl and use either a fork, knife, or spoon when asked.

3. After demonstration, the child can feed, water, and clean the home of classroom pets whenever asked.
4. On request, the child can verbally state the basic classroom rules and give a reason why.
5. In a structured classroom activity, the child will accept the decisions of the person in authority without leaving the activity.
6. Within the school environment, when the teacher exhibits a positive verbal or physical response toward the child, the child's attempts to cooperate will increase.

PRIMARY LEVEL

1. Given a new situation, the child will respond with a behavior commonly acceptable in the situation.
2. Given a daily assigned chore at school, the child will be able to perform the task without complaining or having to be reminded.
3. Given the responsibility of checking out a library book the child will return the book at the stated time to the stated place.
4. Given adequate previous training or experience in a specific exercise, the child will be able to lead others in the exercise.
5. In an unstructured situation, the child will demonstrate that he identifies the rights of others by allowing them to make choices and decisions and to express themselves.
6. During free time, the child will join an activity of his own volition and/or invite other children to join him in a play activity.
7. When shown ten pictures showing interaction among people, the student can differentiate those who show cooperating behavior from those who do not.

INTERMEDIATE LEVEL

1. The student can participate in a group project without arguing or fighting.
2. Upon request, the student can verbally state five ways school experiences help people prepare for everyday living.
3. Upon request, the student can verbally state five reasons why he should practice good health habits.
4. Upon request, the student can verbally state five reasons why he should practice good habits of grooming.
5. Upon request, the student will be able to say the names of the school principal, teacher, nurse, and secretary.
6. Given an academic task that the child fails, he will not physically or verbally abuse or disrupt others but rather will seek assistance in an acceptable manner.
7. Upon receiving a reasonable request for help from a peer for a classroom task, he will fulfill the request.

PREVOCATIONAL LEVEL

1. Given a situation in which the rights of another are being violated, the student will recognize that the rights are being violated, be able to determine an appropriate course of action, and take definite action that will defend those rights.
2. Given a set of school rules he is capable of following, the student will be able to abide by them without having to be reminded of them more than once.
3. Given a classroom situation where other students are involved, the student will be able to demonstrate an interest in the activity of others as demonstrated by taking part in the activity without distracting or disrupting those involved.
4. In group discussions and gatherings, the student will voluntarily contribute at least one idea, thought, or feeling during the time of the meeting.
5. Given an assigned work task involving two or more students, they will work together until the task is completed.
6. During a structured situation in which two students who have expressed a dislike for each other must work next to each other, the student will be able to work without teacher correction.
7. Given a competitive situation, the student will be able to contribute as a member of a team by demonstrating his ability to follow the rules of the game.

VOCATIONAL LEVEL

1. Given a social situation, the student will be able to select the clothing proper for the occasion and verbally offer two reasons to support the selection.
2. Upon request, the student will be able to state verbally five principles of grooming and relate them to employment or social situations.
3. In a given social situation, the student will be able to state verbally the appropriate graces called for and defend his selection of the behaviors named.
4. Upon request, the student will be able to define honesty, truthfulness, and tolerance, and cite examples of each.
5. Upon request, the student will be able to state a set of moral standards and explain and defend them.
6. Upon request, the student will be able to explain and demonstrate his understanding of the need for sharing in maintaining good relations with fellow employees.
7. Upon request, the student will be able to explain verbally the differences between the role of leader and worker in an employment situation.
8. Given a situation, the student will be able to set up committees and other groups necessary for organization in order to accomplish a goal.

Specific units of instruction devoted to the outcomes will be necessary to insure coverage of the skills, but the effectiveness of the learnings will depend to a much larger degree upon the awareness of the teacher in reinforcing desired behaviors in all classroom activities.

The Home, Neighborhood, and Community

Social competence as demonstrated by the development of an adequate self-concept and appropriate behavior in school has its final validation by the transfer of these behaviors to home and community actions. While the supervision of these behaviors outside the school is difficult except in vocational settings, the school is the principal institution which can provide both instruction and some practice in developing the correct behaviors. Outcomes desired are:

PRESCHOOL LEVEL
1. Given an assigned home task that he can perform, the child will accomplish it to the satisfaction of the parents and will be able to state when he has done it well.
2. Given a written note or a verbal message the child will deliver them to the designated person.
3. Upon request, the child will be able to state verbally three things about the work of his father, mother, or surrogates.

PRIMARY LEVEL
1. Upon request, the child will be able to tell the location of stores and public buildings with reference to his house.
2. Upon request, the child will be able to prepare a simple breakfast of cereal, milk, and toast.
3. Upon request, the child will be able to use a vacuum cleaner, dust pan and broom, can opener, dust cloth, mixer, mop and scrub brush, and stove.
4. Upon request, the child will be able to state reasons for starting work on time and putting things away when home chores are finished.
5. In role playing, the child will be able to ask a stranger for directions while maintaining a cautious distance and cordial behavior.
6. Upon request, the child will be able to state verbally two behavior rules that apply to each situation of being at the movies, riding on a bus or subway, in a restaurant, swimming pool, or library.
7. Upon request, the child will be able to describe at a simple level the need for each of the community helpers: police, firemen, garbage collector, bus driver, or subway conductor.

8. Upon request, the child will be able to describe at a simple level the need for each of the family service persons: doctors, dentists, nurses, clergymen, druggists, welfare worker.

INTERMEDIATE LEVEL

1. Upon request, the student will be able to find the telephone numbers of the Police Department and Fire Department in the local telephone book.
2. Given a public transportation system, the student will be able to describe which bus or subway he would use to go from his home to a downtown shopping area.
3. Upon request, the student will be able to name five local businesses, five occupations, and five different jobs people perform.
4. Upon request, the student will be able to name five historical figures and describe the contribution of each.
5. Upon request, the student will be able to name the mayor, governor, and president.

PREVOCATIONAL LEVEL

1. Upon request, the student can verbally state three responsibilities of a wage earner in a family.
2. Upon request, the student can verbally state five responsibilities of a homemaker in a family.
3. Upon request, the student will be able to supply three effects companions have on each other.
4. Given a map of the state, the student will be able to identify and briefly describe each of the major geographical areas.
5. When a state government division is named, the student will be able to tell its major function.
6. Upon request, the student will be able to identify each of the major utilities that serve houses.

VOCATIONAL LEVEL

1. When questioned, the student will be able to state his obligations as a family member and cite examples.
2. Upon request, the student will be able to differentiate between benefits and nonbenefits of neighborhood life.
3. Given either pictures of traffic signs or the signs themselves, the student will be able to describe their meaning.
4. Given a road map, the student will be able to identify the directions north, south, east, and west.
5. Given a road map, the student will be able to produce a route from any given point to another.
6. Upon request, the student will be able to identify agencies providing

help in cases of specific family emergencies and describe how to secure the help.

7. Upon request, the student will be able to cite examples of behaviors that reflect the responsibilities, duties, and rights of citizens.
8. Upon request, the student will be able to plan and prepare a proper breakfast, lunch, or dinner.
9. Given a bundle of dirty clothes, the student will be able to sort and wash the clothes, using the appropriate settings for kinds and colors.
10. Given a basket of newly washed clothes, the student will be able to iron them, using the proper settings for each item of clothing.

Teaching Social Competencies

It has been suggested that child rearing in a democracy should start with the premise that all children will grow up to be productive citizens. Such an approach implies that each child should be expected to exercise self-discipline because that kind of behavior is essential to democratic living. It would be further expected that each child is held responsible for his behavior, acceptable as well as nonacceptable. Finally, each child would be expected to achieve to the best of his ability. He would be a contributing member of society.

Such a climate of expectation and treatment should be part and parcel of the special education program. The tone should be set by the teacher through the reinforcement of acceptable acts from the moment a child enters the program. The teacher must interact with the child as a person who is worthwhile.

Units of experience lend themselves to both teaching social competence and providing practice in the implementation of the concepts in social situations. Since no formal period for teaching social competencies is provided, units should be planned that teach the concept and the use of behaviors specifically. Chapters 10 and 11 include units that are designed to foster social competencies. These units, however, may need to be augmented by specific attention to behaviors that are especially troublesome. A mechanism for attending to this problem is through sociodrama.

The technique of sociodrama is, in reality, a substitute for actual training in social situations where correct behavior is rewarded and incorrect behavior is not. Obviously few schools are equipped to provide all the social opportunities that may be encountered by the youngsters. One advantage of sociodrama, however, is the opportunity to explore alternative behaviors for the evaluation of each one's consequences. That is, in a given social situation a person reacts. The actions change the situation in a manner that cannot be altered. In sociodrama, a reenactment, perhaps several, allows an examination of the consequences of words or acts and a chance to decide what the best course of action may be. For this reason, the use of sociodrama is highly recommended.

Self-management implies an activity that most people seem to learn incidently but which retarded youngsters often do not. This activity is self-role playing. It is vividly illustrated by a child who talks to an imaginary playmate, assigning one kind of behavior to himself and another to his alter ego. This is not far different from an adult's talking over a problem with a friend who "plays" the part of the boss, wife, or whomever. Similar is the common tendency for an adult to practice what he will do or say as he anticipates an anxiety-provoking encounter. "When he says to me, 'Keep away from me,' I will say to him— 'Gladly.' This will make him stop because he will not expect me to say that. Then I will say . . . ." Often this self-dialogue will be stopped, altered, reversed, or discarded, but it is essentially intrapersonal socio-drama used to examine alternative behaviors that may be used if the circumstances demand it. For many people this kind of intrapersonal discussion is a vital aspect of social behavior. It is a fine example of a defensive strategy for protecting the self-concept by using a controlled offensive maneuver—namely, preplanning. As such it has great utility.

Mentally retarded youngsters probably have an even greater need to do preplanning because of their great vulnerability, and perhaps they can learn this strategy of intrapersonal dialogue, but this seems quite unlikely in view of their limited thought processes. However, group sociodrama can partially compensate for their inability to solve social problems through preplanning by attending to commonly encountered problems and evaluating alternative solutions. In this way they will have at least some behavior strategies in their repertoire.

At the preschool and primary levels sociodrama can be effectively used in an uncomplicated way. If, in the usual pushing and grabbing practiced by children, an accident occurs caused by antisocial behavior, a teacher can teach an immediate lesson through role switching. Placing the injured (superficial) child in the role of the injuror and the injuror in the victim's place gives the teacher a chance to have the children re-enact the accident for evaluative purposes. "How do you feel when someone bumps you?" "How do you feel when you bump someone?" "Did Jimmy do the best thing?" "What is the best thing to do?" Having the children switch roles certainly is a start toward developing empathy from an actual encounter. At older age levels more formal attention to social problems is indicated. The vehicle may well be planned sociodrama.

There are five aspects of sociodrama, each with special considerations that require attention. First, a social problem that is relevant to the youngsters must be identified. The problem must be stated in terms that are amenable to behavioral interpretation. Action themes meet this criterion, philosophical or value questions do not. Thus problems that emerge from an encounter or activity are best suited for sociodrama. The questions should, however, have an ethical or moral base such as those represented by the Boy Scout laws. Although it is not feasible to talk about or dramatize trustworthiness, it is feasible to role-play a situation like, "Ozzie, my supervisor, said I could take home meat scraps from the market." In like manner, any of the other laws take on meaning. As a general rule, however, the sociodrama should deal with immediate social problems in the home, school, neighborhood, and community and not be systematically contrived to fit any list of ethical or moral concepts.

Second, the problem should be explored by the teacher and students to identify the circumstances and the cast of characters. The assignment of roles should be made with a full character delineation of each person. Questions that probe, such as "What kind of a man is the boss?" "How would you describe him?" or "You are going to pretend you are the boss; how do you feel?" can help to pinpoint the direction the drama will take.

Third, the actual dramatization should start with a re-enactment of the encounter that precipitated the original problem. Although spontaneity is desirable, it is not the key to successful sociodrama, so it is often necessary for the teacher to interject thoughts, directions, and even dialogue.

Fourth, the evaluation of the sociodrama should be made by the whole class in order to arrive at alternative solutions that are then examined to see which is the best solution. This may require role-switching. For example, have a recalcitrant child play the harried mother's role so he may get some feel for the tribulations of being the mother of such a troublesome child.

Fifth is the search for metamessages—the hidden motivation behind words. Understanding the underlying meaning in the communication between people is a subtle art not mastered by many. Yet it is an important social skill and one that distinguishes the sensitive from the insensitive person. Questions like "Why do you think he said that?" or "What did he really mean when he said you were different?"

can help to focus discussion on underlying motivation and disguised meanings. This probing must be teacher-directed. It is an important but very difficult skill to teach, yet it may be vital to the future social survival of the youngsters.

It is possible that retarded individuals will learn proper social skills only with partial success. The difficulty with trial and error thought processes that they exhibit argues against their being able to generalize principles of behavior to new situations in an effective manner. The school therefore, can only partially compensate by providing experiences in role-switching, role-playing, and intrapersonal dialogue dealing with social problems that seem likely to be encountered by the youngsters both in and out of school.

New materials that support affective development appear almost daily, most with little empirical data to validate their use. Two that have been somewhat studied are DUSO and the Social Living Curriculum.

DUSO (Developing Understanding of Self and Others) consists of a kit, quite similar to the Peabody Language Development Kits, in which a wise dolphin character does most of the moralizing so personal identification is possible, but nonthreatening also. A series of stories of incidents on tape, records, filmstrips, and pamphlets describe occurrences that pose a problem which has several possible alternative solutions. The major strength of the series, however, is probably in the suggested activities questions. These question why principal characters behaved in the ways described, whether the behavior was justified, and whether it accomplished the purpose intended. Pupils must do a considerable amount of thinking to come up with answers to any of these kinds of questions, but of most importance is the consideration of alternatives and the need to evaluate each as a way of solving the problem. This achieves much the same end as role-playing. It should be cautioned that the DUSO materials are designed for children between the levels of kindergarten and sixth grade so teenagers often find them babyish. An additional problem is that there may be a tendency for some teachers to use the DUSO kits in place of role-playing. While it is quite possible to do so, the techniques really complement each other and thus enhance social development. As difficult as it is to reach the behavioral objectives in this area, any extra help should be welcomed, not rejected.

The Social Living Curriculum materials were developed by Herbert Goldstein and tried out experimentally by teachers in the New York area. The research data are more of a formative nature than product; that is, the teachers were more concerned with ways of using the materials than with whether they accomplished the advertised purpose. In this regard the reports were generally encouraging. The teachers found the materials helpful and the youngsters found them absorbing and real. Since they are designed to be used by teenage youngsters and young adults, this means they can be used at the prevocational and vocational levels.

CHAPTER 7

Motor Skills and Recreation

Motor Skills

Ever since Seguin prescribed a motor activity program to improve the functioning of neural pathways so sensations could be better imprinted on the brain, the relationship of cognitive functions to motor performance has received attention by professionals in mental retardation.[1] Most recently, Delacato has advocated a motor activity program that is aimed at establishing neuromuscular patterns of a more intact nature than those that would develop without special training.[2] Kephart, on the other hand, used motor activity as a basis for developing stable perceptual organizations or motor information on the nature of things in the world.[3]

Whether neural functioning is directly or even indirectly influenced

[1] Edward Seguin, *Idiocy and Its Treatment by the Physiological Method* (New York: Bureau of Publications, Teachers College, Columbia University, 1907).

[2] C. H. Delacato, *The Diagnosis and Treatment of Speech and Reading Problems* (Springfield, Ill.: Charles C Thomas, Publisher, 1963).

[3] N. C. Kephart, *The Slow Learner in the Classroom* (Columbus, Ohio: Charles E. Merrill Books, Inc., 1960).

by motor acts has never been empirically demonstrated. However, the influence of motor performance on employability has been found to be substantial.[4] Therefore, a program of motor development emerges as an important aspect of the total development of retarded youngsters.

Research on the relationship of mental retardation and motor performance has been well summarized by Malpass[5] and Stein.[6] Nearly all of the findings are consistent in indicating that the degree of motor incoordination is roughly equivalent to the degree of retardation demonstrated. Studies by Cratty[7] and by Rarick and Francis[8] have indicated that the proficiency of retarded youngsters closely approximates their mental ages, but the degree of motor deficiency ranges from none to a great deal, with an average of about 10 percent less than average children. It should be noted, however, that some retarded individuals have demonstrated remarkable skill in specific athletic activities. From the research findings, it seems safe to conclude that motor performance looms as a most crucial aspect of employability, and that retarded youngsters are potentially capable of nearer normal performance in this area than any other.

A systematic program promises such great dividends that it cannot afford to be ignored or left to chance. It must be carefully planned and executed throughout the entire school career of each youngster. Such a statement could not have been made as recently as 20 years ago. Prior to that time, almost no research had investigated what results could be expected from systematic training programs. Howe in 1959 compared the performance of normal and retarded boys and girls after only 10 days of instruction in three motor activities.[9] The striking

[4] Fount G. Warren, "Ratings of Employed and Unemployed Mentally Handicapped Males on Personality and Work Factors," *American Journal of Mental Deficiency*, LXV (March 1961), 629–633; and Jerry D. Chaffin, "Production Rate as a Variable in the Job Success or Failure of Educable Mentally Retarded Adolescents," unpublished doctoral dissertation, University of Kansas. Lawrence, Kansas, 1967.

[5] Leslie F. Malpass, "Motor Skills in Mental Deficiency," in Norman R. Ellis (ed.), *Handbook of Mental Deficiency* (New York: McGraw-Hill, Inc., 1963).

[6] Julian V. Stein, "Motor Functions and Physical Fitness for the Mentally Retarded: A Critical Review," *Rehabilitation Literature*, XXIV (August 1963), 230–242.

[7] Bryant J. Cratty, "Perceptual-Motor Abilities of Mentally Retarded Youth," Los Angeles, Calif.: University of California at Los Angeles, Department of Physical Education, 1966. Pamphlet.

[8] Lawrence Rarick and R. J. Francis, *Motor Characteristics of the Mentally Retarded*, Cooperative Research Monograph No. 1 (Washington, D.C.: U.S. Department of Health, Education, and Welfare, 1960).

[9] C. Howe, "A Comparison of Motor Skills of Mentally Retarded and Normal Children," *Exceptional Children*, XXV (April 1959), 352–354.

finding was that both groups showed similar patterns of improvement, even though the normal youngsters were superior in their performances. Similar studies by Stein and Pangle,[10] Corder,[11] and Oliver,[12] while rather limited as to the amount of instruction provided, have reported encouraging results.

While it is presently difficult (because of lack of research) to stipulate even minimum levels of motor skills that should be achieved at specific developmental levels (preschool, primary, intermediate, prevocational, and vocational), it is certain that each child should be exposed to a developmental and a recreational program that provides maximum opportunity for motor growth.

Kephart has suggested that the massed-differentiated-integrated developmental theory developed by Coghill and applied by Kirk to reading (see Chapter 4) is applicable to motor skill development. It is the thesis of this theory that motor skills develop from gross to fine through two principles: (1) the cephalo-caudal principle, which suggests that development proceeds from head to feet; and (2) the proximal-distal principle, which suggests that the development proceeds from the body midline out to the periphery. In Kephart's explanation, future stable perceptions depend upon the youngster's developing integrated motor patterns having to do with laterality and directionality. Cross-lateral coordination and the proper understanding of left-right, up-down, and front-back, depend upon adequate motor explorations by the developing youngster. Whether the theory is correct or not, laterality and directionality can be demonstrated to be intimately involved in efficient coordination skills. Therefore, it would appear that complete physical education programs could well begin with the development of lateral and directional differentiation, using the massed-differentiated-integrated theory as a guide for instruction.

In 1965, the writer and his colleagues analyzed 46 jobs done by retarded young adults to determine what skills were necessary for successful performance. Although the procedure of analysis was both crude and subjective, it was possible to identify that three basic attri-

[10] Julian U. Stein and Ray Pangle, "What Research Says about Psychomotor Function of the Retarded," *Activity Programs for the Mentally Retarded*. Reprinted from the *Journal of Health, Physical Education and Recreation*, April 1966.

[11] W. O. Corder, "Effects of Physical Education on the Intellectual, Physical, and Social Development of Educable Mentally Retarded Boys," unpublished Special Project, George Peabody College, Nashville, Tenn., 1965.

[12] J. N. Oliver, "The Effect of Physical Conditioning Exercises and Activities on the Mental Characteristics of Educationally Subnormal Boys," *British Journal of Educational Psychology*, XXVIII (June 1958), 155–165.

butes were required—strength, speed, and coordination—and that each involved the fingers, hands, arms, legs, and back. Repetition of the analysis in Cheyenne, Wyoming, on 1240 jobs confirmed the 1965 findings.[13] The Peterson and Jones job analysis provides a similar list but is more extensive in its analysis.[14]

From the foregoing, it would appear that a developmental physical education program should proceed from the gross to the fine, start with directionality and laterality, and culminate in integrational activities. All should contribute to the development of strength, speed, and coordination. Perhaps the most complete program is one developed by Ernie Davis at the Crowley Special School, St. Paul, Minnesota.

Testing Mobility

Davis suggests beginning with a mobility testing program involving crawling, stand-up mobility, balance, dominance, and counter moves as follows:

1. *Crawling Mobility.* Flat on his belly, have the child crawl the length of a 15-foot mat. Check which leg drags or moves only halfway when crawling. Note the arm pull on those dragging legs and whether the counter moves are appropriate. The test is scored with a "1" for satisfactory through "5" for unsatisfactory, but could be just as appropriately scored only qualitatively. That is, since the test is essentially diagnostic, the information that is really critical to good programming involves noting which aspects of crawling are not satisfactory. Remediation is individual—exercising to correct the incorrect movement. A quantitative score does not really contribute much to programming. This also holds for the other four tests described.

2. *Stand-up Mobility.* Have the child walk at a normal pace toward you. Watch for the left arm to advance with the right leg or vice versa. The head should move in the direction of the advancing hand. The same counter motions should be observed when the child is asked to trot. In a sprint, look for the knees to be brought high and the advancing leg to reach in the stride. Ask the child to side skip in a circle. Heels should be brought together and then opened. Check for leg drag. Reverse the direction. Have the child walk up and down steps. Head should be up and chin level with the floor. Children

---

[13] Wilma Hirst, *Occupational Needs of the Socioeconomic, Disadvantaged, and Other Handicapped Youth of Laramie County School District Number One, Phase One*, June 1, 1967.

[14] R. C. Peterson and E. M. Jones, *Guide to Jobs for the Mentally Retarded*, rev. ed. (Pittsburgh: American Institute for Research, 1964).

should learn stand-up mobility skills so they need not watch their feet when going up steps or walking.

3. *Balance.* Have the child hop for 15 feet, change legs and return; check for dragging and watching the feet. Have the child mark two of his own body lengths on the floor. He should then do two standing broad jumps in succession, turn and do two returning jumps. Check for feet kept together, arms working together, and the distance jumped. With a same-sized partner, have the child do a walk, knee dip, turn, and return. Children should be side by side with arms in back of the partner at the waist. Check for coordination of movement and balance in the dip and turn. Without a partner, have the child repeat the walk, dip, and turn. Check balance particularly.

4. *Dominance.* Have the child throw a ball in his preferred hand. Then have him bowl a ball. Look for proper counter moves. Have the child strike at a ball or target. Note handedness. Have the child do a side kick, a running place kick, and a punt. Note which foot is used and balance in follow through. Have the child pretend to aim a gun or shoot an arrow. Note which eye is the aiming eye. Eye and hand preference should coincide.

5. *Counter Moves.* Every motion has a counter move. Check to make sure that each motion has a proper counter move.

From the diagnostic tests, the instructor can identify the deficiencies exhibited by each child that need special attention. These should be given individual attention through calisthenics and muscle development exercises. An excellent source book of exercises for specific muscle groups and movements has been written by Schurr.[15]

Motor and Recreational Skills

Although both motor and recreation skills are grouped together, the motor skills are more basic and should be emphasized earliest. However, each area supports the other area and neither should be sacrificed. Outcomes to be developed are:

PRESCHOOL LEVEL

1. Given a row of children standing one behind the other, the child will make a verbal indication of his presence within 10 seconds of the time the person in front of him has verbalized his presence.

2. Given a ball 6 inches in diameter, and thrown from a distance of

[15] Evelyn L. Schurr, *Movement Experiences for Children* (New York: Appleton-Century-Crofts, 1967).

5 feet, the student will catch the ball so that it does not touch the floor.

3. Given a ball 6 inches in diameter, the student will throw the ball with an overhand motion a distance of 8 feet.

4. Given a 20-inch bat and a 4-inch ball thrown from a distance of 5 feet, the student will hit the ball while it is still in the air, causing the direction of the ball to be altered.

5. Given toys appropriate to the child's functioning level and time to play by himself, the student will play without making a fuss for a period of 20 minutes.

6. Given a model and a simple finger play, the child will imitate the finger movements of the model.

7. Given a ball 12 inches in diameter and a smooth solid floor, the student will throw the ball down and proceed to catch it as it comes back up to him.

PRIMARY LEVEL

1. Given a set of vertical climbing bars, the student will climb up one side of the bars, cross over, and climb down the opposite side.

2. Given a set of "hand over hand" bars 5 feet off the ground, the student will hang by both hands from the first rung, reach one hand forward to the next rung, and bring his second hand forward, without falling.

3. Given the direction to do a forward somersault, the student will perform the task without falling to either side.

4. Given a stable floor, the student will stand on one foot for a period of 10 seconds, without putting down his other foot.

5. Given a balance beam 4 inches wide and 6 feet long, the student will walk along the balance beam, placing one foot in front of the other, heel to toe.

6. Given a weight of at least 5 pounds with a handle, the student will bend at the knees to grab the weight, keeping his back straight, then pick up the weight by straightening his legs, until he has reached a vertical standing position.

7. Given only the level ground, the student will jump with both feet together so that both feet reach a level of 2 inches off the ground.

8. Given either the left or the right foot, the student will move from a position of standing on one foot and hop forward, landing on the same foot, without falling over.

9. Given the direction to move in a sliding movement, the student will step forward with one foot, then slide the second along the ground to meet the first.

10. Given an object thrown or rolled toward him from a distance of at least 8 feet, the student will move so that the object does not hit him.

11. Given a prostrate position with arms at the sides and legs together on the floor, the student will roll over in either direction at least four times, keeping his hips centered along a straight line.
12. Given a ball 3 inches in diameter, or a beanbag, and a target 1 foot in diameter at a distance of 8 feet, the student will toss the ball or beanbag with an underhand motion, so that the ball or beanbag hits the target.

INTERMEDIATE LEVEL

1. Given a ball 12 inches in diameter and a smooth solid surface, the student will bounce the ball at least three times, so that his hand hits the ball between each time it hits the ground.
2. Given a 10-inch ball, thrown from a distance of 5 feet, the student will catch the ball using only his hands and fingers.
3. Given a 10-inch ball, being rolled from a distance of 8 feet, the student will step forward and kick the ball so that it returns in the general direction of delivery.
4. Given simple folk dances, with distinct verbal "calling," the student will follow the steps and directions called for in the dance.
5. Given structured games with up to five rules, the student will participate in the games in accordance to the rules.

PREVOCATIONAL AND VOCATIONAL LEVELS

1. Given clubs appropriate to the student's interests and open to him, the student will join and participate in such clubs and organizations.
2. Given the opportunity, the student will voluntarily participate in sports activities on both the individual and team level.
3. Given bingo, simple card games, and checkers, the student will demonstrate his ability to play and verbalize how he could become involved in such games.
4. Given the basic dances appropriate for the geographical area, the student will demonstrate his ability to perform the dances appropriate to the music provided.
5. Given the games baseball, football, hockey, and basketball, the student will explain the scoring system of each.
6. Given a supine position on the floor, with knees bent and feet flat on the floor, the student will bend from the waist, raising his head to a position where he can touch his chin to his knees, then return to the starting position a total of (x) number of times (sit-ups).
7. Given a supine position on the floor, with arms extended out along the floor and perpendicular to the body, and with legs pointed in the direction of the ceiling, the student will move his legs together, from side to side, touching the floor on each side and always keeping his legs perpendicular to his body (hip twist).
8. Given a supine position on the floor with elbows propped against the

floor and hands under hips, the student will raise his legs to a position above his body and move his feet and legs in a pedaling motion (bicycle).

Teaching Mobility

Materials from a variety of different sources have been collected into an easy to use series of lessons by Robert Valett.[16] These start with activities that require nothing more than a little space in a classroom and no more materials than usual classroom furniture. The materials include a mobility test similar to that of Davis, but the test has teaching lessons that correlate with the test so they can be applied to each child's individual problem.

The diagnostic test and the remedial programs cover a variety of activities. The principle motor skills are those of rolling, sitting, crawling, walking, running, throwing, jumping, skipping, dancing, balance and rhythm, body spatial organization, dexterity, tactile discrimination, directionality, laterality, and time orientation. The 228-page loose leaf notebook covers a number of other areas also such as perceptual discrimination. Certainly one of its strengths is the fact that the notebook allows a teacher to add new materials as appropriate in each section.

In addition to the pure movement activities, the need for youngsters to learn game skills so they can participate with their peers in athletic games looms as an overriding concern. Foremost in these skills are those of throwing, catching, and striking. One way to teach these skills has been described by Davis. In preparation for nearly all his activities, Davis[17] taught his students how to "fall in" in military formation according to height and to count off by twos. This technique makes it possible to form two teams of about equal size simply by grouping the ones and the twos. A dividend is that pairs of about equal size can be formed by taking each 1 and 2 in sequence.

To throw and catch a ball, the students start with about a 10-inch ball for each pair of children. The students in each pair kneel facing each other no more than 10 feet apart. The students then roll the ball between partners. The real trick to rolling and stopping the ball is in the finger position. The youngsters should be taught to point their fingers down and move their hands, arms, and finger toward the target

[16] Robert Valett, *Remediation of Learning Disabilities* (Palo Alto, Calif.: Fearon Publishers, 1968).

[17] "The Ernie Davis Lesson Plan Book" (St. Paul, Minn.: H. M. Smyth Co., 1965).

from the back of the ball. The partner should be taught to stop the ball with hands together, fingers pointed down. Once this rolling and stopping has been mastered the youngsters should be taught to bounce the ball while still kneeling. Now they should learn to keep their fingers pointed up. The ball should be pushed so it falls about half way between partners and bounces about chest high. The key to ball handling is that the ball is caught and pushed with fingers pointed down when the ball is below the waist and with the fingers up when the ball is above the waist.

After the children have learned to catch and push with partners they need to learn to bounce and catch alone. Here, the key is to extend the fingers forward with the hands together. The movement is a pushing down movement, not a drop or slap. When mastered with both hands, the children should then learn to push down with one hand. This, of course, is dribbling, a skill that takes an enormous amount of practice to perfect. Obviously using balls of different sizes, materials, and resiliency characteristics provides nearly an endless opportunity for variety.

Throwing one handed is a complex skill, but can be taught using some of Davis' suggestions. First, the child needs to learn how to shift weight. The child can be instructed to stand with the left foot ahead of the other by about 18 inches or so. He should then be instructed to put his right thumb in his right ear. Then he should point his forefinger forward as he moves his weight to his left foot. When the movement has been mastered, a ball (tennis) should be put in his right hand. Then he should put his right thumb in his ear, shift weight, and throw from that basic position.

Striking a ball may consist of either kicking, hitting with the hand or with a bat or racquet. For kicking or hitting with the hand, the feet position and weight shift just described is basic. First the children should learn to hit a ball that is motionless on the ground or a tee and later a ball that is rolled, pitched, or on a tether of some kind. Timing is crucial and requires much practice to perfect.

Hitting a ball with a bat is somewhat different, but some of the skills used in throwing one handed can be used. Putting a large ball on a tee that is waist high, the child should be positioned to stand with his left side in the direction he wants to hit. Have him put his right thumb in his right ear. Place the bat in his hand and have him grip below his right hand on the bat handle with his left hand. The weight shift should be on the right foot when the bat is held and shifted forward to the left foot as the bat is swung forward to meet the ball on the tee. After practice the ball can be made smaller, pitched, bounced or swung on a tether so greater skills can be developed. Although there are many other skills that will need to be developed, the basic ones just mentioned can go a long way toward allowing the children to participate with others in cooperative as well as competitive games.

In addition to the foregoing suggestions, the American Association for Health, Physical Education, and Recreation (AAHPER) supported a project on physical activities for the mentally retarded. In 1968 they published their report, which is available from AAHPER, along with a series of newsletters called *Challenge*, which describe new techniques and materials for use in physical education and recreation.

All of these can be highly recommended because they have been tried out on retarded youngsters.

At the preschool level, after the youngsters have been tested for any motor skill deficiency, the class period can start with having the youngsters "fall in," "dress right," and "open ranks." The next few minutes should be devoted to calisthenics. Skill training followed by organizational games which use the skills taught could be scheduled for the final 20 minutes of the period. For example, if the youngsters are just learning to roll and catch a ball, they could roll the balls between partners for 5 or 10 minutes and then play dodge ball for the final 10 or 15 minutes of the period. For variety, one or two days each week can be allowed for free play after the calisthenics and skill training have been completed. If free play is allowed, a large number of items should be available to play with. Every playground should have jungle gyms, monkey bars, balance boards, tether balls, shuffle boards, jump ropes, and basketball hoops adjusted for the height of the youngsters. Sand boxes, culverts, slides, and obstacle courses are desirable. If physical education is held indoors, the same kind of equipment should be provided with the addition of tumbling mats and other gymnastic equipment.

Too many schools treat the physical education period as a recess. It is here contended that physical education is an important class and should be planned with equipment provided to cater to the developmental needs of the children. Haphazard activity does no credit to the school, and contributes virtually nothing to the children's development.

Games suitable for the teaching and practice of skills of turning, dodging, stopping, starting, twisting, turning, catching, and throwing can be used at the preschool, primary, and intermediate levels with few modifications for the different groups. Julia Molloy of the Orchard

School, Evanston, Illinois, has described a large number of games suitable for both indoor and outdoor play. Most require very inexpensive equipment and may be played in places where space is limited.

Under the auspices of the Kennedy Foundation and in cooperation with AAHPER, a project on recreation and fitness for the mentally retarded was initiated in 1965. Pilot programs for the retarded were supported in various parts of the country. The reports from these programs contained descriptions of games developed to teach specific skills to the retarded youngsters. These descriptions are available from the project headquarters.[18] In addition, a listing and description of games was prepared by C. C. Franklin. This booklet is available from the same source. Especially useful descriptions have been prepared by the Seattle, Washington, Public Schools; the Memphis, Tennessee, Public Schools; the Boulder Valley Public Schools, Boulder, Colorado; and the Hamilton, Ohio, Public Schools. These are also available from the AAHPER headquarters.

Teaching Swimming

One program that needs special discussion is that of teaching swimming to the retarded. Whether the instruction is done as part of the school program or a recreation program, every youngster should have the chance to learn to swim and to receive the attendant water safety instruction.

Ernie Davis has described a step-by-step program of swimming instruction for retarded youngsters.[19] Essentially the program starts with the youngsters standing in waist-deep water. Next, each child puts a washcloth over his face and wipes his face up toward and over the top of the head. Then the child blows air through the washcloth while it is held on his face. Then they hold the washcloth on the face, bent forward, and blow air through the cloth into the pool water. Still using the washcloth, they put their faces in the water, remove the cloth, and hold their breath while under water. They are then taught to windmill their arms while walking on the bottom. They are instructed to watch the leading arm. This teaches head turning for proper breath control later on. After the arm crawl stroke, the flutter kick is added to the pattern and swimming occurs. Other aspects of different strokes and general water safety are taught as the youngsters mature

[18] The address is 1201 16th Street, N.W., Washington, D.C., 20036.

[19] Information may be obtained by writing him at the Crowley Special School, St. Paul, Minnesota, 55107.

in their skill. The technique is easy to use and applicable in any instructional program.

Physical education at the prevocational and vocational levels can well be patterned after the Ernie Davis lessons. In addition, recreational skills should be programmed. If the school systems have a full-hour physical education program, at least two days each week should be devoted to recreational skill training. Included should be those individual and small group games that are mentioned in Chapter 10. Games ranging from croquet to solitaire to social dancing need to be a part of the leisure time skills and cannot be assumed to have been taught to the youngsters in their own homes. In a nation that prides itself on the shortening of the work week, it seems most unwise to provide a training program that will equip a youngster to work but gives him no tools to cope with the increasing amounts of nonworking time with which he must learn to live.

Recreation[20]

Organizations

Many organizations exist that cater to youth—Boy and Girl Scouts, 4-H, YWCA, Boys Clubs, and a host of others. Most of these clubs have programs that encourage some kind of achievement activity for true membership. Since many retarded youngsters have difficulty in meeting the competitive achievement standards of some organizations, most of the organizations have ignored the retardates as youngsters who did not really have much to contribute to them, nor did the organizations have much to contribute to the youngsters.

Under the urging of the National Association for Retarded Citizens, the Boy Scouts of America reexamined its offerings relative to the retarded. The result of this reassessment has been a major effort to provide scouting experiences for retarded boys. In May 1966, a handbook was issued by the National Council of the Boy Scouts of America that details the commitment of the organizations to the retarded. The excellently done handbook describes the steps to be taken in organizing a unit, the rules and regulations for membership and advancement, and provides detailed instructions concerning procedures designed to allow the retarded Scout to advance through the Scout ranks in a legitimate, meaningful, and rewarding manner.

[20] A more comprehensive list of recreational skills is suggested in Chapter 12.

This effort emerges as a giant stride in public understanding and concern by a large and influential youth organization. Certainly every teacher should support the program by referring eligible members and offering whatever help is sought by the organization's leaders. Equally important is the opportunity of interested teachers to use the example and materials of the Boy Scouts to awaken other organizations to the potential benefits of their programs to retarded children and young people. Public support may also be needed, but teachers are in a unique position to urge provisions for the retarded in city, county, regional, state, and national recreational programs and should do so whenever possible. The Boy Scout example is an excellent one to emulate.

Camping

Many school systems have camping programs available to them. Quite often there is some confusion over whether a camp program should be educational or recreational in nature. The confusion seems unnecessary when the camp environment is considered in terms of what it lends itself best to in meeting the needs of youngsters. The best setting for teaching work skills, for example, is in a business or industry. The best setting for teaching academics is in a school. A camp, however, is eminently suited to teaching the social skills of cooperation and developing individual responsibility. The immediate and natural consequences of encounters with a primitive (relatively unimproved) environment provides rewarding or punishing consequences of a most understandable sort. If you do not gather wood, you have no fire. No fire, no warm food. Such lessons are simple, yet vivid.

Effective camping experiences need planning and execution just as surely as any other learning experiences. And, as in other aspects of the program, enumerating the developmental outcomes can provide guidelines for the planning. In the social development areas, Baumgartner[21] has provided a sequence that is a hierarchy of skills to be developed:

1. Social Participation
   a. Isolates himself, works or plays alone
   b. Plays or works near another child, but not necessarily with him
   c. Begins to attend to activities in a group situation (for example, around a campfire)
   d. Becomes secure to the extent that he will attempt a new activity
   e. Operates comfortably on the fringe of a group

[21] Bernice B. Baumgartner, *Helping the Trainable Mentally Retarded Child* (New York: Bureau of Publications, Teachers College, Columbia University, 1960).

    f. Works or plays cooperatively with one or more
    g. Works as a contributing group member
    h. Initiates activity
2. Developing Responsibility
    a. Observes others carrying out individual or group tasks
    b. Begins to help with a task when helped by someone
    c. Needs some assistance in carrying out a task
    d. Volunteers to carry out a task, but needs some help
    e. Shows increasing independence in performing a task but will ask for help when necessary
    f. Assumes responsibility for carrying out a task
    g. Shows others how to accomplish a task with which he is familiar

The camp program has a wide range of activities available. It is an excellent environment in which to assign groupings of children with like developmental characteristics, so they may work on tasks that will elevate their behavior to the next developmental level in each of these social skill areas.

To make a camping experience functional, a director should be responsible for the administration and direction of all other personnel and programs. He may need an assistant director, if the camp is large, to be in charge of all of the activities of the program. In each activity—housing, meals, nature, games, arts and crafts, riding, and waterfront—it may be desirable to have experts directing the activities. In smaller camp programs these functions may be handled by counselors or junior counselors.

The programming should be geared to the developmental levels of each group. With young children (6 to 8 years old) no more than five youngsters should be assigned to any one counselor. As the maturity and social development increase, more youngsters can be grouped together. Often a senior counselor with junior counselors (volunteers from high school or college) can handle up to 20 youngsters if the ratio of campers to junior counselors remains about 5 to 1.

The camp program should provide for about 30 minutes to an hour for each activity, and the groups should be rotated so no one activity for each is overloaded while others are vacant. A schedule such as the following may be set up for group one, with group two, and the others, starting different activities as the first group begins its first activity:

6:30– 7:00 a.m.	Rise and wash
7:00– 7:30	Breakfast
7:30– 8:30	Clean up camp
8:30– 9:30	Nature hike

9:30–10:30	Waterfront
10:30–11:30	Skill games
11:30–12:00	Lunch preparation
12:00– 1:00 p.m.	Lunch and rest
1:00– 2:00	Arts and crafts
2:00– 3:00	Riding or skill games
3:00– 4:00	Waterfront
4:00– 5:00	Campfire preparation (wood, skits, program)
5:00– 6:00	Dinner
6:00– 7:00	Free time
7:00– 9:00	Campfire
9:00– 9:30	Bed preparation
9:30	Lights out

All manner of modifications can be made relative to the camping facilities provided. The key to good experiences, however, involves using the camp to aid the social and personal development of the youngsters through well scheduled and planned activities.

A national clearinghouse for information on camping and outdoor recreation for the retarded has been established at Little Grassy Lake, Carbondale, Illinois. Much valuable information may be obtained from that source.[22]

[22] It is called Information Center, Recreation for the Handicapped, Little Grassy Facilities, Southern University, Carbondale, Illinois, 62901.

CHAPTER *8*

Esthetics

It may seem incongruous to include a chapter on art and music in a book that espouses the twin program goals of independent living and work competence and stresses the need to strip from the curriculum those experiences which do not seem to contribute to those two goals. Additionally, research evidence concerning the contributions of music and art to skills of independence in working and living seems not to exist.

Yet the fundamental premise of this book is that the image of the world developed by each individual is not only uniquely his own, but it determines the standards on which his behavior is dependent. This image is presumed to be the chief source of the self-concept of each person. As such, what a person knows and how he feels determines which stimuli will be meaningful to him. In short, his expectancies are largely determined by his interaction with the environment. Central to this theme is that mental retardation is a condition that is characterized by significant difficulty in accepting information, classifying and storing that information in the form of perceptions and concepts, and processing those perceptions and concepts because of restricted thought processes. By extension, it appears that art and music can make a contribution to the life style of an individual in the form of increasing the sources of pleasure open to him, precisely because music and art can be appreciated at various levels of sophistication. Again by extension it seems that enjoyment may materially affect an individual's self-concept. Thus, although research evidence in this area is nonexistent, esthetics is included as a potentially significant aspect of the total program.

Both art and music have been presumed by many people to contribute to the mental health, social adjustment, language development, and physical development of the retarded. They have also been credited with the capacity to promote learning about places, people, history, geography, cultures, values, and feelings. Perhaps such claims are valid. Even if such validity was granted, a question might still be raised regarding the necessity for such learnings or whether they may not be learned as readily through less remote activities.

A way of avoiding a fruitless debate is to simply accept that esthetics is part and parcel of everyday living and therefore cannot be ignored. Granting that premise, the problem of how best to include art and music experiences in the program must be faced.

It seems well established that there are many levels at which art and music can be enjoyed and used. At the simplest level is perception of the stimuli. This is exemplified by listening to music that is pleasing or seeing art objects that are enjoyable. An understanding of the elements used by the artist or composer to express his feelings can probably provide a higher level of enjoyment. For this level of enjoyment, it is probably necessary to know about themes, contrasts, and elements of construction. Critical appreciation is an interpretative process that depends upon perception and understanding, but that also calls upon the viewer or listener to make an interpretative judgment of the communicative skill of the artist or composer. Such interpretation is probably beyond the capability of the retarded—perhaps beyond most people. It is, however, possible to teach for perception and understanding.

This is essentially sensitivity training. By contrast, much of the art and music experiences evident in programs for the retarded have been of the rhythm band and "Maybasket-for-Mother" variety. While it may be justifiable to do things for the enjoyment of other people, it is here contended that art and music can enrich the lives of the retarded themselves and that this is potentially a more pressing function of the esthetics program.

Esthetics is the appreciation of beauty. Central to this appreciation is an understanding of what beauty is. Beauty is an abstract concept, but like all concepts, it is comprised of essential perceptual elements that combine in a variety of forms to meet the criteria of the concept. Most people have some vague notion of things that they see as beautiful. The vast majority, however, have little notion of what the elements are that contribute to the notion, or what effect rearranging the elements would have on their judgment of what is beautiful.

Teaching esthetics to the mentally retarded often has been confused with providing experiences of an artistic or musical nature. They are not the same thing. One can easily learn to play a musical instrument or draw lines, for example, without any understanding or even concern over whether their production has any elements of beauty. The intent of the esthetic experiences provided should be to teach the appreciation of beauty through the medium of art and music. Even though art and music may not necessarily be beautiful, the understanding of their elements is essential to appreciation.

Art

Visual perception has been extensively discussed in Chapter 4. But the discussion was primarily concerned with those visual-perceptual skills required for learning to read. The perceptions required for the understanding of art are not general. They are specific to the perceptual elements that are involved in the artistic production. Thus art education must teach the child what to attend to. It is not a matter of telling the child to look at a picture or sculpture or print, but rather what to look for. Art education should concentrate on the elements of expression and should do so in a systematic manner.

Art Elements

The elements used in the creation of anything artistic are lines, shapes, textures, light and color, and space. It is these elements that children must first learn to recognize if they are to understand art. The manner in which the elements are used identifies the technique of the artist. The principles that guide the artist are balance, contrast, emphasis, subordination, opposition, transition, repetition, rhythm, and variety. How these principles are employed determines the meaning of the art production. If a person will learn to appreciate art, he must be taught to recognize the manner in which the artist employs the principles of organization in arranging the elements to convey his idea or feeling intended. This kind of learning is complex, but can be approached in fundamental steps—that is, inductively. Furthermore, the materials of instruction are concrete and the children can be actively involved in the learning process. Thus art education fits the learning characteristics of the retarded (inductive method, concrete materials, and active participation) and can become a legitimate and meaningful part of the curriculum.

Line   Line is the fundamental element in most artistic creations. Lines may be broken to convey interruptions, straight to convey strength, curved to convey warmth, heavy to convey boldness, light to convey delicateness, or zigzagged to show motion. Human emotion symbolized by lines is readily understandable when interpreted to children with examples of art objects used as demonstrations. The teacher can use pictures that use lines to convey different emotions to demonstrate what lines can do. Then the children can be told, "We are going to be artists. An artist tries to tell people how he feels or thinks about something by drawing lines. Here is a picture by an artist who is angry. What are the lines like?"[1] After some discussion about the use of lines, tell the children that they are not going to be just any old artist, they are going to be angry artists. Provide them with finger paints and let them pretend to draw angry pictures. Emphasize the use of bold strokes or any other technique used in the demonstration pictures, but, most important, the children should understand that their own finger paintings express their own emotions of anger.

On succeeding days, introduce emotions of gaiety or joy, exuberance, concern, sadness, and love, and the qualities of strength, weakness, and uncertainty or confusion. Pictures by recognized artists should serve to introduce the moods or qualities to be depicted and the children should be taught to identify the ways the artists use lines to express themselves. Displaying their own drawings and telling what they felt (not what they were trying to draw) helps them realize that a picture may not need to look like something—it may just represent how one feels. In this kind of activity failure is virtually impossible. Everyone is a success.

Color   Color is another way in which emotions are expressed. Warm colors are those that seem to expand or move toward you.

[1] Otto G. Ocvirk, Robert Bone, Robert Stinson, and Philip Wigg, *Art Fundamentals* (Dubuque, Iowa: William C. Brown Company, Publishers, 1962). This book deals with the nature of art, form, line, shape, value, texture, color, space, and forms of expression. It contains illustrations and 10 problems plus pictures for each lesson. It sells for about $6.00. In addition Mary C. Rathbun and Bartlett H. Hayes, Jr., *Layman's Guide to Modern Art* (New York: Oxford University Press, 1954), is an excellent reference for the art novice.

These are the reds, yellows, and oranges. Cool colors are those that seem to contract or recede. These are the blues, greens, and purples. Black, white, and brown are neutral colors to emphasize the warmth or coolness of the other colors. Pictures that use both line and color to convey emotions and qualities should be displayed and discussed with the children. The children should then be given a chance to draw pictures of different moods and characteristics, combining both color and line. Discussion of the finished product should center on the method of representation, not whether it looks like something.

When a color is introduced, the children should be given a color wheel that demonstrates the primary colors of red, yellow, and blue and the secondary colors of orange, green, and violet, with the explanation that secondary colors are made by mixing equal parts of the primary colors. Repetition of the qualities of warmth and coolness should be used by the teacher whenever the colors are discussed or employed. This will help to associate feeling with color.

Many different media can be introduced at this juncture. The most common are crayons, chalk, and charcoal, but brushes, pencils, tempera, water color, oils, and ink are equally appropriate. Mood or quality pictures using many different colors, lines, and media can provide almost endless experimentation and ensuing discussions of the effectiveness of expression achieved through the various materials.

Shape   Shape is the third element that can be introduced. Pictures that use both geometric and biomorphic (related to nature) shapes— either alone or in relation to line and color—to express ideas should serve as demonstrations. The use of shapes to represent an attitude, an expression, or an image can be illustrated and discussed. Often the children achieve a more realistic understanding when they play-act moods by assuming different postures. Acting as models for the other children to draw is usually fun for the model as well as the rest of the class.

Balance   Guiding principles used to evaluate art should be introduced after some experimentation by the children with line, color, and shape. The most fundamental one is balance. This should be illustrated with pictures that demonstrate both symmetrical and asymmetrical organization. Balance can then be extended to show that a large dull color may be balanced by a smaller bright color, one bold line by several delicate lines, shape by color, and color by lines or shape. Experimentation in achieving balance, with discussion of the results, will serve to reinforce the idea that the principles of balance can be achieved in many different ways. The teeter-totter concept can be effectively used to explain balance.

Space   The element of space should be introduced with a demonstration of perceptual perspective, first in geometric line drawings, and then with figures obscured by other objects and distinct objects versus indistinct ones. Illusions are an excellent method of demonstrating perceptual distortion. The principles of contrast, emphasis, and subordination will begin to take on meaning as they are related to the elements of line, color, space, and shape and the principle of balance. Experimentation, demonstration, and discussion are absolutely mandatory if understanding is to be achieved. Opposition and transition should be explained as methods of emphasizing an interest point by using lines that come together at right angles. This can then be demonstrated with color and shape or any other elements.

Texture and Light   The elements of texture and light lend themselves to demonstrating the principles of repetition and rhythm. Prints are especially useful for clarifying both the elements and the principles. Metal, wires, cloth, and different kinds of beads and paper may help to demonstrate the effects that can be achieved by different usages of the various materials. It should be constantly pointed out that feelings or ideas are being conveyed by the artist. That is, the artist is an interpreter and commentator. If only a flat reproduction of the world were desirable, a photograph, by the same token, would be superior to any work of art.

Figure drawing may be introduced at any point that seems appropriate. It should be remembered that figures are representational, but that proportionality and perspective are essential to the drawing of figures. The *Art Guide for Teachers of Exceptional Children*, Northern State College, Aberdeen, South Dakota, has excellent illustrations of how to teach proportionality. In addition, it has detailed instructions on the preparation for art lessons using various media.

Exposure to art objects should be provided at all times. Visits to art galleries should never be guided tours. Instead, preparation for viewing specific examples that illustrate the exquisite use of particular elements and principles can greatly enhance the instructional and appreciational value of gallery visitations. The classrooms should be a constant gallery of both the children's productions and the works of recognized artists which feature changing themes or elements and principles. Art should enrich the lives of all of us, but looking at art with no understanding of what is being seen is apt to be barren.

Outcomes

From the art activities of the program, certain specific outcomes can reasonably be expected. These are:

PRESCHOOL LEVEL
1. Upon request, the child will be able to select the primary colors of blue, red, and yellow.
2. Upon request, the child will be able to select the secondary colors of green, orange, and purple.
3. Given a request to use colors to express an emotion, the child will select dark colors for anger and light colors for joy.
4. When shown a picture in which lines are used to express emotion, the child will be able to associate (select) heavy lines for boldness and zigzagged lines for action.

PRIMARY LEVEL
1. Given a choice of symmetrical and nonsymmetrical art objects or pictures, the child will be able to select those which are symmetrical from those that are not.
2. Given finger painting materials, the child will be able to express an idea or emotion by a picture representation.
3. When shown pictures in which geometric shapes are used, the child will be able to point to and identify the different shapes.
4. Given a choice of different sized art tools such as brushes, scissors, etc., the child will select those that are appropriate for the task to be done (e.g. picture painted).
5. When presented with different kinds of textured materials, the child will be able to select those that are rough, smooth, sticky, wooly, or furry.

INTERMEDIATE LEVEL
1. Given the proper materials, the child will be able to draw a picture of a simple subject such as a tree or vase.
2. When presented with the following art materials, the child will be able to demonstrate at least one use for each: charcoal, pencil, tempera paint, print blocks, clay, and yarn.
3. When shown a picture in which perspective is used, the child will be able to verbally state two ways in which perspective is achieved.

PREVOCATIONAL AND VOCATIONAL LEVELS
1. Upon request, the student will be able to identify an example of balance in a piece of art work.
2. Given a picture in which balance is achieved by apposition (offsetting

line with color, etc.), the student will be able to identify the elements used.
3. Given an art object in which rhythm is dominant, the student will be able to pick out the pattern in the art object.
4. When asked to distinguish between repetition and variety, the student will be able to identify examples of each.
5. Given a display of art work done by his peers, the student will be able to select the best work and verbally explain the reasons for his choice.

Teaching Resources

A teacher who has had little exposure to art understanding need not feel inadequate to conduct a meaningful and rewarding art program. The *Colorado Art Guide, K-12*, prepared by teachers in Colorado for the State Department of Education, Denver, has a remarkably clear explanation of what art is, the use of elements, and the place of principles in art. It is illustrated with beautifully done pictures and good lists of media and preparation hints. Although the purpose of the *Colorado Art Guide* differs from that of the author's, it is an excellent booklet for every teacher of retarded children.

A most useful book for illustrating the function of elements and principles is *The Meaning and Wonder of Art*, by Fred Gettings, the Golden Press, Inc., New York. This book illustrates composition, lines, measurement, light, color, and other aspects of art technique with pictures by acknowledged artists to give meaning to the discussion. It is easy to read, understand, and use. Bates Lawry's *The Visual Experience*, Prentice-Hall International, London, discusses the art elements and principles with excellent illustrations. Of particular interest is the section on the "critic" which discusses in understandable terms how art is judged.

Although esthetic appreciation should be uppermost in the art program, products and processes certainly have a place. Most children like to do things. Art periods should give them opportunities to make things, to experience different media, and to experiment with different techniques. Drawing, painting, crayons, paper construction, modeling, chalk, printing, stitchery, mosaics, and murals should be included in the program with special emphasis always directed to the use of elements and principles to produce a particular effect.

To many retarded youngsters, the world may be seen as sometimes hostile and menacing and nearly always drab. Art can be an enriching agent. The dimensions it can add to human enjoyment are much too substantial to be casually dismissed.

Music

Music should function in the lives of the retarded as a way of making life richer. If it does not enrich the scope of their living, the youngsters are being denied one area of experience that has great potential for nearly everyone. The outcomes at each level are designed to reflect an increased awareness of the part music can play in the lives of everyone. In addition, the outcomes are designed to assure that each child will have an opportunity to learn about the wide variety of kinds, styles, and uses of music. These are:

PRESCHOOL LEVEL
1. When records of different time are played (march, waltz, rock) the child will be able to keep time to the music by clapping his hands or marching.
2. When clapping to a tune, the child will be able to sing or whistle along.
3. When asked, the child will be able to identify songs or tunes he prefers over other songs or tunes.

PRIMARY LEVEL
1. Upon request, the child will be able to identify simple musical terms such as note, rest, staff, and time.
2. Given an accompaniment of a record or instrument, the child will be able to sing the words of at least three different kinds of songs.
3. Given a record player and record or a tape deck and tape, the child will be able to play them properly.

INTERMEDIATE LEVEL
1. When two songs are played, the student can distinguish major from minor melodies.
2. When songs are played, the student can recognize: soft rock, country and western, soul, and acid rock.
3. Given a tune played for him, the student can distinguish between pop, salon, and classical music.
4. Upon request, the student can verbally explain the difference between brass and stringed instruments.
5. Given some practice, the student will be able to play in a rhythm band.

PREVOCATIONAL AND VOCATIONAL LEVELS
1. Upon hearing a musical number, the student will be able to identify brasses, strings, percussions, and tell which group has the lead.
2. Upon hearing a vocal musical number, the student will be able to tell whether the number is a solo or group and distinguish between a small group and choir.

3. Given a vocal solo, the student will be able to identify a ballad from rock and soul.
4. Upon request, the student will be able to verbally indicate his preference in music and defend the choice.

Reichard and Blackburn[2] have developed a system of instruction in the basic competency areas that employs music as a basic instructional tool. It is the contention of these authors that: music in a variety of forms can be used to support nearly any teaching activity either directly or indirectly. Teaching a concept directly would be exemplified by having the children learn to sing the song "Little Green Traffic Light" as a way of teaching the colors red, green, and yellow. Indirect use might be teaching the child to march to the tune of four quarter time. In addition they point out that music can function to elicit, sustain, repeat, or reinforce any of a variety of outcome behaviors.

Their book is largely made up of series of lessons in which specific outcomes in each of the competency areas are taught using music as a vehicle for the instruction.

In addition one section describes band instruction techniques that can be used to help children develop those musical skills necessary for playing in a band.

While it is very desirable to use music as an aid to instruction, there is every reason to also include some basic instruction in music also.

As in any esthetic area, understanding music is an essential. The elements and principles of music must be learned in much the same manner that elements and principles are learned in art. It is desirable therefore that an instructional program that is systematic be used. Fortunately, such a program exists. It is called *Threshold to Music*.[3] The first three years of the program consist of lessons and accompanying charts that can be used by any teacher whether he is musically sophisticated or not.

Part One is made up of five chapters of instruction with 43 accompanying charts. In Part One, the children are taught to "feel" rhythm and its parts, to read beats and rhythmic patterns, to recognize and read intervals, to read and sing the major second, the perfect fourth, and the tonic chord. They are introduced to the pentatonic scale and to

---

[2] Cary L. Reichard and Dennis B. Blackburn, *Music Based Instruction for the Exceptional Child* (Denver, Col.: Love Publishing Co., 1973).

[3] It was developed by Mary Helen Richards and can be obtained from the Fearon Publishers, Inc., 2165 Park Boulevard, Palo Alto, Calif., 94306.

rests. The method for doing so involves the children in rhythmic activities of participation which are step-by-step and make use of natural behaviors. At the conclusion of Part One, the children should:

1. Have a strong feeling for beat and rhythmic patterns
2. Be able to perform simple rhythmic exercises using both hands
3. Be able to sing a tune while clapping or walking the beat
4. Be able to read the tones—*do, me, sol,* and *la*
5. Be able to read simple songs that contain the tones of *do, me, sol,* and *la*

Thus the elements of beat, rhythms, high and low tones, and phrases are all introduced through participation activities. Songs that use the beat, rhythms, and pentatonic scale are listed in the song bibliography for supplementary instruction with the children.

Part Two uses four chapter lessons and 44 charts to teach reading rhythm patterns, meters, and time signatures and octaves. By the end of Part Two the children should:

1. Be able to sing rounds and canons
2. Read notes and patterns
3. Be able to figure out notated tunes
4. Be able to take musical dictation
5. Know ordinary musical terms

Elements are combined into increasingly complex principles during the second part. However, the continuing involvement of children in the musical activity keeps this from becoming an exercise in abstraction. It is concrete and purposeful throughout. A bibliography of songs suitable for supplementary activities for Part Two is included. The songs are generally strong, tuneful, and have great appeal.

Part Three uses three lesson chapters and 34 charts to teach the movement of tones, majors and minors, and the major mode. All of the previously learned skills get frequent repetition in a variety of exercises for reinforcement purposes. By the end of the third part, the children should have:

1. Learned about major and minor sounds
2. Learned the major diatonic scale
3. Learned half steps
4. Learned notation and signatures
5. Experienced improvisation and syncopation

Frequent reference to songs and records that supplement the lessons help provide variety in repetition.

Should the music program in the school adopt the Mary Helen Richards system, the three-part basic program is extended through two additional books, *The Fourth Year* and *Songs in Motion.* It is quite probable that twice as much time (and supplementary material) will be needed by retarded children to master the elements and principles. In this case, the first three parts would be expected to span the pre-school and primary levels, the intermediate would be involved in the fourth-year program, and perhaps would venture into the *Songs in Motion* part of the program.

Implementing Art and Music

Throughout this book it has been stressed that skills and knowledges should be taught and that opportunities to use the skills and knowledges in meaningful situations must be provided. This principle includes art and music activities. Every opportunity should be seized that is judged to be made richer by esthetic supplement.

Unit work provides excellent opportunities to illustrate the elements of art in nearly every situation imaginable. In addition, an alert teacher can help the youngsters identify art elements that permeate everyday things. Too often, people do not notice because they do not take the time to look or are not aware of what to look for. Sensitizing the youngsters to pleasant combinations of line, color, form, space and texture in the natural setting of everyday events can be most rewarding.

Additionally, units can become more meaningful if they are augmented by displays, mock-ups, murals, and the like, as supporting or culminating activities. The medium used is not so critical as the opportunity to employ a wide variety of techniques. Care should be taken to allow each child to be an active participant in developing the product being developed. It does little good to teach skills that are practiced only by a select few. All the children need to use their skills in creative activities.

Music has an even wider applicability for enrichment, perhaps because it seeks us out rather than waiting to be discovered as does art. Because of its "seeking out" quality, many classrooms use music for background to other activities. A quiet record can be listened to during rest, lunch, seat work, cleanup, and similar activities, with a generally tranquilizing effect. For hyperactive youngsters, a few minutes of pleasant listening may have a quite remarkably soothing effect.

Unit work can be augmented by music as well as art, and should be. The wide variety of music available makes it possible to find something for nearly any subject being studied. As in art, music that reflects the emotions being visually illustrated can be an excellent supplement. Pop songs have the added virtue of familiarity, but classics conveying joy, gladness, anger, despair, happiness, sadness, and serenity can easily be introduced as correlatives to illustrate the emotions. A happy circumstance of music is that even the unusual becomes familiar through repetition. Thus as creative art plays a significant part in unit activities, music can conveniently strengthen the impact of the art. Songs can also play an important role in helping youngsters to understand other people, races, times, and customs. Most native songs are sung or played for a purpose: to tell a story, represent a feeling, create a mood, or accompany a celebration. This is true in nearly all civilizations, including the early historical eras of the United States. Furthermore, nearly all public and many school libraries have quite excellent record collections that are free. While it takes time to seek out specific records and tapes, the contribution of music may be well worth the effort.

If it is deemed desirable to teach more technical aspects of music, this can be done as a part of the music program. Individual instruments of the string, brass, percussion, and woodwind variety are easily obtained but should be played either in person, or via films. Additionally, there seems no reason why retarded youngsters should not be encouraged to pursue instruction in piano, voice, strings, instrumentals, drums, or guitar, should they evidence interest. There is no necessary relation between impaired intellect and creative skill or sensitivity. In any case, however, unless the youngsters have pleasant and repeated exposures to art and music, whatever talent they may possess may never develop and a potentially important aspect of human experience may be denied them by default.

CHAPTER 9

Health and Safety

Whatever may be the life style or socioeconomic circumstances of the children, the twin and often interrelated problems of personal health and safety will have an impact upon them throughout their lifetimes. Conceptually, the areas are similar since any program of instruction in either area is aimed at the prevention of harm. That is, the health program should be designed to avoid illness and the safety instruction to avoid accidents. While these goals are stated in negative terms, the programs are quite positive. They should teach the children what to do rather than warn them into a state of hypochondriasis or immobility. A good program should provide knowledge of the realistic nature of disease such that the children will not become victims of imagined illnesses. At the same time they should be sufficiently competent in the prevention of accidents and care of the injured to be able to participate in zestful activities with considerable confidence.

In the area of health, the children should be started on what to do first and later on the reasons why the activities are important. Outcomes to be pursued are:

PRESCHOOL LEVEL
1. Given the need to go to the bathroom, the child will indicate his need, complete the task, flush the toilet, and wash and dry his hands.
2. Given a sink, toothbrush, and toothpaste, the child will brush his teeth after each meal.
3. Given a sink, soap, and washcloth, the child will wash his hands and face before and after each meal.
4. Given a class of boys and girls, the child will separate the class into groups according to sex.

PRIMARY LEVEL
1. Given the task of dressing himself, the child will put on clean socks and underwear each day.
2. Given the instruction to go to bed, the child will proceed to his bedroom and get into bed.
3. Given only a verbal command, the child will point to the major parts of the body.
4. Given the need to blow his nose and a box of tissues, the child will remove one tissue, blow his nose into it, then throw the tissue in the wastebasket.
5. Given the need to cough or sneeze, the child will place at least one hand over his mouth during the actual cough or sneeze.
6. Given pictures of sloppy and neat appearances, the student will verbalize five characteristics of a neat appearance and five characteristics of a sloppy appearance.
7. Given three different weather conditions, and a variety of clothing, the student will choose the appropriate clothing for each condition.
8. Given a variety of food items, the student will verbalize whether the item is usually eaten at breakfast, lunch, or dinner.
9. Given an empty sink, dirty dishes, soap, and a washcloth, the student will put soap in the sink, add hot water, place the dishes in the water, use the washcloth to wash the dishes, rinse the soap off the dishes, and place them into the drying rack.
10. Given a personal problem, the child will verbalize the problem to the teacher, to a degree that the teacher understands what the problem is.

INTERMEDIATE LEVEL
1. Given the question, "Why do we brush our teeth?" the student will verbally state five reasons why teeth should be brushed.
2. Given a comb and mirror, the student will comb his hair.
3. Given the question, "Why is bathing important?" the student will verbalize five reasons why it is important to take a bath.

4. Given a can of deodorant, the student will apply the deodorant to the appropriate body parts.
5. Given a scale graded in pounds, the student will read the scale, and distinguish between lighter and heavier weights.
6. Given a thermometer measured in degrees Fahrenheit, the student will read the thermometer and verbalize whether the reading indicates warm or cold weather.
7. Given a picture of five major vital organs, the student will name the organs and verbalize the functions of each (heart, lungs, brain, kidney, stomach).
8. Given the question, "Why do we need rest?" the student will verbally state three reasons why rest is important to health.
9. Given pictures of many different foods, the student will choose five specific foods that should be eaten every day.
10. Given a question concerning the preparation of specific foods, the student will include in the answer the process of cleaning or washing that food.
11. Given several pictures of foods, the student will identify those foods that require refrigeration.
12. Given several pictures of foods, the student will separate them into categories of fruits, vegetables, and meats.
13. Given the proper ingredients and verbal instructions, the student will prepare a simple meal.

PREVOCATIONAL LEVEL

1. Given a thermometer, another student, and a watch with a second hand, the student will place the thermometer in the second student's mouth and leave it there for 2 to 3 minutes, and read it to the nearest whole number.
2. Given a schedule of bathing every two days, the student independently will adhere to the schedule.
3. Given the question, "When should we call the doctor?" the student will verbalize three cases that would warrant calling a doctor.
4. Given examples of burns, cuts, and broken bones, the student will verbalize what medical attention is needed.
5. Given the question, "How are babies born?" the student will verbalize the basic process of human reproduction.
6. Given the question, "What is meant by good personal hygiene?" the student will verbalize that good personal hygiene involves the proper care of teeth and hair, and keeping their bodies clean and well fed.
7. Given a list of health agencies, the student will verbalize how often the services should be used, and what service is provided by which agency on the list.

8. Given a list of eating habits, the student will distinguish which are appropriate to his individual needs.
9. Given a self-recording chart, and a list of eating habits, the student will record his own eating habits.
10. Given the eating habits recording chart, the student will verbally relate the data to his own body needs.
11. Given a chart of the four basic food groups, the student will indicate the proper number of servings required daily for each group, in order to maintain a well-balanced diet.
12. Given a list of foods the student has eaten for a given week, the student will classify them according to food group, compare this to the chart of required daily servings, and indicate which areas his diet was deficient in.
13. Given a recipe and necessary equipment, the student will read the recipe and follow the directions in order to produce the expected food product.
14. Given a question concerning physiological changes of the body during puberty, the student will verbalize three changes that occur during this period.
15. Given the list, parents, siblings, peer group, other adults, employer, and other employees, the student will verbalize the type of role or relationship he would have with each person or group.

VOCATIONAL LEVEL
1. Given a list of foods the student has eaten for a period of two weeks, the student will classify the foods according to the four basic food groups, and the reasons for the choices made.
2. Given a schedule of bathing every one or two days, the student will maintain the bathing schedule and keep a record of it.
3. Given a period of two hours per day for leisure time activities, the student will plan activities of rest and recreation to fill those two-hour periods for an entire week.
4. Given a question concerning the care of children, the student will verbalize five basic elements of child care.
5. Given a model of appropriate dress for a specific occasion, the student will produce a similar effect from his own clothing.
6. Given soap, bandages, ointment, and a minor cut, the student will clean and bandage the wound.
7. Given a complete meal, the student will demonstrate his ability to eat properly.
8. Given the need for immunization shots, the student will keep and follow a record of when the shots should be given.
9. Given a question concerning the dangers of contagious diseases, the student will verbalize what those dangers are.

10. Given a question concerning the proper use of drinking fountains and rest rooms, the student will verbalize the proper use of each.
11. Given a question concerning the disposal of trash and garbage, the student will verbalize at least three procedures.
12. Given a question concerning self-medication, the student will verbalize the dangers of its use.
13. Given a problem of health, the student will verbalize where the problem is located, when it began, and what caused the problem.
14. Given a question concerning the dangers of smoking, alcohol, and drugs, the student will verbalize three dangers of each.
15. Given a question concerning the importance of liquid to a diet, the student will verbalize two reasons for drinking fluids.
16. Given four different situations, the student will verbally identify the person or agency to approach for guidance or counseling.
17. Given an emotional state such as fear, joy, loneliness, and sorrow, the student will expound on this feeling verbally.
18. Given contact with peer group, teachers, and other adults, the student will demonstrate his ability to establish acceptable personal relationships.

Teaching Health

Although it appears that the germ theory of disease would be too abstract to be grasped by youngsters who are retarded, such does not seem to be the case. It is difficult to pinpoint just why, but one guess is that television commercials, which stress the need for mouth wash, deodorant soap, underarm sprays and the like, emphasize the relationship between germs or viruses and health. Thus the terms and relationships are quite familiar even though the actual theoretical relationship is never mentioned. What is even more likely is that the ads imply a direct relationship between cleanliness, food, regularity, and rest, and how people feel. Thus feeling good is associated with being healthy and being healthy is tied directly to personal cleanliness, proper food, excretory regularity, and adequate rest. Probably the germ theory of disease may never be fully grasped, but the direct relationship of what things influence good health and feeling good is quite apparent.

At the preschool and primary levels every morning a health inspection should be held. This can involve the activities of questioning the children about their tooth brushing, combing hair, washing, using deodorants, toileting, regular bathing, food intake, and the hours of sleep obtained. Discussions of what the children did relative to each of the activities and how they feel helps get across the idea of the positive relationship between taking good care of themselves and feeling good. The emphasis should be on good health habit training, not necessarily on the reasons why. In this connection, using gold stars or points or graphs to reward good habits can be very useful. In addition, the modeling behavior of the teacher may be more important than is generally thought. That is, a demonstration of concern for good health habits by teachers can go a long way toward convincing the children of the importance of the activity.

At the primary and intermediate levels, units that are specific to certain activities may be called for. Chapter 11 suggests several units that deal with health habits, food groups, and grooming and clothing and can be used to deal with particular kinds of knowledges or behaviors in which the children are deficient. These can be extended or supplemented as the need arises but always should emphasize the relationship between feeling good and being healthy as influenced by the way we take care of our bodies.

At the prevocational level, the Biological Sciences Curriculum Survey (BSCS) group has developed a program called *Me Now* which is marketed by the Hubbard Company.[1] It is a part of the sciences program for the mentally retarded in which the functions and structure of the life sciences are explored. The entire program has participation activities in which the children become involved in learning by doing. Because it was extensively field tested with mentally retarded children, it has excellent validation information to support the content, materials, and methods described and the enthusiasm of children for the activities.

Unit I, "Digestion," follows the fate of food in the child as it enters the mouth and moves through the body via the digestive process. Growth, health, and food groups and their relation to body parts all receive careful attention. In addition, the circulatory system as a vehicle for distributing the digested food is explained.

Unit II, "Respiration and Excretion," explore breathing including suffocation and drowning, oxygen and carbon dioxide, wastes and internal body processes, the excretory processes, and the functions and locations of the organs involved.

Unit III, "Movement, Support, and Sensory Perception," deals with the role of muscles, bones, brain, nerves, and sensory receptors. The functions of each, names and locations, and interrelationships become primary study activities.

Unit IV, "Growth and Development," treats the growth and develop-

---

[1] Hubbard Scientific Company, Box 105, Northbrook, Ill. 60062.

ment of a human being from the moment of conception through old age. Since it deals with human reproduction, some school officials may wish to preview the materials and content before using them. However, they have been successfully used in many schools and are quite appropriate to the understanding of prevocational-aged mentally retarded youngsters. Differential growth rates in individual differences and the role of heredity in physical characteristics are also included.

The comprehensiveness of the coverage and the extensiveness of the research undertaken to develop good activities, materials, and sequences are rarely encountered in materials designed for mentally retarded children. The BSCS Life Sciences Curriculum for the Mentally Retarded can very well stand as a model for formative research which other materials developers could copy with profit.

At the vocational level the intensive study of the effects of tobacco, alcohol, and drugs is virtually mandatory. Nearly every publisher of social studies materials for regular classroom use will have films, film strips, slides, cassettes, and printed materials that can be examined for suitability. However, the major theme to be emphasized remains the one dealt with throughout the chapter, namely, that our bodies reflect what we do to them. If we care for them, they will serve us better than if we abuse them; and if we abuse them, we will ultimately destroy ourselves.

This principle also applies to our own mental health. That is, we are responsible for how we view the world. Other people can contribute to our happiness or unhappiness, but we are the final arbiters of what we do in periods of well-being or adversity. This acceptance of the reality of personal responsibility for behavior is closely related to the principles of self-discovery discussed in Chapter 6, Social Competencies. Thus, mental health is seen as closely related to social competence and whenever possible, such a relationship should be identified and discussed.

Despite our best efforts, some problems may become too difficult for any of us to handle without help. In these instances community agencies are available and can be called upon. Unfortunately many of the youngsters may not be aware of what help is available or how to go about getting aid. This most important information should be directly dealt with so they will know where to go, what to do, and how to use the sources of help available.

Obviously when studying community agencies that exist to help with mental health problems, those that deal with physical health can also be studied. Hospitals, clinics, therapy centers, convalescent homes, and the like should be studied not only from the point of view of their contributions to health, but also in terms of possible kinds of employment. Many of the youngsters may someday work in those places so this simply adds another reason for learning about them.

Safety

Probably no other area cuts across every other area so much as does safety. Virtually every other activity is laced with cautions designed to protect people from harming themselves or others. In addition to the specific dangers included in those areas, there are general kinds of behaviors that affect a person's life style and may mean the difference between a person who lives rather safely and one who could almost be considered accident prone. Behaviors that need to be mastered are:

PRESCHOOL LEVEL
1. Given the teacher, bus driver, and crossing guard, the child will follow the directives given by these persons.
2. Upon hearing a fire alarm in school, the student will follow the teacher out of the building and stay within 5 feet of the teacher.
3. On the school bus the child will remain seated from the time he gets on to the time he is supposed to get off.
4. Given household dangers such as knives, pins, matches, medicines, and poisons, the child will not touch them.
5. Given a tricycle and the freedom to ride, the child will ride only on the sidewalk or within his yard.
6. Given a body of water, the child will stay away from the water when not accompanied by an adult.
7. Given the offer of a ride or candy from a stranger, the child will refuse any such offer.
8. Given an animal unfamiliar to the child, the child will remain physically separated from the animal.

PRIMARY LEVEL
1. Given a question concerning the danger of streets and alleys, the child will indicate at least one danger of each.
2. Given the traffic signals appropriate to the area, the child will indicate under what conditions he must wait.
3. Given the words "STOP, CAUTION, GO, DANGER, FIRE EXIT, POISON, WALK, FLAMMABLE, and DO NOT ENTER," the child will read the words and verbally indicate an understanding of each.
4. Given a question concerning the dangers of lakes, pools, and rivers, the child will verbalize one such danger.

5. Given a question concerning bike safety rules, the child will verbalize five rules.
6. Given a bodily injury, the child will name four persons he could approach with the problem.
7. Given a question concerning the dangers of medicine, the child will verbalize at least one such danger.
8. Given scissors, ruler, saw, screwdriver, hammer and nails, pliers, pins, tacks, paper clips, staples, record player, and cassette, the child will demonstate the appropriate use of each.
9. Given pictures of safe and dangerous situations in the home, the child will identify which are safe and which are dangerous.
10. Given a designated set of school behaviors, the student will play in accordance with those rules while at school.

INTERMEDIATE LEVEL

1. Given pictures of safe and dangerous situations in the home, the student will indicate which situations are safe and which are dangerous.
2. Given the conditions of overloaded electric outlet, bare electric wire, clutter on a stairway, broken step ladder, frying pan unattended on stove, can of gas near a fire source, and a young child near an unattended power saw, the student will take the steps necessary for correcting each situation.
3. Given a role-playing situation, the student will demonstrate the proper procedure for reporting a fire or accident.
4. Given the signals of a yellow, red, and green traffic light, the student will verbalize the meaning of all possible combinations of the traffic light.
5. Given a bicycle, the student will indicate the proper hand signals for a right and left turn while riding the bicycle.
6. Given a street diagram, the student will locate and mark the proper side of the street to ride a bicycle on.
7. Given the situation of being lost, the student will verbalize which agency he would call for help.
8. Given a car parked parallel on the street, the student will demonstrate the proper procedure for getting in and out of the car.

PREVOCATIONAL LEVEL

1. Given a question concerning the proper care of tools, the student will verbally state three reasons why tools must be kept in repair.
2. Given a question concerning the care of appliances, the student will verbally state three reasons why appliances must be kept in repair.
3. Given a question concerning the care of furniture, the student will verbally state three reasons why furniture must be kept in repair.
4. Given a question concerning the proper use of appliances, the student

will verbally state three reasons why appliances must be used only for their designed purpose.

5. Given a variety of inflammable materials, the student will properly demonstrate their use.
6. Given a model of an electrical fuse box, the student will properly remove the old fuse and install a new one.
7. Given a question concerning the dangers of a power lawn mower, the student will verbally state five such dangers.
8. Given a request to call the police or fire department, the student will demonstrate his ability to complete the task.
9. Given a question concerning common fire hazards in a home, the student will verbally state five common examples of fire hazards.
10. Given a hypothetical example of an accident, the student will demonstrate his ability to keep the injured warm, keep crowds away from the scene, and contact the police.
11. Given a body of water large enough to support a person, the student will float or tread water for two minutes.
12. Given a Red Cross dummy, the student will properly demonstrate the method of artificial resuscitation.
13. Given a picture or model of poison ivy and poison oak, the student will identify which is which.
14. Given pictures of plants or snakes common to the locality, the student will identify those that are poisonous.

VOCATIONAL LEVEL

1. Given a hypothetical case of a fire, the student will discuss and demonstrate methods of putting out a fire.
2. Given an example of a hazardous situation, the student will describe ways to eliminate the hazard.
3. Given the heavy equipment and power tools of the school, the student will describe the hazards to be avoided in using this equipment and tools.
4. Given a motor vehicle, the student will demonstrate his ability to drive safely on any given course in traffic and to obey the traffic laws.
5. Given an accident report form, the student will fill out the form to meet the standards of the insurance or police agencies.
6. Given a car maintenance manual and car, the student will verbally state when the car should be brought to a garage for care.
7. Given a swimming pool and the Red Cross Swim Test, the student will pass the test to the level of beginning swimmer.
8. Given a situation of a drowning person, the student will describe the appropriate life-saving measures.
9. Given a job involving machinery, the student will keep his hair covered.

10. Given a question concerning safety rules of a specific plant, the student will list the rules.
11. Given a specific occupation, the student will explain the danger signals and symbols of that occupation.
12. Given a question concerning the qualities of his friends, the student will explain what the qualities of his friends are that led to that friendship.

Teaching Safety

The natural curiosity, friendliness, and lack of experience of any child are potential sources of danger which need to be dealt with at the preschool and primary levels. Probably the first most important lesson to be learned is that certain adults—parents, teachers, crossing guards, police, firemen, and the like—play a regulatory role and enforce certain rules that protect children and prevent people from being hurt. The recognition that rules help them live more securely may be a rather difficult understanding to achieve, but it is absolutely fundamental to the whole area of safety and must be taught. Some of the units in Chapter 11 may be helpful, but there is no substitute for direct instruction in following rules. A permissive classroom or work area is not very conducive to teaching recognition of the need for rules and the necessity of having to enforce rules, so the task becomes easier if the rest of the learning environment is orderly. Furthermore, children are more likely to honor rules voluntarily if they were involved in establishing those rules in the first place. While such a cooperative attitude does reduce the job of the person enforcing the rules, more importantly, it aids in beginning the development of a favorable attitude toward self-directed behavior, which is so necessary to successful adult living. It also gives the youngster practice in identifying dangerous things and situations himself so his protection will not be solely in the hands of other people.

Learning to recognize things that are dangerous is another important skill. Somehow the children must learn to guard against things that are pointed, sharp, hard, or irregular. Things that are not under control such as fire, open water, wind, or hurtling objects are or can be equally dangerous. Finally, they must be taught to make the delicate judgment as to whether unfamiliar and unknown people, things, and events are helpful, harmless, or harmful. While the general rule of beware of those things that are sharp, uncontrolled, or unfamiliar may be a good one to follow, being overly cautious in everything is not a very fulfilling way to live. Somehow the children will need to temper curiosity, friendliness, and naiveté with caution, but not to the extent that they are completely inhibited. Thus, specific lessons dealing with common dangers should be provided.

Another way of reducing danger is to let the children learn how things work in order to make the unfamiliar become familiar. At the primary and the intermediate levels lessons in science that deal with everyday machines and appliances can go a long way toward supplying this knowledge.

At the prevocational level, the BSCS group has developed a program called *Me and My Environment.* It too is marketed by the Hubbard Scientific Company.

Unit I, "What Is My Environment," deals with activities involved in investigating the visible environment, using landmarks in the visible environment, sensing the invisible environment, and looking at the invisible environment. The activities provide a high degree of involvement of the children, with experiments making up the bulk of the activities.

Unit II, "Me as a Habitat," explores the world of microbes, diseases, drugs, alcohol, and smoking.

Unit III, "Energy Relationships in My Environment," introduces the children to energy, energy flow through food chains, and food making in plants.

Unit IV, "Transfer and Cycling of Materials in My Environment," treats the transfer of materials and energy, decomposers, and problems of garbage.

As in the other BSCS materials, there is a high degree of student involvement in each lesson and the exercise of inference and judgment is provided but within the capability of the youngsters.

The opportunity to become familiar with a wide variety of things in the environment is certainly an aid to safer living, but accidents still happen. Therefore, every person should have a basic knowledge of first aid. To be sure, a knowledge of first aid can enable a person to help others, but it can be of value to the person himself, not just in being able to direct others when one has been injured, but in the peace of mind that comes from knowing what to do. Also there is a great comfort communicated by a person who seems to know what to do for those in need of help. Certainly other reasons can be identified also, but not the least of the values is that of helping a person to become safety conscious in his habits.

Nearly any good book on health will have good suggestions for first aid practice, but the standard work for many years is the handbook on first aid distributed by the American Red Cross. Detailed instructions on how to care for wounds, shock, suffocation, breaks, sprains, burns, heart attacks, and other common problems are explained with pictures and diagrams that are easily understood. Having the youngsters practice on each other with splints and bandages can be fun as well as instructive.

In addition to the specific instruction certain general principles need to be emphasized. The youngsters need to learn that they must act quickly in cases of severe bleeding, cessation of breathing, and suspected poisoning. They need to learn not to move the injured, to keep them warm, and to send for a physician. They should know better than to give fluids to unconscious people or to pick people up by the head and feet at the same time. Such information is basic for everyone, but there is a very good chance that if the retarded youngsters do not learn these things in school, they may not learn them at all. This is too important an area to be ignored or omitted.

In every area of living there are safe and unsafe ways to do nearly everything. Since it is patently impossible to cover every single instance, the best that can be done is to deal with those which are most likely to be encountered in as straightforward a manner as possible and to reinforce the principles of caution: beware the hazardous, uncontrolled, and unknown.

CHAPTER 10

Vocational Competencies

For many years the avowed purpose of programs for the retarded was vocational in nature. Even judging the worth of programs was usually tied to follow-up studies and based on the number of former students who were found to be gainfully employed. In the early programs, no real preparation for teaching vocational skills was ordinarily provided teachers in their own teacher preparation experiences. Furthermore, most state departments of special education or the equivalent made no distinction between certification to teach the retarded at the lower age level and at the prevocational and vocational levels. Any successes scored in the vocational training of the retarded was certainly not to be credited to the training programs of the colleges and universities or to the enlightened guidance of state departments of education.

In 1952 the Federal Vocational Rehabilitation regulations were liberalized to allow that agency to recognize mental retardation as a serious obstacle to employment. This meant that vocational rehabilitation counselors were permitted to provide agency services to this very large group of people who had previously been excluded from this source of help. The actual extent to which service was supplied was limited at first, but dramatically increased when the State of Texas, under the leadership of Charles Eskridge, began to assign vocational rehabilitation counselors to work with the schools in the training, placement, and supervision of mentally retarded young people in community jobs. This innovation caught on nationally for two reasons: first, job placement and supervision were now being done by people trained to do that work rather than by people trained as teachers of academic subjects; and second, additional personnel were added to school faculties (at least as adjunct staff) to do a critically important job at no, or very little, additional cost to the school. The service has become so widespread that nearly every school that has a vocational program and is located near a local office of vocational rehabilitation is likely to have some kind of service arrangement with that office. It has been a nearly universally mutually rewarding arrangement.

As programs at the vocational level grew, research data on the vocational success of the retarded began pointing up a serious problem of underemployment among the retarded. This showed up in several ways, but was most noticeable in industrial areas where many retarded persons were found to be working successfully at semiskilled and skilled jobs within only a few years after leaving school. One of the suspicions that came from this finding was that the training provided by the schools was not geared to employment in skilled jobs, but the abilities of the retarded were, in many cases, sufficiently high to allow them to learn these skills on the job. Therefore, the schools were undertraining the youngsters. In order to correct this condition, in 1963 Congress passed the Vocational Education Act, which allowed mentally retarded youngsters to enroll in regular vocational education programs in the schools, and in 1968 the amendments which enlarged and clarified the mechanics of this kind of inclusion and provided that 10 percent of the Vocational Education funds were to be spent on the handicapped and 15 percent on programs for the disadvantaged.

The consequence of these occurrences means, practically, that professionals in special education can work as equal partners with vocational educators in training retarded teenagers and young adults for jobs, and can count on vocational rehabilitation counselors to at least participate in and often take the leadership for job finding, placement, and supervision after the students have been trained. It also assures that funds to support the efforts will be made available. Of even greater importance is that since the 1968 amendments apply to all handicapping conditions, it is not necessary for a youngster to be designated as mentally retarded in order to qualify for help. This allows schools who do not use specific categorical labels to serve youngsters who need help under an amorphous umbrella term such as educationally handicapped or disadvantaged. This essentially means that large numbers of youngsters who need the services but have been precluded by failing to qualify for inclusion under a specific label, such as deaf or mentally retarded, can now be included in the program and provided with the extra help they need to insure success.

The 1968 amendments changed the concern and responsibility of vocational education in rather dramatic fashion by emphasizing services to groups of people who generally had not been served in the traditional vocational programs of the past. They also recognized the fluid nature of life styles in America, which emerged after World War II. No longer did people who were born in one area grow up, work, marry, grow old, and die in that same area, nor did people remain for a lifetime at a single job. More likely, an individual would have a succession of jobs throughout his employment career, some of which might not have even existed in his youth and many in parts of the world a long way from his birthplace. This recognition spawned a new conceptualization of vocational education as just one element in the total career of a person and launched vocational educators into some new areas with few precedents to guide their efforts.

Unfortunately, the concept of career education has often been misunderstood by people who insist on equating it with vocational education. The two terms are not synonymous. Hoyt (1974) has attempted to clarify the concept.[1] He defines education as "all those activities and experiences through which one learns," and career education as "all those activities and experiences through which one learns about work." Career is the totality of work a person does in his lifetime, whereas a vocation is the primary work role a person has at any given point in time. An occupation is paid work, but a vocation does not necessarily have to be paid. It is possible to have a vocation without an occupation, but it is not possible to have an occupation without a vocation.

Work is a concept that is restricted to human beings in that it is a conscious effort aimed at producing some benefit and is something one chooses to do. Labor may also produce benefit, but the element of choice is missing. Labor is forced, work is not. People, therefore, work because they want to in order to fulfill some rather basic human need. Principally, people work to earn money to purchase goods and services that are related to living. This is a basic reason given by many people when asked why they work. But there are other reasons too. Our com-

---

[1] Kenneth B. Hoyt, "Career Education and the Handicapped Person," unpublished paper, c. 1974.

plex societies simply could not survive if most of the people in the society did not work. Indeed, some people equate good citizenship with work by contending that one who does not work is not contributing a benefit to others and is not, therefore, a worthy citizen. Children can be tolerated because they will work and the aged because they have worked, but able-bodied people of working age who do not contribute are considered bums. A third reason people work is psychological. This generally means that people need to feel that their contribution is of some benefit to the world and makes them needed. It makes a person feel that his life is worthwhile, that it matters whether he lives or dies because he is contributing something to make the world better than it would have been had he not been here.

Hoyt maintains that career education encompasses all three basic reasons for working; economic, societal, and psychological. It is this breath of the concept that mandates that work be considered a human right and not just a societal obligation.

Career education has been described as consisting of three main functions: awareness; exploration; and preparation. These functions have both vertical and horizontal dimensions which often operate simultaneously. The vertical thrust begins at the kindergarten level as children learn about the world of work. They find out what work is, that it is necessary and important, that it can become a major source of identification and satisfaction, and that people earn a living in many ways.

In the upper elementary grades they further learn that jobs fall into families related to different kinds of activities. The U.S. Office of Education has identified 15 of these families, arranged in clusters of jobs, each of which has many different jobs in it.[2] Among these jobs there exists a hierarchy arrangement from those that require very little skill or training to perform, to those requiring skill training and college attendance considerably beyond the college bachelor's degree level.

At the prevocational or junior high school level, some career exploration may occur, either by families of jobs, by level of complexity, by proximity, or some other arrangement. Usually the twin questions of personal interest and personal talents become of paramount importance in this phase and many potential jobs are eliminated because a child is neither interested nor capable of performing satisfactorily in the job.

[2] Kenneth B. Hoyt, Rupert N. Evans, Edward F. Mackin, Garth L. Mangum, *Career Education* (Salt Lake City, Utah: Olympus Publishing Co., 1972).

At the senior high school or vocational level, job preparation involves the training in the school on a job site or both which will equip an individual with those minimal skills that permit entry into a job. The goal of the preparation phase is the development of entry level skills in some suitable job for every child in the nation's schools at the time he either leaves school or graduates from high school.

The horizontal thrust of awareness, exploration, and preparation is presumed to be of increasing importance as the child progresses through school. As a youngster becomes more sophisticated in his career knowledge, he becomes aware of many more jobs than he knew of at younger age levels. This opens up more avenues for exploration and eventually preparation in specific areas as time goes on. Particularly at adult ages, people engage in the awareness, exploration, preparation sequences more and more as they pursue career advancement or career changes. Since the average person is predicted to experience three or more job changes in his lifetime, those skills needed for the functions of awareness, exploration, and preparation become very important for each person to master during his formative years.

For professionals working with mentally retarded youngsters, the concept of career education certainly poses no threat since it is perfectly consistent with what has always been the format of services to the retarded. Although called by different names, the curricular experiences have been anchored around the awareness—exploration-preparation sequence for many years. Thus, the career education movement not only is compatible with the goals and objectives of the special education movement, but has led to the development of a host of materials that can be used to assure the career development of the handicapped—many of them with very little modification.

Those skills and knowledges that comprise vocational skills are made up of learnings and behaviors that have their origins at an early age. Specific understandings of the world of work are largely attitudinal. Thus it is proposed that attention be given to the development of attitudes concerning the dignity of work, beginning at the preschool level. The program at the preschool, primary, and intermediate levels should concentrate on experiences and incidental learning that emphasize calling attention to occupations in the scope of adult activities, developing skills that are vocationally directed, and learning behaviors which will contribute to future occupational placement and job retention. These should focus on career awareness.

At this awareness level a number of people have used job surveys to identify potential jobs that the youngsters can be made aware of

through especially prepared materials. The State of Wyoming, for instance, sponsored the development of decks of cards with microfilm
information on jobs. The project is called WORK, an acronym for
Wyoming Occupational Resources Kit. Each card has a picture of the
job and information about the job including the family, level, requirements, skills needed, pay, fringe benefits, availability, and location of
the job. Some include a kind of self-test to let the student decide
whether the job description fits his own interests, needs, and talents.
Similar materials published by educational publishing companies appear almost daily. Many of these materials include written, pictorial,
cassette tape, and other multimedia presentations. Almost uniformly
they are of very high quality but vary considerably in their suitability
for the handicapped.

At the prevocational level and continuing at the vocational level,
the individual should be exposed to carefully graded and supervised
work experience of increasing complexity. The accompanying study
should deal with instruction designed to further his skills, knowledge,
and positive attitudes, toward helping him find his place in the world
of work.[3] The prevocational program (usually housed in a junior high
school building) should provide for up to a half day of work exploration
experience and the remainder of the day devoted to related instruction.
This should begin about age 14 or 15 and preferably somewhat earlier,
if possible. The initial introduction to work should be of a sheltered
variety. That is, it should be under the control and supervision of the
school. This may be obtained by purchasing evaluation services from
an already-established sheltered workshop, by assigning the students
to a school-operated sheltered workshop, to school campus jobs in the
cafeteria, to janitorial, office, or garage duties, or to the establishing of
simulated work stations in a classroom (Chapter 12 contains a more
complete listing and description of campus work stations).

The exploration phase has generated its share of new materials
also. Of principal interest are those systems developed principally for
the retarded. The Jewish Employment and Vocational Service (JEVS)
in Philadelphia, Pennsylvania, evolved from the need for activities
that were suitable for people of rather limited abilities to determine
what kinds of training activities might be best to utilize in the prepara-

[3] Oliver P. Kolstoe and Roger M. Frey, *A High School Work-Study Program for
Mentally Subnormal Students* (Carbondale, Ill.: Southern Illinois University Press,
1965); and Lotar Stalacker, *Occupational Information for the Mentally Retarded* (New
York: The John Day Company, Inc., 1967), include more detailed information on work-
study programs.

tion of the person for employment either in a sheltered workshop or in competitive industry. It consists of 110 work samples carefully selected for their relevance to jobs done by the retarded. Normative information on what is competitive performance is provided for each task. This makes JEVS a very useful system.

The Singer Graflex Corporation[4] has developed a series of film strips with accompanying narration on cassette tapes which are auto teaching devices that guide a youngster through the exploration of a job. Each job has a work station setup with appropriate tools and with real or simulated job tasks which the youngster performs on instruction from the tapes and film strip. Since both of these are under the control of the child, he can proceed through the exploration at his own rate and with minimal supervision from the teacher. The job explorations include the use of the Dictionary of Occupational Titles, basic tools, bench assembly, cooking and baking, cosmetology, data recording, drafting, electrical wiring, engine service, masonry, medical service, office and sales clerk, refrigeration, heating and air conditioning, plumbing, sample making, sheet metal, and soldering and welding, and new ones are continually being developed. Perhaps one of their strongest features is the individual nature of the experiences. At the same time it could be construed to be a weakness since only one person can use each station at any one time.

One aspect of the exploration phase that has received too little attention is the determination of a student's vocational interest. One major aim of this phase of the program has grown out of the discovery of how little most of the youngsters know about the incredible variety of ways people earn a living. The consequence of this condition is that most of the youngsters have vocational interests in only a few areas because they know about very few jobs. The aim of the program has been to try to broaden the knowledge about jobs and therefore the interests of the youngsters.

Since reading is not always a reliable medium to use to get information for many retarded youngsters, efforts to determine the vocational interests of the retarded have centered on picture representations. One of the first attempts was reported by Parnicky, Kahn, and Burdett (1965).[5] By use of uncomplicated drawings of people

[4] Vocational Evaluation System, Singer Education Division, 3750 Monroe Avenue, Rochester, New York, 14603.

[5] Joseph J. Parnicky, Harris Kahn, and Arthur B. Burdett, "Preliminary Efforts at Determining the Significance of Retardates Vocational Interests," *American Journal of Mental Deficiency*, 70 (November 1965), 393–398.

working, the authors attempted to determine the relationship of the youngsters' interests and experiences. Not unexpectedly they found interest and experience related, but they were unable to make any predictions from the inventory. Subsequent standardization of the instrument named Vocational Interest and Sophistication Assessment (VISA) on some 3000 subjects confirmed their earlier hopes for developing a stable instrument, but still provided only minimal predictive validity.[6] A somewhat different technique was presented in a multiple choice picture interest inventory developed by Becker.[7]

The Reading-Free Vocational Interest Inventory (RFVII) consists of pictures presented in triads to 6400 subjects in various parts of the country. A forced choice technique required the respondents to choose only one of the three pictures in each triad (55 for males and 40 for females). Although the reliability and concurrent validity seem good, there is not enough information on the predictive quality of the inventory to be confident that it is a good instrument. However, both VISA and RFVII appear to be worth trying since they offer some choices the youngsters may not otherwise be aware of. The history of interest inventories is short, but it is much too promising an area to ignore.

The preparation phase typically is housed in a high school building because the youngsters are ordinarily at least 16 years of age. If in the prevocational phase they may have identified an area in which they have an interest or a talent, they may wish to start their training for placement rather soon. This is not a real problem. On the other hand children who are rather immature or undecided may wish to be allowed somewhat more time to find themselves. This also should not be seen as a real problem, although it is likely to be so viewed by a great many teachers.

In the preparation phase, many schools are now making better provisions for serving the handicapped in their ongoing vocational education programs than they did in the past. Ideally, these programs provide modification within the regular offerings so the handicapped are not unduly penalized by their disabilities. At the very least, special sections can be offered which enroll mostly those youngsters who manifest some problems in full participation but can, with time and help, develop the requisite skills required for entry level in an area.

---

[6] Joseph J. Parnicky, Harris Kahn, and Arthur B. Burdett, "Standardization of the (VISA) Vocational Interest and Sophistication Assessment Technique," *American Journal of Mental Deficiency*, 75 (January 1971), 442–448.

[7] Ralph L. Becker, "Vocational Choice: An Inventory Approach," *Education and Training of the Mentally Retarded*, 8 (October 1973), 128–135.

In 1975 the Bureau for Education of the Handicapped in the United States Office of Education published a technical manual that described successful practices in many different aspects of career education programs for the handicapped.[8] Although the manual describes a great many practices that have been found to be successful, not all are equally applicable to every program in every part of the country. Some things are. Successful programs universally were staffed by people who were genuinely concerned about the welfare of the youngsters being served. However, good intentions were not enough. In addition, every good program was characterized by the care that went into each element of the program and the internal program integrity. That is, each part of the program fitted neatly with every other part. Finally, every good program spent as much effort preparing the community to accept their students as they did in preparing the students to work in the community. How they did this varied from place to place, but some elements were present in nearly all. These included some kind of initial work experience, an on-the-job training phase or job tryout and some kind of permanent placement with appropriate supervision and follow up.

Initial Work Experiences

Since the purpose of the work-study experience is the development of acceptable standards of work skills, the important aspect of the initial work experience is to help the student learn what acceptable work standards are, and help him achieve these standards through sequential experiences. By controlling the initial work experience, it is possible to introduce standards in such a manner that the students will not be traumatized nor unrealistic in their expectations. This is done most easily in a sheltered setting, but also can be accomplished in campus jobs and simulated work stations.

Most sheltered workshops engage in a variety of work of a subcontract, reclamation, or manufacturing type. Well-organized workshops provide evaluation, training, and extended work sections that may be separate areas or may overlap. Since the school program is a training program, only the evaluation and training areas are of concern. Evaluation is done in various ways in workshops. The most common, however, requires the student to take a series of tests and to engage in

[8] "Career Education Programs for the Handicapped," (Washington, D.C.: U.S. Govt. Printing Office, 1975).

a number of work or work-related tasks for specified periods of time. Standards of "normal" performance are used to evaluate the tests and tasks so the vocational strengths and weaknesses of the individual are revealed. A training program is then initiated which is based on the evaluation profile of the individual.

Training follows sequentially arranged experiences of increasing complexity of performance, and increasing quantity and quality of production. In well-established workshops, differing kinds of supervisory conditions may also be programmed, ranging from benign to highly authoritative. The student in the training program can be introduced gradually into succeedingly more demanding work stations, and increasingly more demanding and harsh supervision. The more realistic the work demand and supervisory relation, the better the experience. Even though this is initial work experience, the conditions should be controlled so they approximate the world of real work as soon as the student can tolerate it.

The use of school campus jobs is probably the easiest to arrange in many school systems. Students are assigned to different jobs in the lunch room, garage, office, or with the maintenance staff. Once the student has mastered a job, he should be removed to another, perhaps more difficult job until he has experienced all the differing jobs suitable to his ability. One problem inherent in campus assignments has been the practice of paying the students an hourly wage regardless of their work skills. Since the goal is to teach people how to work, the reward conditions should be tied to work skill. To accomplish this, it is necessary to set performance standards and tie rewards to the degree to which the students meet the performance standards. If the going rate for washing dishes is $1.00 per hour, for example, performance standards should indicate the number of dishes to be washed per hour. Should that be 100 dishes, and the student washes only 50 per hour, his pay should be 50 cents for his work. Similarly, if a good janitor cleans a certain number of rooms per hour and a student cleans the same number, but forgets to arrange the chairs, his pay should be reduced in proportion to the amount of time chair-arranging takes. In short, both quantity and quality can be included in pay calculation. The important consideration, however, is that standards of performance govern the issuance of rewards.

Simulated work situations are sometimes used alone or in conjunction with campus work stations. Although there are a variety of ways to set up the stations, one quite satisfactory method has been to ask industrial firms for work tasks or evaluation or training equipment that they no longer need. Often the industries willingly donate both machines and materials to schools. It is not necessary that only industries in the immediate location be solicited. Any representative type of work in the region or in nearby large cities can be used. Generally, one work station for each student should be secured. Given this situation, students can be rotated on the jobs at regular intervals and as their skills warrant. One advantage to soliciting work samples is the availability of production standards for each job. These make it possible for students to have their production compared with industrial standards that come from the work world. This adds a note of realism to what would otherwise be essentially an artificial situation.

Initial work experience should be continued until the students are ready to enter the competitive work world on a trial basis. Usually this occurs at about the age of 16, but could be delayed if necessary. Initial work experience should be planned for from two to three years with work-tryout planned for another two to three years.

Work Tryout

Work tryout, sometimes called work adjustment training, on the job training (OJT), or job tryout, is handled in a variety of ways by different work-study programs. Fundamentally, it is designed to provide a bridge between sheltered work and the competitive labor market and so can be viewed as semicompetitive or semisheltered—the semantics are not as critical as the concept. Most often, job tryout involves the use of businesses and industries in the community as appendages of the school. Employers and supervisors actually function as adjunct instructors in the work-study program. Students are assigned for work experience to the work stations on a rotating basis for from two to six months. In most cases, the student spends one-half day on the job and one-half day in school. This pattern continues for from one to four years, or until the job skills of the student are good enough to warrant seeking full-time employment for the student. For most students, experiences on four or more different kinds of jobs should be provided before permanent placement is sought.

Permanent Placement

Permanent placement should be searched for as the culmination of the special program for the mildly retarded. This is the test of the effectiveness of the rest of the program. In some school systems, graduation for the students hinges on successful full-time work experience for one year, during which time the students attend discussion seminars held in the evenings, late afternoons, or Saturdays. Several dividends accrue from this requirement. First, a diploma automatically enables a person to be eligible for some jobs for which he would otherwise be disqualified. That is, regardless of a person's ability to perform in a satisfactory manner, he may not even apply if he does not have a diploma. In dollars and cents, it is conservatively estimated that the diploma is worth at least $1000 per year in enabling an individual to apply for better-paying jobs than those he might be restricted to without a diploma. Second, the seminars enable youngsters in full-time employment to discuss problems and behaviors that are crucial to their employment and living success. Third, their full-time work experience is cushioned by school personnel who are available to trouble-shoot in emergencies. Fourth, the youngsters will retain student status so they can participate in school activities as performers or spectators while they are establishing themselves as adult citizens. Fifth, the seminars can act as a safety valve for those who experience job failure. Some schools support an "open" campus plan, in that any former student who loses his job or is in need of further job training may re-enroll in school as a postgraduate student. He may then repeat any part of the training program but must participate in the seminars. This is an excellent type of postschool program since it allows the student to feel free to contact the school for help whenever necessary. Thus the school, which may have been a positive force in their development, can continue to provide support when needed. Such security insurance is difficult to evaluate in dollar value but may be priceless in individual cases.

Although vocational competence is the ultimate competence sought by this program, outcomes from the analysis of occupations, the development of vocational skills and the development of individuals for occupational placement and job retention can also be specific.

Analysis of Occupation and Job Finding

The development of positive attitudes toward work and the understanding of the contribution of work in our social structure seems to be an area that needs special attention with retarded children. Many come from homes supported by welfare funds, so the model of productive work is not present. Others may be from homes where work is an accepted way of life, but they have never been made aware of their own probable involvement in work. To develop positive attitudes toward work, it is necessary to begin attending to work at an early stage and to continue to make the children aware of this vital force. Outcomes that should be pursued are:

PRESCHOOL LEVEL
1. When questioned, the student will be able to state the occupation of his mother and father.
2. When questioned as to what his parents receive for working, the student will indicate or state that it is money.
3. When asked, the student will be able to identify two people outside his immediate family who work.
4. When questioned, the student will be able to name three different jobs performed by school personnel.
5. When questioned, the student will be able to name three different types of jobs.

PRIMARY LEVEL
1. When asked, the student will be able to name three occupations of the helping professions.
2. When asked, the student will be able to verbally state how the helping professions help people.
3. When asked, the child will be able to describe two chores performed in the home and tell who is responsible for them.
4. When asked, the student will be able to name three businesses operating in his community.
5. When questioned, the student will be able to name three kinds of stores and tell what they sell.
6. When questioned, the student will be able to name two community utility services.

INTERMEDIATE LEVEL
1. When asked, the child will be able to name two ways in which people help others through their work.
2. When questioned, the student will be able to describe the tasks performed by different members of the family.
3. Given pictures of a fireman, policeman, electrical worker, nurse, doctor, factory worker, the student will correctly identify the occupation of each.
4. Given pictures of a police worker, factory worker, store clerk, gas station attendant, mail carrier, and farmer, the student will be able to name three things each worker does as part of his job.

PREVOCATIONAL LEVEL
1. When asked, the student will be able to discuss the differences between leisure time and work time.

2. Given ten labeled pictures of various work situations, the student will be able to correctly match them with ten pictures of different kinds of dress.
3. In a verbal discussion of various occupations, the student will be able to identify one occupation he would like to engage in and one he would not like to work at.
4. Given an uncomplicated job application form, the student will be able to fill in all the blanks correctly.
5. When questioned, the student will be able to tell about opportunities for jobs that are peculiar to his locality.
6. When questioned, the student will be able to discuss two services of the Employment Agency.

VOCATIONAL LEVEL
1. When questioned, the student will be able to name two skills needed for the successful performance of a given job.
2. When presented with a given job, the student will be able to fill out a job analysis form.
3. When questioned, the student will be able to name three sources of information about employment opportunities.
4. Given a role of job interview, the student will be able to conduct himself properly.
5. When questioned, the student will be able to name the major provisions of the wage and hour law.
6. When questioned, the student will be able to state verbally the provisions of unemployment compensation.
7. When questioned about fringe benefits, the student will be able to name the benefits of hospitalization, insurance, vacations, and social security.
8. When questioned, the student will be able to discuss the requirements for union membership and name two advantages of belonging.

Surveying the community to locate possible jobs is made a good deal easier when existing sources of help are used. Certainly the one agency most in touch with current job needs in a community is the Employment Service. Records for the federal Department of Labor originate with the employment service requests not only for the kind but also the number of employees needed in an area. This simply means that the records are not only meticulously kept, they are also current. Quite often the work placement counselor can get a very good picture of the employment trends by looking at the records for the past year or two. This provides excellent clues as to where to look for jobs. At the same time, becoming acquainted with the Employment Service personnel goes a long way toward securing good services for the youngsters in the school program. Not that they will be given any preferential treatment, but rather that the people who run the service will better understand the strengths of the students, and not just be concerned with their weaknesses so placements are apt to be better than they might ordinarily be. Obviously, every youngster should be registered with the employment service before he leaves school.

A second source of job information is the want ad section of the daily newspaper. Whether this is used in the classes or just by the placement counselor or work experience coordinator, the requests reflect current conditions and need to be looked at daily. The follow up should be preceded by a telephone call, but that in turn is fruitless until a personal visit is made. Fundamentally, the personal contact is the key to successful job finding and placement. The bromide that "the work counselor who wears out the seat of his pants before the soles of his shoes ain't a good work-counselor" has a good deal of truth to it.

Developing the Individual for Occupational Placement and Job Retention

The actual placement of the individual on a job and his ability to hold a job is a combination of his skills, knowledges, ability, attitudes, and probably other things. The individual does not emerge full-blown for employment through the magic of metamorphosis. The development of an employable person is the culmination of his slowly developed abilities over an extended period of time. Therefore, it is not too early to pay attention to job placement development, beginning with the pre-primary experiences of the child. Outcomes to be developed are:

PRESCHOOL LEVEL
1. Upon request, the child will be able to discriminate between his belongings and those of other children.
2. Given a group of common objects, the child will be able to categorize them by use.
3. Given three different instructions, the child will be able to follow them.

PRIMARY LEVEL
1. When given a group of objects of different kinds, the child will be able to sort them by shape, color, or size.
2. When asked, the child will be able to explain warning and direction signs.

3. Upon request, the child will be able to verbalize classroom rules of conduct.
4. Given an assigned classroom chore, the child will carry it out without being reminded by the teacher.

INTERMEDIATE LEVEL

1. Given an assortment of hand tools, the child will be able to name them on request.
2. Given a task to do in a group activity, the child will be able to complete his assignment in a satisfactory manner.
3. Upon the completion of a task, the child will be able to describe two reasons for taking pride in a job well done.
4. Upon request, the child will be able to name three activities of a good worker.

PREVOCATIONAL LEVEL

1. Given the opportunity, the child pays for his lunches and transportation from his earnings.
2. Upon request, the child will be able to recite his vital statistics.
3. Given a problem involving wages and hours worked, the child will be able to explain the relationship.
4. When criticized for poor work, the child can explain the reason why the criticism is warranted.
5. Given a job to do, the student will be able to function without supervision.

VOCATIONAL LEVEL

1. Given a job situation, the student can converse with fellow workers using the correct vocational vocabulary.
2. Given a job assignment, the student will be able to work alongside other employees without interfering with the work of his peers.
3. Given a job assignment, the student will be able to work a full day with no appreciable drop in production.
4. Upon finishing a task, the student will be able to start a new task without having to be directed to do so by his supervisor.
5. Given a task that requires a sequence of movements for completion, the student will be able to perform successfully each of the acts in the correct order.
6. Upon request, the student will be able to describe the appropriate dress for each of three different occupations.
7. Upon request, the student will be able to name three advantages of working for the company or business for which the student works.
8. Upon request, the student will be able to explain three job requirements of a supervisor.
9. Upon request, the student will be able to describe verbally what a worker must do to be promoted in his job.

All these skills and attitudes are critical to successful employment, but they emerge as a result of years of preparation. Since employability is the desired end product of the entire program, the concentration on specific behaviors is built on top of the program of general development. Thus the prevocational and vocational experiences are provided in work settings and are supplemented by experience units provided in the school setting. Units that have been found to be useful are included in Chapter 12, but the teacher should be constantly aware of the need for developing skills and attitudes throughout the entire program.

Part III

UNITS
OF
INSTRUCTION

CHAPTER 11

Preschool, Primary, and Intermediate Units of Instruction

Teaching educable retarded children is at best a difficult though rewarding task. Given an individual with poorly organized perceptions, inadequate intellectual skills available to evaluate already poor perceptions, and who has difficulty in forming meaningful concepts, the teacher is faced with the necessity of developing an educational program that will facilitate perceptual organization, concept development, and intellectual processes. A further restriction is imposed by the limited adult roles open to the retarded. The program, therefore, becomes one of trying in every possible way to develop a limited person into an adequate human being who can maintain a satisfactory level of living and working in society. The challenge is substantial, but the rewards are enormous when one considers the alternative of a probably dependent person versus an independent citizen.

Not only must the teacher arrange a learning environment that teaches skills and knowledges, but he must also arrange opportunities for the child to use these skills and knowledges in meaningful situations. Furthermore, the lessons and experiences must be presented in such a manner that they are consistent with the learning levels and characteristics of the children. Many authorities have described the

217

learning characteristics of the educable retarded.[1] There seems to be general agreement that certain principles of presentation are more effective than others. Most stress the need for simplicity, brevity, sequence, success, overlearning, and meaningfulness. In addition to rather formal instructional procedures, units of instruction need to be developed to reinforce and give meaning and utility to the learning tasks.

The term "unit" has been used to describe a wide variety of activities. In some, the emphasis is on content, others emphasize student participation. Some units are largely developed by teachers, while others grow out of experiences of the students. In this section, a unit may be thought of as a series of learning experiences organized around a central theme or problem area. The unit therefore cuts across subject areas and may at different times emphasize one area more than another. It should serve the purpose of reinforcing learning skills, and providing an opportunity to use those learned skills in meaningful activities.

Suggestions for possible units are arranged according to levels and presented in this and the next chapters. The list is far from definitive but is perhaps broad enough to give some idea of the scope that should be included. Obviously each teacher, each group of youngsters, and each locality will exert a considerable influence on what areas are actually covered.

In developing units it has been found to be a good idea to keep the unit in a plain file folder on which the name of the unit (or subject covered), level, ages of the children, and amount of time needed to cover the unit are written. Inside, the unit outline, materials used, references, resources, work sheets, vocabulary lists, and evaluations or suggestions for improvement can all be gathered.

The unit outline should start with a statement of the goal of the unit, followed by a listing of the enroute objectives to be achieved in reaching the goal. For example, if the goal is to teach the children the makeup of a family, the enroute objectives might be: (1) upon request,

---

[1] See Samuel A. Kirk, "Research in Education of the Mentally Retarded," in Harvey Steven and Rick Heber (eds.), *Mental Retardation: A Review of Research* (Chicago: University of Chicago Press, 1964); John W. Gilbaugh, *How to Organize and Teach Units of Work in Elementary and Secondary Schools* (San Francisco: Fearon Publishers, Inc., 1957); *A Program of Instruction for Elementary School Children with Retarded Mental Development* (Kansas City, Mo.: Kansas City Board of Education, June 1959); and Herbert Goldstein and Dorothy Seigel, *A Curriculum Guide for Teachers of the Educable Mentally Handicapped* (Springfield, Ill.: State of Illinois, Circular Series B-3, No. 12, 1858).

have the child identify the members of his family by name; (2) upon request, have the child identify the members of his family by role; (3) have the child identify members of the family by age. Each of the enroute objectives will require a series of experiences supported by materials and activities that lead the child directly to the behaviors specified.

How the unit will be introduced should be carefully thought out and described. Some good ways have been through field trips, a resource person, films, film strips, a weather change, a game, pictures, TV treasure hunt, a bulletin board or some unusual pupil interest. At this stage the teacher needs to do some good research and thinking about the unit. Looking in encyclopedias, magazines, books, films, tapes, library collections, picture stacks, commercial catalogs, and music collections is a good way to start. One often overlooked resource is your colleagues and also your friends. Sometimes it is surprising to discover how knowledgeable these people are.

As you record your unit plans, it is a good procedure to put the related ideas close together:

Objective	Teaching Procedures, Pupil	Activities, Worksheets	Materials Needed
1.	1.	1.	1.
2.	2.	2.	2.

In addition, it is useful to list the materials used directly as well as the resource materials that may be supportive of the activities and materials employed. For example,

Materials used directly:

1. Experience chart
2. Experience chart paper
3. Black crayon or grease pencil
4. Calendar
5. Flannel board and flannel objects
6. Flash cards of vocabulary and spelling words
7. Flash cards of capital letters

Resource Materials:

1. Bulletin board
2. Books
3. Magazines

4. Film or film strip
5. Resource person
6. Field trips
7. Transparencies, overhead projector
8. Teaching aids
9. Collections

Often it is worthwhile to write out a sample experience chart story (or save those from previous units related to the one being planned) so a tentative vocabulary or spelling list can be developed. The final list can then be made up as new words are identified that need to be learned by the children. Tentative worksheets can also be prepared which help a child to learn basic skills that are related to the other competency areas. That is, each unit should be examined to determine how it will relate to the other skill areas. Each unit should contain a planning sheet that relates these skills. Figure 1 is an example.

FIGURE 1

Name of Unit _____

Goal of Unit _____

Concepts Included 1._____

2._____

Communication Reading Listening	Arithmetic Facts & Processes Time	Health and Safety
Oral Written	Money Measurement	Motor & Recreation
Social	Vocational	Esthetics Art Music

Other

Upon completion of the unit some tangible product or activity should result. This may be a display, a booklet, some art object, a party, a play, some trip or visit, or some event or thing that ties all the elements into some synthesis. Whatever it is, it should leave the children with a sense of accomplishment in which they can take some pride.

The final act of the teacher is an evaluation of the unit itself. While there may be many ways to do this, the following questions, answered conscientiously, will provide a good picture of the strengths as well as the weaknesses of the effort.

1. Did the unit fit into the overall curriculum?
2. Was the unit suitable for the ability level of the children?
3. Was the unit of interest to the students?
4. Did it make good use of community resources?
5. Did the unit fit into a balance between the different competency areas?
6. Did the unit fit into a logical sequential plan for development?
7. Was the unit feasible in terms of time?
8. Was the unit properly challenging without being too difficult?
9. Did the unit deal with a topic of importance?

Any question answered negatively should be followed by how the unit could be improved next time and thus become an important aid to improving teaching.

Although the unit may develop from an item of current interest, a newspaper story, radio, or TV, or any of a variety of sources, the unit may generate somewhat more interest if it arises out of the current experiences of the students. Field trips, movies, resource people, or other sources may be used by the teacher to stimulate the development of a unit which has relevance to the children's needs and interests.

Experience charts can be used as the mechanisms around which units function. Several reasons prompt this suggestion. First, experience charts grow out of the activities of the children. Thus, there can be a high degree of personal commitment on the part of the child to the work represented. Second, the subject represented may be presented in a variety of ways from very simple to quite complex. This flexibility allows specific control of subject, vocabulary, and concepts commensurate with the achievement level of the children. Third, the development of the chart is a group project. Skills of social interaction may be taught and emphasized in the context of a real and vital activity. Fourth, the chart does not interfere with the use of any kind of supporting resources. Visual, written, spoken, or manipulative materials can be searched for and used to enrich the unit. Fifth, the chart lends itself to a variety of uses. It can be used to introduce new words, to teach spelling, to teach writing, to teach matching, or it can be the basis for making one's own book. Sixth, the chart fulfills the requirements indicated as contributing to the learning of the retarded. It is simple, brief, has sequence, provides for success, lends itself to overlearning, and it is meaningful.

To develop an experience chart, the teacher should introduce the unit in any of the ways that will spark the interest or enthusiasm of the youngsters. These include using news items, visitors, field trips, movies, TV, or any item of current meaning to the children. From the ensuing discussion, the children can dictate their own story or stories which are printed on blackboard by the teacher. The stories at the pre-school levels should be simple—not more than two or three lines with not more than three or four words per line, and with a great many repetitions of words.

The teacher can next print the story from the blackboard on a chart. This provides recognition in a slightly different setting, but the same story is used. Then the teacher can print each sentence on cardboard and insert the sentences in a tag board while the children "read" each sentence. The sentences can be mixed up to aid in teaching sequencing with the children—helping to put the sentences in the correct order. The sentences can then be printed as phrases or individual words to be inserted on the tag board for additional practice. The stories can be traced by the youngsters for seat work or the words or sentences can be dittoed so the children can make their own books by pasting the sentences or words in the correct order.[2]

One inexpensive item of equipment that has been used by many teachers to give added interest to experience charts is a Polaroid camera. Pictures taken of the children, points of interest from trips, and things of meaning or uniqueness can be pasted on the experience charts. The pictures not only aid in recall and recognition, but have the added characteristic of providing personal identification for the children. Furthermore, for many children this may be the only opportunity they have of securing personal mementoes. In all, the $20 or more invested is well worth the money. Parenthetically, color film is much more effective than black and white.

At the primary, intermediate, prevocational, and vocational levels, the experience chart system is used, but the stories become progressively more complex and precise. Perhaps most critical of the uses of the experience chart is that of teaching thought processes. On the premise that mental retardation involves limited thought processes, every opportunity should be afforded to develop the thinking of the youngsters.

Guilford[3] has indicated that five processes make up the intellectual operations. These are memory, cognition, convergent, divergent, and evaluative thought. Memory is the process of recalling previously

---

[2] For a fuller discussion of the use of experience charts see Kirk, *Teaching Reading to Slow-Learning Children*, pp. 85–92.

[3] Guilford, Chap. 1.

learned material. It is exercised by answering a question like *"What did we write a story about yesterday?"* or, *"What did we see on our trip?"* Cognition is the recognition of previously learned material. It involves choices from among alternatives and answers the question of *"Which* of these is the one we used yesterday?" The *"what"* and *"which"* questions are the most frequently used in school situations. Of less frequent use are questions of convergence, divergence, and evaluation, so these processes need special attention. Convergent thought is elicited in response to questions concerned with *"How* many other ways could we do this?" Such questioning presumes a "correct" method, and is therefore inductive since all methods lead to a single solution. Divergent thought is called into play when questions of the "what if" variety are posed. This is essentially a deductive process in that there is no "correct" answer, only possibilities or alternative approaches. Evaluative thought answers the question of, "What is the *best* method?" To answer this question, criteria of use must be established since "best" always implies the question, "Best for what?"

Units of instruction lend themselves to providing practice in all five thought operations, but since the lessons are largely structured by the kinds of questions teachers pose, it is possible to concentrate somewhat less on questions of "What?" and "Which?" in order to provide training and exercise in those thought processes that emphasize "How?", "What if?", and "Which is best for our purpose?" Since these questions are equally appropriate and important for children at all levels of development, from preprimary to vocational, no unit should be considered complete unless provisions are made for convergent, divergent, and evaluative thought.

Even though units arise from the interests and experiences of children, a good teacher usually has an arsenal of topics that provide sequence and order to the core of each area. These may be used sequentially according to a rigid schedule, but such a procedure does violence to capitalizing on student enthusiasm and the units are seldom timely. In order to facilitate teacher planning, units can be scheduled in three-week blocks of 15 daily lessons each. Seldom does a unit fit such a schedule. Some never really get started, some run neatly for the allotted time, and some extend for six weeks or more. There is nothing sacred about a rigid schedule, but a flexible schedule is required for systematic teaching. There is, therefore, some justification for sticking to the core, and there is every prudent reason for having more topics than probably will be covered.

Given units of three weeks, 12 units would be needed for each academic year's work. At the preschool and primary levels, this would mean some 36 units, each dealing with aspects of the home, would be needed. At the intermediate level, 36 units on the city, borough, region, or state would have to be planned. At the prevocational and vocational levels, 72 units dealing with the youngster in the role of a worker, resident, and citizen in the home, neighborhood, city, borough, region, state, and nation will be needed. In total, 180 units will be required to supplement the formal instruction in readiness, academics, vocational exploration, and vocational experience to fill a total program. While no one list of 180 units could possibly fit the needs of each class or school, the following units and materials that support the units can be used as a base for the development of units more suitable to a local situation.

Preschool Level—The Home

As the primary social unit of our society, the home probably is responsible for more elements of living and learning than all other societal institutions. Units at this level have as a common goal not just capitalizing on that social institution most familiar to the child, but introducing attitudes concerning cooperative living which have counterparts in all other societal relations. The units should deal with both structure and function, always identifying the interrelationships as they are relevant to the developing child. Units that can be used are:

The Child

1. *Name, Address, Telephone, Number.* This unit is a good one to use at the beginning of school, since it gives both the teacher and the children an opportunity to get to know each other as well as learn vital information. The unit should provide for both the oral recognition of the child's name, address, and telephone number, and also the written recognition. Chart stories for each child can be reduced to card size to be carried for identification.

2. *Age.* Not only should the child know his age, but this unit allows the child to learn the importance of age as it relates to the age for starting school, and the age for entering activities such as the YMCA programs, Scouts, Little League baseball, and the related admission cost of movies.

The Family

1. *Members of the Family.* Mother, father, brothers, sisters, grandparents, relatives, and roomers may all be included. Pictures, either

real or symbolic, cut from magazines allow the children to make their own family albums. The real utility of the unit, however, lies in the children's opportunity to learn that families are more or less alike and that each person in the family is worthy of recognition and support.

2. *Mother's Work.* The complexity of home management and family roles can be taught by considering the work of different members of the family. Mother's role can be identified relative to cooking, cleaning, washing, sewing, shopping, dressing, and caring for children, instruction, spiritual training, and, perhaps, working.

3. *Father's Work.* Father's work involves not just working out of the home to support the family, but also household maintenance, sharing in household tasks, and child rearing. In homes where no father or mother resides, the work must be done by someone else.

Children's Work

Children's work can be introduced both as self-care and contributions to the family. Since the influence of the school can be directed toward the children, several units on *clothing care, personal grooming,* and *health* can be used.

1. Clothing care involves learning the kinds of clothing such as outside wraps—hat, coat, overcoat, raincoat, sweater, and jacket. Undergarments such as different kinds of underwear and socks, and outer wear such as dresses, slacks, blouses, and skirts should be learned. The appropriateness of various outfits can be stressed. Personal care and hygiene should also be emphasized.

2. Putting on and taking off clothing may involve practice with buttons, hooks, eyes, snaps, zippers, belts, and lacing and tying shoes. Specific items representing each kind of fastening are most helpful for practicing.

3. Care of clothing involves hanging up wraps and coats, cleaning and polishing shoes, and putting them in their proper places. Activity of a shoe-polishing nature is generally great fun.

4. Grooming units may be combined or dealt with individually. Care of the skin by washing, bathing, and diet receive great support from TV commercials.

5. Care of the teeth through regular brushing can be supported by movies from the county dental society and/or lectures by a dentist or the school nurse. More important is the provision of tooth brushes, toothpaste and an available sink for morning, noon, and after-snack tooth brushing. Prizes or stars or awards for faithfulness and competence are effective.

6. Care of the nails, fingers, and toes may accompany units on washing or be independent. It is necessary that both cleanliness and neatness be stressed. Proper equipment should be made available and properly demonstrated. The imaginative use of a Polaroid camera (before and after pictures) can help to reduce possible embarrassment.

7. Care of the hair through washing, combing, cutting, and arrangement can be a source of fun for all through demonstration. Classes that include children of different races provide the opportunity to discuss individual differences in a positive manner.

8. Units on the proper attire for seasons, weather, and occasions lend themselves to reinforcing the importance of all areas of grooming as they contribute to one's appearance. Magazine pictures are excellent for illustrative purposes.

9. Toilet activities—when, where, and how—can concentrate on the importance of the functions. In addition, washing the hands, and adjusting the clothes are necessary concomitants. The proper use of a handkerchief or tissue for coughing, sneezing, and nose care is correlative to toileting. In addition, razor blades, poison labels, and similar items lend themselves to units on first aid.

10. The importance of good food identifies the contributions of various food groups. Milk and dairy products, vegetables, fruit, cereals, meats, fish, eggs, and poultry each has a different contribution to a balanced diet. The National Foods Council and the American Dairy Association have free materials and movies that can be used to support this unit.

11. Good eating habits of washing before eating, cutting small portions, and thorough chewing lend themselves to the teaching of the uses of dishes, cutlery, napkins, discarding dropped or unclean food, and proper table manners. Lunch period is an excellent opportunity to tie the unit to a real situation.

12. A unit on rest should stress the value of rest at night and during the day. Counting the pulse rate before and at rest is a dramatic method of demonstrating the value of rest. Rest habits that stress a regular time and place, loosening of clothing, removing shoes, and rearranging clothing after rest can be demonstrated. Ways of relaxing without actually sleeping can be included—counting sheep, thinking black, and thinking of one's "heavy" fingers, toes, wrists, arms, legs, and torso.

Functions of the Home

1. *Shelter.* How the home furnishes nourishment, rest, safety, recreation, enjoyment, and privacy can be elicited from this unit. Many

children simply do not associate these functions with their own homes. Therefore, a movie on animal homes is an excellent way to introduce this unit.

2. *Rooms.* Not just the rooms in the home, but the function of the kitchen, dining room, bedrooms, living room, bathroom, basement, attic, and garage can be used to illustrate appropriate role behavior of different family members. Pictures from magazines can graphically illustrate different kinds of room sizes, furnishings, and functions. These may range from the children's own homes to the palaces of kings.

3. *Heat.* Different kinds of fuel—wood, coal, oil, gas, and electricity—and different systems of heating lend themselves to the realization that all homes have in common the function of heating, but in many differing ways. The heating system of the school makes an excellent contrasting study.

4. *Furniture and Appliances.* Lights, lamps, toasters, irons, washers, dryers, stoves, vacuum cleaners, and sewing machines make excellent demonstration devices. The variety in each appliance area can be capitalized upon to show both commonalities and differences. Magazines are a rich source of pictures. Correlative furniture can also be most illuminating in developing both perceptions and concepts.

5. *Comforts.* The function of TV's, radios, phonographs, and telephones is excellent for teaching both the use and abuse of these luxuries. An excellent method of approaching this unit is to write stories about the consequences of misuse.

6. *Manners.* The misuse of luxuries can often lead to a unit on courtesy in the home toward members of the family, visitors, and on special occasions. Practice in the right and wrong ways of behaving are especially adaptable to role playing or skits.

7. *The House.* This unit may be taught as a single unit or several units. Of importance is the identification of parts of the house—roof, windows, doors, chimney, porch, sides—the materials from which houses are made—brick, boards, stone, cement, stucco—and the types of houses—one-family, apartments, trailers.

8. *Safety in the Home.* A single unit or several units on safety can deal with accidents that happen in the home. The National Safety Council has both free materials and movies that are effective for illustrating dangers. In addition, dangers from fighting, pushing, sharp and blunt instruments, matches, and electrical and gas appliances need to be included.

9. *Fun Times with the Family.* Many children are not sufficiently aware that the family unit can be a source of enjoyment. One or several

units dealing with family activities such as picnics, birthdays, vacations, and holidays which include where to go, what to do, and how to enjoy the activities can be beneficial in developing the notion that planning is a requisite for having an enjoyable time.

Friends

1. *How To Make Friends.* The social skills of getting along with people start with making friends. A unit that deals with this subject becomes an important part of the preparation for good interpersonal relations. Such fundamental behavior as smiling and talking with others about subjects of mutual interest, finding good things in people, and telling them good things in a sincere manner can be practiced in the class group. Role playing and skit presentation are effective methods of presentation and learning.

2. *Why We Want Friends.* The human needs for companionship and understanding can be emphasized in this unit. More important, however, the mutuality of friendship and attendant responsibilities should receive major attention. Stories about "my friend" can be used with profit.

3. *Where We Find Friends.* To reinforce the lessons of how to make friends, consideration of the effect of behaviors on people the children meet in school, at church, and in the neighborhood can be emphasized. Stories on "how I met my best friend" can be a source of personal and lively discussion.

4. *How We Select Friends.* Calling attention to the things that attract us to people—appearance, manners, fair play, mutual interest, behavior, and leadership qualities—also serves as a springboard for discussing the kinds of behaviors to avoid or which are repelling. Of concern should be a discussion of people to avoid, including those with bad reputations and antisocial tendencies. One or several units may be desirable and useful in this area.

School as Part of Home

Units that treat the school as a counterpart of the home can be most effective in relating societal institutions to each other. Just as the home is a primary social organization, the school is closely related in its structure and functions. Units which emphasize these relationships form a good beginning for role identification needed for adult living. The units closely parallel those of the home.

1. *Members of School Family.* Classmates, teachers, administra-

tors, counselors, custodians, cooks, other teachers, and other classes can be identified as members of the school family. Books with pictures, real or symbolic, serve the purpose of providing tangible comparisons.

2. *Work of Teacher in School Family.* It is often surprising to children to find that teachers work. Even the daily activities of the teacher are often overlooked or not noticed. Snapshot pictures of the teacher at work provide an excellent method of documenting the varied tasks of the teacher. When the pictures are taken by the children, the results may be hilarious.

3. *Work of Children in School.* Not only are children often surprised that teachers work, they are surprised to discover that they do many things in the course of a school day. Candid snapshots to illustrate experience chart stories give the opportunity to point out both good and bad examples. The chance to identify with the activities and the stories helps to personalize the unit.

4. *The Work of Other Members of the School Family.* Administrators, secretaries, custodians, cooks, other teachers, and other classmates are fair game for candid camera work. One or several units that document the activities of people who contribute to the running of the school provide an excellent means of relating the resemblance between the home and the school.

5. *Rooms in School.* The comparison of rooms in the school with rooms in the home can be extended to include function as well as furnishings. It is sometimes quite illuminating to compare the function and furnishings of a gymnasium with the function and furnishings of a living room.

6. *Fun with School Family.* These units may provide the opportunity to introduce children to activities denied them at home. Trips, parties, picnics, and holiday celebrations require planning and execution with specific divisions of labor. These units are especially useful for an exercise of divergent and evaluative thought processes. Other units which are suggested by units on the home may include what schools are made of, safety in the school, and any of the other units covered. Comparison is an excellent method of instruction.

Primary Level—The Neighborhood

The neighborhood is broadly defined as the areas outside the home that the children are likely to have a need to contact. In a small town, this may include the entire community. In a big metropolitan area, this may include a four- or five-block area plus specific stores, recreation, or other points of interest. Units which can introduce the child to this expanding environment should serve to identify those elements that are of importance to him. In each school or class, these will probably differ, but they have in common the recognition of the needs of the children to become systematically exposed to a widening life space.

What Makes Up a Neighborhood

1. *Neighborhood Make-Up.* This unit is similar to the unit on the members of a family. It can deal with the homes, stores, streets, and families that comprise the neighborhood. The use of simple maps to orient the children is an especially helpful technique.

2. *Living in the Neighborhood.* What different people and families do and how they earn a living can be presented by pictures and stories on experience charts. If these are related to maps, this makes the study both personal and meaningful.

Neighborhood Services

1. *Community Helpers*
   a. Helpers Who Keep Us Safe
      (1) Safety Patrol. Not only the boys and girls or men and women who serve on safety patrol, but also the signs and rules and the reasons for them can be used as resources to support this unit.
      (2) Policemen. One or several units can be used to discover what policemen do, the different kinds of policemen and what the children can do to help the policemen in their work. The curriculum guide from the Kansas City public schools, page 630, has especially good suggestions for activities and materials to give vitality to these units.
      (3) Firemen. The work of the firemen, how they learn to do their work, the kinds of equipment being used, the kinds of clothes they wear, and life at the fire station can be studied in whatever depth is appropriate. Experience-chart stories help to reinforce how the children can help the firemen to do their work. What to do in case of fire, and how and where to turn in an alarm should be included.
      (4) Life guards. Pool or beach life guards, their work, how they become qualified, and what prompts the rules and regulations can make this study vital. The reciprocal responsibility of the children to these helpers should be emphasized.

b. Helpers Who Guard Our Health
   (1) Doctors and Nurses. Both preventative and corrective medical practice should be emphasized. The nature of illness is a good source of discussion, especially if one of the children has had a recent experience with illness.
   (2) Dentists. Coupled with good oral hygiene practice, a visit to a dental office and laboratory can make this a very personal unit.
   (3) Street Cleaners. The function of the street cleaners in the total health and sanitation program of the neighborhood is often overlooked. The equipment used is often fascinating to boys.
   (4) Garbage Collectors. A trip to the city dump, with an explanation of the fly and rodent control programs and various methods of disposing of different kinds of refuse often turns out to be unforgettable.
c. Helpers Who Provide Us with Food.
   (1) Milkmen. Those who deliver as well as those who supply the stores and the dairy itself can be studied. A trip to a dairy to see the equipment and the processing of milk and other dairy products can lend support to this unit.
   (2) Grocers. The variety of grocery stores, stocking, storage, displays, selling, delivering, and the people involved provide a variety of items of interest. Using comparative ads from newspapers is an excellent way of introducing this unit.
   (3) Butchers. If a butcher shop is available, this makes an interesting trip. Cold storage lockers, meat cuts, displays, and packaging are all aspects for study.
   (4) Bakers. The preparation, equipment, packaging, and displays are all part of the complex business of providing the children some notion of the effort involved in providing good things to eat. A trip is a most rewarding experience, especially if it culminates in free cookies.
d. Communication Helpers
   (1) Postmen. One or several units can be devoted to the postman, mail clerks, and a trip to the post office. Writing a class letter that is followed through the process from mailing to sorting and sacking lends realism to the unit.
   (2) Newspaper Boys. Not only the delivering or selling of papers, but the whole process of preparing and printing papers can be more meaningful if the children are introduced to a news item that is being gathered and prepared by a reporter. Any school news item can serve this purpose.
   (3) Telephone Workers. Linemen, installers, switchboard operators, and supervisors can be included for study. A trip to the

telephone company makes this unit more meaningful. Telephone use and courtesy can be easily incorporated through role playing.

(4) Radio and TV. If various kinds of stations are available, this unit can become an interesting comparative study. Viewing a live radio or TV show is often an unusually enlightening experience.

(5) Telegrams and Cables. These rapid means of communication are good media for extending the environmental limits of the children in a nonthreatening manner. The mechanics as well as the function are explainable at an easily understandable level.

e. Transportation Helpers

(1) Automobiles. Both the convenience and responsibilities of auto ownership should be emphasized. Different styles of cars through the years make this an excellent unit for historical learnings.

(2) Taxis. The function of taxis becomes a good introduction to this complex operation. In a large city, fleet headquarters makes an excellent field trip.

(3) Trucks. The various kinds, sizes, and functions of trucks can be well documented by collections of pictures on experience charts. Riding in the cabs of trucks is an additional dividend often provided by trucking companies.

(4) Buses. Planning a short bus trip, purchasing the tickets, and taking a special trip is often the first real experience in travel of this nature for many children. In addition, the types of buses —school, transit, and cross-country—may be included.

(5) Trains. The taking of a short trip on a train may be profitably explored. Barring this possibility, stories and pictures and a trip to the local station or a station or terminal in a nearby city can make this unit personal. Being able to climb up into an engine cab can often be arranged.

(6) Airplanes. This unit is best managed by a trip to an airport. If one is not available, pictures and movies may have to suffice.

(7) Boats. From pleasure boats to barges to freighters to liners, pictures can be of help to make this study interesting. Port cities provide a bonanza for experience of related activities such as docking, loading, and unloading, and cruises.

f. Helpers Who Guide Us

(1) Parents. Manners, behavior, and courtesy can be tied to an exercise in what parents want children to be and do when they grow up. Understanding parental concerns and responsibilities is an essential area for exploration.

(2) Teachers. The hopes of teachers for the future living of their pupils can be the basis for this study. It is an extension of what teachers do in their daily work. The emphasis is on the future, not the present.

(3) Clergy. Different kinds of clergy and churches may make an excellent display through pictures and visits. The functions of churches in youth activities can be pointed out.

(4) Club leaders. YMCA, recreation youth club, Scout, and other leaders may be called upon to explain their programs. Children involved in various clubs can be a rich source of support for this study.

Observing Special Days and Holidays

1. *Children's Birthdays.* The meaning of the gift of life can be brought home to the children by a "birthday day" each month in the classroom. The wise use of one's talents is an excellent theme to pursue.

2. *Halloween.* Not only parties, but the meaning of Halloween and ways of celebrating it can be studied.

3. *Thanksgiving.* A simple explanation of the origin of Thanksgiving is most appropriate. Skits, plays, and contests between "Indians" and "Pilgrims" lend realism and some historical perspective that is easily understandable.

4. *Christmas.* The similarity of Christmas and the Jewish Hanukkah, as well as the differences between these simultaneous holidays, can be pointed out in a positive manner. Traditional customs, songs, and practices can be pictured or demonstrated. Doing things for others is a dominant theme.

5. *Lincoln's Birthday.* His life and work stand as splendid examples of humanitarian compassion. Pictures, movies, or shrine visits when possible are excellent activities. A penny makes a good introductory aid.

6. *St. Valentine's Day.* Either historical perspective, or making valentines, or both can make this a fun occasion.

7. *Washington's Birthday.* The "father of our country" theme with pictures and skits may provide some understanding of our political heritage.

8. *Easter.* The seasonal rebirth of plants can make the study of Easter and other seasonal holidays of spring take on meaning. Nearly every major religion celebrates spring in some fashion. These similarities are important and may be dramatized with profit.

9. *Mother's Day.* Making gifts can be a concrete method of calling

attention to the importance of mothers of all kinds. Procreation of the species can be an interesting line of pursuit in animals, birds, plants, and people.

10. *Summer Holidays.* Memorial Day, Independence Day, and Labor Day celebrations vary from community to community, but some acquaintance with why and how these holidays are celebrated may serve to introduce the children to these customs.

At both the preprimary and primary levels, an excellent source for materials and ideas is *A Program of Instruction for Elementary School Children with Retarded Mental Development*, developed by the Kansas City, Missouri, Public Schools. This excellent guide has ideas, units, methods, and materials in all areas of instruction developed by teachers under the direction and guidance of Mrs. Nell Dabney, and may be obtained from the administrative office of the Kansas City Schools.

The General Aniline and Film Corporation[4] has published *Language Development for Pre-School, Kindergarten, and Early Primary.* The teacher's handbook and transparencies cost about $300, but are remarkably good aids. The set consists of 62 transparencies (many with overlays) and 62 lesson plans covering eight units. Unit I is called "About My Classmates and Me." Represented are Negro, white, Oriental, and Spanish-American children. Unit II, "The Family," has transparencies of a white family in an automobile, grandma and grandpa stepping off a train, a Negro family, an Oriental family, and a Spanish-American family. Overlays make it possible to include or exclude specific family members. Unit III, "Different Ways of Living," pictures suburbia, a cold-water flat, a large mid-city, and a rural town. Children are shown playing on streets, in alleys, in a backyard, and in an apartment court. Unit IV, "Parts of House," shows a suburban house, a two-story house, and rear views, cross sections, and split levels. Unit V, "Rooms in a House," shows a living room, dining room, kitchen, bathroom, bedroom, and furniture. Individual pictures of a bed, a chest of drawers, and a closet allow the use of overlays to call attention to specific functions. Units VI and VII, "Things We Do Around the House," Parts A and B, picture appliances, setting the table, washing clothes, different kinds of clothes lines, ironing, doing dishes, working around the house, father's work, mother's work, children's activities, including care of pets, an apple tree through the seasons, a picnic, and play equipment. Unit VIII, "Evaluation," pictures a utility closet, a birthday party, and children going to school. The excellence of the transparencies and the

[4] Their address is 140 West 51st Street, New York, 10020.

usefulness of the lessons promise great utility. The company is developing units on the extended environment including driver training and occupational information. These should be well worth considering in any school program for the educable retarded. Even though the school may not be able to buy the transparencies discussed, the concepts should be taught by using magazine picture substitutes.

Intermediate Level—City, Region, and State

Since the children at the intermediate level will be chronologically between about ten and fourteen years, they should have developed enough academic skills to use resource materials, books, magazines, and periodicals to supplement experience charts and field trips in their unit work. The experience charts should still be the basic teaching media in the unit, but functional academics should be stressed in the pursuit of information on the expanding environment experiences of the children.

Community Organization

1. *Sections of Town.* A large map of the entire community can be cut into smaller sections which represent the chief areas: business, industrial, residential, and shopping centers. Pictures of buildings enhance the map study work. In large cities, bus tours are very interesting field trips.
2. *Street Numbering Systems.* Nearly every community has an order of some kind in their designation of streets, avenues, and boulevards. Finding the order and using it can be a good mystery or "Where am I?" game activity.

Community Institutions

1. *Churches.* The identification of churches by locations and design is a good way to call attention to the different groups.
2. *Health Centers.* Medical buildings such as laboratories, offices, hospitals, clinics, and veterinary services can be pictured and located while the kinds of services rendered are explained.
3. *Recreation Centers.* YMCA's, clubs, health centers, private golf courses, and the like may help to establish the many ways people spend leisure time.

Government Services

1. *Schools and Colleges.* In cities of above 15,000, a variety of educational institutions may be found. The services offered by many of these have direct relevance to the lives of the children.

2. *Parks and Playing Fields.* Most communities provide some kind of publicly supported park or playground facility. Quite often the children are not acquainted with how to use them. Swimming pools may be part of the services provided. In some communities, rural parks such as mountain parks or seashore areas are maintained by the community.

3. *Libraries.* Library services have been extended to include tapes, recordings, and art displays in many places. Obtaining and using a library card may be part of this unit.

4. *Art Galleries.* Galleries may range from private collections to metropolitan institutions, but most communities have something that serves this function. If necessary, movies or trips can supplement communities which lack the facility.

5. *Museums.* This is similar to the study of art galleries—in both units, the reasons communities have art galleries and museums can be stressed.

6. *Water.* The collection, processing, and distribution of drinking water, and collection of wastes can be included in a comprehensive unit or series of units devoted to this vital service. Comparative systems can serve to enliven this area.

7. *Light.* Generation, distribution, control, and repair are some of the areas that may be explored. Comparative amounts of electricity for differing uses can be demonstrated.

8. *Sewage.* The collection and processing of sewage can lead to some understanding of both water and air pollution. Legislation and news items lend timeliness.

City Governmental Offices

1. *Mayor or City Manager.* What the chief official does, how he is selected, and the relevance of these functions to the children can be gleaned from a visit to city hall.

2. *Councilmen.* A unit similar to that on the mayor and a visit to a council meeting may make this subject meaningful.

3. *Judges.* Federal, state, or local judges in the community may provide a different slant to the law than that experienced by some of

the children. Seeing a judge hold court is a good experience, especially when one is not the defendant.

4. *Chief of Police.* Both the man and the office can be an interesting subject for study. A visit, pictures, and news items lend immediacy.

5. *Fire Chief.* Similar to the study of the chief of police, a visit to the headquarters or district quarters helps support this unit.

6. *Public Health Office.* The work of this office is often misunderstood. Attention to why the regulations are enforced can be most revealing. A visit to the laboratory, if one is available, is an interesting trip.

Regional Government

1. *What the Region Includes.* Maps of the region or state can be used with pictures to represent the surrounding area. Farm areas, mountains, seashores, lakes, parks, significant community monuments, industries, and points of interest can be identified and studied in one or several units. Trips are most effective but in their absence, movies, pictures, resource pictures, collections, and visitors serve to demonstrate almost as well.

2. *Regional Services.* Country Governmental officials can be studied just as city officials were. These become real when individuals such as commissioners, the sheriff, and others are used as focal points of study.

3. *Transportation.* Railroads, highways, waterways, and skyways can be studied both on a regional and state basis. Maps and pictures can combine to make this personal to the children.

State Government

1. *The Governor.* Both the person and the office combine to emphasize the interrelationship of the two. One or a series of units can serve to point up the importance of this office.

2. *The Legislature.* News items can help to make this study timely. Relating the function to the city commissioner or county commissioners often helps to explain the function.

Departments of Government

Units dealing with these departments can be selected for their relevance to the children. Among the departments which can be supported by movies or free materials are:

1. Mental health
2. Public instruction
3. Highways
4. Fish and game
5. Welfare
6. Public health
7. Finance (tax collections)

History and Geography of the State

Many units devoted to geological and geographical aspects of the state can be pursued. Economic, recreational, esthetic, and topological aspects of any area or region can be explored if they have relevance to the children. The key to selection is meaningfulness.

CHAPTER 12

Prevocational and Vocational Units

Prevocational Level

The instructional program for the mildly retarded changes in a significant manner at the prevocational level. In most school systems, this program is housed in a junior high school. Regular students no longer spend their time primarily with a single teacher. They may have homeroom assignments, but they are usually scheduled for different classes in different parts of the building. Each period of the day they must pass to another room, sometimes in different areas of the building.

Schedules

The usual junior high school schedules eight periods per day, two of which are physical education and lunch. This leaves six periods for classroom work. Patterns of scheduling, of course, vary from school to school, but the eight-period day is quite a usual one. For retarded youngsters, this strange new schedule can be quite upsetting, yet it is often even more upsetting to be in a self-contained program when other students are not. It is therefore recommended that schedules similar to those of the regular students be designed for the special class youngsters.

239

The schedules should include blocks of time for initial work experience (sometimes called occupational information and occupational exploration) as well as the other classes in the day. The program schedule should and will need to be modified to fit a particular school, but a typical program could be:

Period I:	Homeroom and occupational information
Period II:	Physical education and recreation (alternating)
Period III:	Occupational exploration
Period IV:	Occupational exploration
Period V:	Lunch
Period VI:	Shop and homemaking skills
Period VII:	Social studies
Period VIII:	Social studies

Variations of this schedule may be made to include a larger block of time for social studies or more time for initial work experience. It may be necessary in some schools that shop courses and homemaking skills be taught by the special class teacher. Whatever the arrangements, the schedule should include the experiences represented by the above list.

Initial Work Experiences

In the absence of being able to secure initial work experiences from a sheltered workshop, or from work samples, school campus jobs can serve the purpose of introducing the students to the world of work. Some jobs that have been used by schools for this purpose are:

1. *Building Maintenance.* The students may assist the custodial staff in a variety of tasks, such as dusting, emptying waste baskets, cleaning windows, arranging desks and chairs, sweeping, mopping, and waxing.

2. *Grounds Maintenance.* This may include picking up litter, raising or lowering the flag, cutting the grass, caring for the flowers and shrubs, and removing snow or ice.

3. *Cafeteria or Food Service.* Unloading and storing food, shelving materials, putting out milk, removing garbage, cleaning tables, filling salt and pepper shakers, supplying the serving line, and serving from the line are some of the jobs that can be learned by students.

4. *Office Services.* Collecting attendance slips, taking messages, unloading and storing supplies, putting stamps on letters, distributing bulletins, distributing locker keys, recording attendance, serving as

hall monitors, running the Mimeograph machine, and simple filing may be done by these youngsters.

5. *Teachers' Aides.* Helping young children with their wraps, assisting at recess, decorating the room, keeping the blackboards clean, and reading stories to children can be of great training worth to these retarded young people.

6. *Stock Room.* Unloading and stocking, storing, delivering, and cleaning are all good training activities.

7. *Library.* Pasting, dusting, mending, caring for magazines, collecting books, and stacking can all be learned by the retarded.

8. *Visual Aids.* Delivering films and strips, setting up the equipment, caring for the equipment, threading and running projectors and collecting equipment are tasks within the capabilities of these youngsters.

9. *Physical education and recreation.* Issuing equipment, inflating balls, setting up equipment for classes, and storing equipment after classes may be some of the tasks these youngsters can do. Being managers of athletic teams is an excellent integrational activity.

10. *Music room.* Setting out stands, storing and getting out equipment, and repairing or caring for sheet music are within the range of work of these youngsters.

11. *Art room.* These young people can assist the art teachers by cleaning and caring for the equipment, preparing clay, running the kiln, and in a variety of other activities. Participating as stage hands for plays may be part of this assignment.

In many school systems, it will be possible to rotate the youngsters so they can gain experience on all of the jobs represented. Within a three-year period, three jobs per year could be covered. Obviously more time will be needed for some youngsters than others. It may be that one job assignment per semester would be a more satisfactory system. Of principal importance, however, is that the youngsters be assigned to work experience as a part of their regular program, and that they be rewarded on the basis of the quality and quantity of the work they do. The close supervision of the work experience by the classroom teacher allows the supporting classroom activities to be much more realistic than they otherwise might be.

Occupational Information

One purpose of the prevocational program is to provide an opportunity to find out about the world of work through study. The occupational information class is designed for this purpose. Although this is specified in the schedule as a single period class, many schools prefer to make this a double period so field trips can be scheduled. The content of the class involves study and discussion pertaining to occupations. Two sources of information are especially good for this class. One is the *Rochester Occupational Series*, marketed by Science Research Associates.[1] The other is *Jobs for the Mentally Retarded*, by Peterson and Jones, Research Center, Pittsburgh, Pennsylvania.

The Rochester series consists of a book of stories made up of five sections. Section I is called "Starting Work"; Section II, "On the Job"; Section III, "Keeping the Job"; Section IV, "Working for the City"; and Section V, "Time Out for Leisure." Each section is a story about some aspect of work. Accompanying the stories are a series of workbooks for the students which reinforce the story lessons. The stories and workbooks are pertinent and interesting. Of greater significance is the fact that three levels of reading are provided for each story and workbook. The easiest level book has a vocabulary demand of about second grade. The middle series has a reading level of about third or fourth grade, and the most advanced has a reading level of slightly beyond fifth grade. Almost regardless of the reading ability of the children, an appropriate book is available to them. Thus a wide range of achievement can be accommodated by the series.

Jobs for the Mentally Retarded, by Peterson and Jones, is a detailed analysis of jobs that can be done by retarded children. In addition to the job analysis, sections on how to train people for the jobs are also included. This book is an excellent study source for the students as well as the teacher. It could be the primary source for study during the second and third years of the program if it is supported by field trips, movies, and films, or film strips appropriate to the job described.

Physical Education and Recreation

The physical education and recreation programs should concentrate on skills and strength developments begun in the preceding levels. In addition, individual skills should be taught in the single or two-man team games. In the program should be time and opportunity to participate in swimming, bowling, croquet, badminton, tennis, handball, square dancing, social dancing, fishing (both fly and bait casting), archery, ping-pong, horseshoes, darts, pool, bird watching, nature study, camping, roller skating, ice skating, miniature golf, and, if possible, water and snow skiing, riding—both horse and bicycle, games such as

[1] The address is 259 East Erie Street, Chicago, Illinois, 60611.

hearts, pinochle, cribbage, checkers, smear, Monopoly, Scrabble, charades, and solitaire.

The same pattern of teaching as used in any unit of instruction applies in the teaching of the recreation and physical education skills. The fundamental rules, skills, and movements should be taught as specifics. Then the use of the movements, skills, and rules should be practiced. In short, both the static and dynamic aspects of the games need attention and therefore should be planned for in the program. Since some skill in these activities may spell the difference between satisfactory use of leisure time and unsatisfactory activities, this looms as a significant part of the prevocational program.

Home Economics

The numerous follow-up studies have consistently pointed out that these youngsters (both boys and girls) will be homemakers. Unfortunately, many of them have home models that provide scant or poor preparation for appropriate adult homemaking roles. If the adult performance of these youngsters depends upon the standards they have learned, the school emerges as the institution that will have the major responsibility for preparing them to be adequate homemakers. Both information and skill in homemaking tasks and supervised practice seem called for in the program. It is therefore proposed that shop and home economics be taught both boys and girls. Whether the activities are presented by semester or are alternated during the week may be a matter of school preference. It should be remembered that the mental maturity of the students will be roughly that of the usual fifth grade normal youngsters and their rate of learning is such that at least twice as much time will be required to teach them as is typically allowed for children in the regular programs. It is therefore proposed that the shop and homemaking programs run for the full three years allotted to the prevocational program.

1. *Food Management.* Food preparation and cleanliness is probably the most important aspect to be stressed. This extends to the kitchen in general as well as the utensils, materials, and the person handling them.

The cooking vocabulary should be introduced in the context of specific activities so that the words will take on the concrete meaning of the activities or things to which they apply. Experience charts can be useful for both vocabulary development and supporting the lessons presented.

The content of units on cooking can profitably explore low-budget, balanced meals as a theme. Proper breakfasts, lunches, and dinners can be taught using basic food groups and related to family nutrition. Then the preparation of specific items from hors d'oeuvres to desserts can be systematically included. The preparation of whole meals and the serving to other classes or people is an excellent culminating activity. Menu planning for a family for a week or several weeks ties well to budgeting and comparative buying. The various methods of food storing and food wasting also need to be demonstrated. Fundamentally, both boys and girls need to learn cleanliness, buying, budgeting, planning, and nutrition as essentials for future home managers.

2. *Clothing Management.* Both boys and girls need to learn the basics of clothing management. As a part of the homemaking program, the youngsters should learn to use both home and commercial laundromat equipment for washing and dry cleaning. Ironing and pressing the clothes after laundering should be a part of the school program, followed by storing on both a seasonal and regular basis. Buying comparatively through the use of ads in newspapers can be an important part of the clothes management program. In this connection, catalogs such as those from Sears, Roebuck, Montgomery Ward, and Penney's are invaluable when used as an encyclopedia to determine what is and what is not a bargain. Quality standards are as much a part of value as are relative prices. These are well discussed in the catalogs and so provide remarkably good guides. Sewing skills are also essential to clothing management. Whether for remodeling, repairing, or basic construction, both boys and girls should learn the basic running stitch, the overcast, and the weave. These can be practiced in repair work first and followed by remodeling and then construction. The youngsters need to be allowed to learn to use machines as a part of their training.

3. *Home Management.* The many elements of home management should be included in all of the prevocational programs. Good management, however, is highly related to system. Not only does system relate to the day of the week (Monday—wash, Tuesday—iron, Wednesday —scrub, Thursday—bake, Friday—clean, Saturday—shop), but this or any other system may change with the week of the month, the season of the year, and a host of other variables. Yet system is the key to efficiency, so emphasis should be given to how to go about developing system. It should be pointed out that it is first necessary to identify what needs to be done. Then the amount of time necessary to do the jobs must be estimated. Then the materials and the equipment required must be secured. Last, the method of starting and the criteria for judging when a job has been finished must be decided upon. Priorities may need to be discussed and agreed upon before a schedule can be

adopted. Even when a schedule is adopted, alternatives need to be identified. If, for example, the Fourth of July falls on a Monday, what do you want to do about washing clothes? Any attention that can be given to this kind of knowledge and practice is time well spent. Furthermore, if a teacher can relate the classroom schedule to a home management schedule, it is apt to take on added meaning to the youngsters.

4. *Child Care.* To many of the retarded youngsters, children in their own families are intruders of questionable worth. Child care study for both boys and girls should stress the value of children in a family setting. Films on the care of the young among different animals offer excellent parallels for discussing the joys of parenthood and the contribution of children to the family. The similarities of child-rearing goals with those of animal families, as well as the differences, make it possible to teach the youngsters their responsibilities as parents for the development of the child into a secure and independent, self-managing adult. By implication, this also defines their expected adult role. It is then possible to study the specifics of child rearing in terms of physical care, emotional care, and intellectual development.

5. *Physical care.* Cleanliness, sleep, nutrition, immunization, illness, clothing, fresh air, and exercise all contribute in a significant manner to the physical development of the child and should probably be dealt with in an individual manner. Developmental norms can be introduced to dramatize this area.

6. *Emotional care.* The need for affection and ways of providing affection as they affect the security of the child can be discussed and demonstrated. Simple stimulus-response-reinforcement explanations related to children's basic needs can be explored. A great many movies on rat and human learning can be used to explore the consequences of emotional deprivation.

7. *Intellectual development.* The effects of environment exploration and language stimulation as they contribute to the learning of a developing child are well documented by movies on child development. In addition, the John Tracy Clinic, 806 W. Adams Blvd., Los Angeles, California, has excellent parental educational materials. Although these materials were designed by and for parents of deaf children, they exemplify child rearing practices beneficial to nondeaf children. Furthermore, they are practical and easily understood.

Shop

Just as home economics was designed for boys and girls, so also the shop offerings should be provided for both and can concentrate on those aspects of home mechanics pertinent to successful home maintenance. Some of the areas to be covered are the following:

1. *Electricity.* This source of power can be studied from its origin at the local light and power company, through transmission lines, meters, and fuse boxes into the home. Simple motors, heat elements, and light elements can be disassembled and/or repaired as a part of class work. The use and misuse of home appliances should be integral to the program.

2. *Plumbing.* The operations of fixtures, their construction, and simple repairs should be presented. Tying the section to both supply and disposal can provide access to community understanding and responsibility.

3. *Home maintenance.* Preventative maintenance should deal with not only the "what" and "how," but also the "why." Both the economic and esthetic considerations should be stressed. Careful attention to learning how to scrub and polish floors, walls, furniture, tiles, and fixtures can stress the difference between long use and replacement. Maintenance schedules should receive top priority.

4. *Lawn care.* Every facet of lawn care from soil preparation, seed selection, fertilizing, watering, mowing, trimming, and flower beds to landscaping can be studied and practiced. Field trips to parks and homes make this section viable. If an area of the school campus lends itself to student care, this makes an excellent project.

5. *Automotives.* Care and maintenance both from an esthetic and mechanical point of view should be taught. An old car, donated or purchased, can become a source of pride as it gradually assumes respectability through rejuvenation by the class.

In all these areas, the trade books such as *Mechanix Illustrated* are excellent source materials—reasonably priced and easily understood.

Social Studies

The social studies time block can be used for a variety of activities that broaden the experiences of youngsters. One area which seems to be of paramount importance is the self-understanding of the emerging adult. It is therefore suggested that a series of units dealing with the theme, "Who am I?" be provided. These units recapitulate the home, the school, neighborhood, borough, city, state, and nations, studied at lower levels with an emphasis on the emerging adult independence role of the youngsters as a center of concentration.[2]

[2] The Frank E. Richards Company, 215 Church Street, Phoenix, New York, 13135, has many workbooks to support the following units.

1. *Biological Background*
   a. Race and origin. Record of accomplishments is not confined to any race or ethnic background. A unit or series of units that explores the lives and achievements of notable persons with backgrounds similar to those of the members of the class may provide models for identification purposes. Pictures or displays can serve to emphasize the tangible contributions of specific persons.
   b. Family history. Identifying the accomplishments of members of the family represented may be used to illustrate the continuity of life from one generation to the next. Family tree displays make excellent projects. A comparison of the material possessions of present generations with those of the past lends itself to detecting progress in civilization and expectations for the future.
   c. Family continuity. The need for continuity of the species can be introduced through films dealing with animal family life. The need for people to transmit life from one generation to the next supports the theme that people are important and that each individual has a role to play in the world. How people's actions affect other people may be explored in this unit or units.

2. *The Self*
   a. Origin. The biology of conception can well make use of a series of 35-millimeter slides prepared by Creative Scope, Inc., of New York. These illustrate sex activities in animals and humans and the products of conception. It may be possible to use the school nurse as a resource to answer questions that might arise. Some schools may prefer to segregate boys and girls for these discussions, but this may depend more upon the character of the classes than upon the nature of the subject matter.
   b. Biological Make-up. Many modern encyclopedias have excellent overlay illustrations of the skeleton, the organs, the muscles, the circulatory system, the digestive system and the respiratory system. In addition, the book *What's Inside Me,* by Herbert Zim, has descriptions written at two vocabulary levels which are accurate and easy to understand. The units illustrate individual commonalities.
   c. Physical Make-up. Difference in height, weight, strength, speed, eye color, hair color, clothing size, shoe size, and other measures can be used to introduce units on other individual differences to point up the uniqueness of individuals.
   d. Personality. Dominance, submissiveness, optimism, pessimism, and other characteristics are illustrated by various personality tests on the market. Value judgments as to the goodness or undesirability of the characteristics should be carefully avoided. The purpose of these units is to understand, not demoralize.
   e. Mental. The nature of individual problems of learning can be illustrated in a nonthreatening manner if it is carefully pointed out

that vocational competence, character, and personality are not related to the ease with which one learns. Some people are excellent athletes while others are not. This does not imply that the nonathletes are inferior people.

f. Emotional. A series of films of the cartoon variety, available from many film companies, can show how emotions affect behavior and what part emotions play in daily living. These films are generally entertaining, informative, and most useful for understanding complex behavior.

3. *Understanding Behavior*
   a. Survival Needs. Every living organism has basic physiological needs that must be satisfied to sustain life. Studying threats to satisfying these needs can be pursued with the aim of understanding each person's own adjustive reactions.
   b. Safety Needs. Closely related to physiological needs are those of safety. These may include any threat to the person of a physical nature, but also include threats to security.
   c. Belongingness Needs. Affection and acceptance as universal needs are as vulnerable to threat as the more basic needs. The reaction of persons to intruders who promise to rob an individual of a boy friend or girl friend can be nearly as violent as threats to life itself. Alternative behaviors that can safeguard or assure the security of sources of affection can be explored through group discussion or role playing.
   d. Self-actualization Needs. Insults as threats to one's feelings of competence, how it is sustained, and alternatives to reduce threat can be most revealing to the youngsters. Discussions of loyalty, integrity, responsibility, and patriotism are natural concomitants of discussions on self-actualization. This can also lead to the study of future adult social roles.

4. *Social Institutions*
   a. The Family. The role of adults in providing for the physiological, safety, affectional, and self-actualizing needs of family members can be explored through re-examining family activities as studied at the preprimary level. In this connection, the role of sex activities between marriage partners can be understood in the context of need fulfillment. Chastity and fidelity become meaningful when identified as security elements.
   b. The Church. The functions of the churches as they relate to the fundamental needs of people can be related to the complexity of adult roles. It should be constantly reiterated that institutions exist because they contribute to the fulfillment of human wants and needs. All churches have this in common so these common functions become the focal point for study.

c. Government. The part played by municipal, county, state, and national governments can be related to need fulfillments at a personal level. A series of units dealing with the various governmental functions studied at the primary and intermediate levels, but related to adult fulfillment needs, can be supported by a series of books by Margaret Hudson on *Being a Good Citizen.* These workbooks provide a rich source for discussion when they are related to personal needs. Through all the discussions should run the theme of individual discipline and responsibility for the rights of others.

Vocational Level

The program at the vocational level is designed to provide articulation between work experience and supportive study. In most schools, the program will be located in the high school building. The students, therefore, should have a program schedule as much like that of the rest of the students as possible, but with up to a half-day of work experience and approximately one-half day in related study. The suggested schedule for the prevocational level lends itself to easy modification to fit the usual high school model. Since the students will be involved in work experiences of various levels of complexity, the study portion of the program should be cognizant of this progression in a supportive manner. Occupational study, occupational experience, and social skills can be assigned blocks of time that are consistent with the school policy. If possible, and profitable, the shop and homemaking experiences begun in the prevocational program can be continued and extended. If this is not possible, the special class teacher may have to develop specific units that can be taught during the social studies period.

Schedules

Although the program at the vocational level is described in terms of units of instruction, some states require the offerings in the special classes to be identified by titles similar to those used in the regular program. In most instances there is no regulation as to the content of the classes, only the title. In such circumstances the program presented can be quite easily adjusted to meet local requirements. Generally, a student must earn 15 Carnegie units to graduate from high school. In these 15, most states require two or three units of English, one of math, one in science, one in social studies, and two years of physical education. The rest of the units may be earned in a variety of courses appropriate to the specialization of the program: college preparatory, business, secretarial, agricultural, distributive education, or whatever.

The foregoing has been interpreted by some schools to mean that each student must take two or three courses called English, one in math, one in science, one in social studies, and two to four years of physical education. Just when the required courses are taken is relatively unimportant. Furthermore, the other ten units may be earned in nearly any combination of course titles. One way of conforming to the 15-unit requirement is through a schedule such as the following:

8:00– 9:00 a.m.	English, one unit credit
9:00–10:00 a.m.	Physical education, one quarter-unit credit
10:00–11:00 a.m.	Occupational information, one unit credit
11:00–12:00	Math, one unit credit
12:00– 1:00 p.m.	Lunch
1:00– 4:00 p.m.	Occupational exploration, one unit credit

During the second and third years of the program, science is substituted for math, and then social studies is substituted for science. Homemaking and shop can also be included if desirable. With such a schedule, the student can earn up to 12¾ units in three years. With two units of credit in the fourth year (one for work experience and one for a problems seminar—which is sometimes called social studies), the student easily fulfills the title requirements for graduation.

The actual content of the courses can be selected from the units of instruction suggested in this chapter.

The concentration of the study program should be on occupations. Students should learn about jobs, how to get jobs, and how to keep jobs. This will necessarily involve many of the social skills needed for adequate independent living. In the area of occupations, the students should be given the opportunity to study jobs at first hand. There are many job analysis forms that suit this purpose, any of which may be modified to fit local conditions.[3]

Materials that may be used to support units at the vocational level are constantly being prepared by publishing companies. Series developed by Lawson,[4] by Hudson,[5] by the Mafex Company,[6] by the Fearon

[3] See Kolstoe and Frey.

[4] The address is Gary D. Lawson, Route 2, Box 2804, Elk Grove, California.

[5] Margaret Hudson, *To Be a Good American Series* (Palo Alto, California: Fearon Publishers, Inc., 1965).

[6] Mafex Associates, Box 114, Ebensburg, Pennsylvania.

Company,[7] and by the Steck Company[8] are available and are suitable for many programs.[9] The Finney Company[10] of Minnesota has developed a series of four units, each containing five volumes which describe 12 jobs each, or a total of 240 jobs. Each job is described as to the kind of job, pay, history, what to expect, working hours, what the employee does, what the job is like, training offered, good and bad things about the job, ways to get the job, sources of free information about the job, free movies, and a self-test that poses the question, "Is this job for you?" The cost is $30 for each volume, so that the entire resource will cost $120.

Fudell and Peck have developed units and workbooks that cover three years of a work-study program which have grown out of their experiences in vocational level programs.[11]

Richard Smith,[12] Dan S. Rainey,[13] and the author developed unit ideas for a three-year program which are not commercially available but which are described in the following section. They are merely suggestive since every program will have unique needs. During the first year:

1. *Orientation to School.* This unit deals with the names and positions of the principal school officials with whom the students are likely to have contact. In addition, school rules, the room locations, schedules, tardiness, available activities, and a discussion of the special program are dealt with. The intent of the unit is to provide some good reasons for the students to commit themselves to the program.

2. *Travel.* Many of the students will need to know how to get from school or home to their various job sites. This unit provides that instruction and practice, but also may include specific study of maps, bus routes, and access to other points of significance.

3. *Grooming.* While elements of grooming such as nails, teeth, dandruff, hair, perfume, cosmetics, and deodorants are subjects for

[7] Fearon Company, Fearon Publishers, Inc., 828 Valencia, San Francisco, California, 94110.

[8] Steck Company, Austin, Texas.

[9] Marian Jones, *How to Tell the Retarded Girl about Menstruation* (Nennah, Wisconsin: Kimberly-Clark Corporation, 1964); and Helen Prevo, *Family Life* (New York: Frank E. Richards, 1967).

[10] Finney Company, 3350 Gorham Avenue, Minneapolis, Minnesota, 55426.

[11] Stanley Fudell and John Peck, *How to Hold Your Job* (New York: The John Day Company, Inc., 1967).

[12] Richard Smith is former Director of Special Education, Carbondale Community School District 96, Carbondale, Illinois.

[13] Dan S. Rainey is Assistant Professor of Special Education, Southern Illinois University, Carbondale, Illinois.

discussion, the main emphasis is on inner versus outer appearance and how to achieve attractiveness. Units here should deal with specific situations such as church, job, and recreation dress. Many cosmetic firms will furnish free demonstrations and samples.

4. *Measurement.* Common objects of standard size are dealt with in this unit. The main content is using physical attributes for common estimation—stride, hand, and finger length, arm length, neck size, height, and weight for reference points. Distance, time, volume, and weight are also considered, but only for estimates.

5. *Getting Along with Others.* Understanding moods and attitudes and difficulties as they are reflected in people's behavior can be important for job adjustment. Role playing is the vehicle for explaining these behaviors.

6. *Banking.* Various accounts such as checking, saving, investments, and loans need explanation because some of the youngsters will have earned enough money to be concerned about carrying it around. A visit to the bank is often called for.

7. *Dating.* The mechanics of even asking for a date are often bewildering to these young people. Where to go, things to do, and costs involved are supporting topics for discussion.

8. *Installment Buying.* Not just the mechanics of installment buying and the interest charges, but rather the purpose of installment buying to make money—as for example, buying a lawnmower which can be used to earn money—is the purpose of this unit.

9. *Planning Summer Activities.* A systematic exploration of possible jobs, programs, hikes, trips, and recreation offerings is the content of this unit. Such a unit may be profitably explored each year.

10. *Job Analysis.* Some three or four times throughout the year, the students and the teacher can analyze selected jobs in the community by use of a job analysis form. The purpose of these trips is to give the students some skill in judging the suitability of specific jobs. For that reason it is well to include at least one job that is beyond their skills level.

During the second year of vocational level work, it is expected that driver training will take up approximately nine weeks of the school year. Some excellent visual aids are available for this training. Standard Oil Company has a series of films that are available free, but the school must furnish the projector. That model costs about $200. The General Aniline and Film Corporation has transparencies that graphically illustrate critical elements of good driving. The cost of the series is about $30.

Three units can very well supplement the driver training program with important information for the students:

1. *Car Care.* The reasons for washing, waxing, greasing, and changing oil, tire care, radiator and battery care, as well as ways these are done on different cars can be explained and demonstrated. Gasoline stations have care charts which can be used to support this unit.

2. *Car Buying.* This unit deals with how to choose a car, how to establish a need for a car, and whether to select a new or used car. An excellent resource is a friendly car salesman who will explain the pitfalls one can stumble into when buying a car.

3. *Car Insurance.* The need for insurance, kinds of coverages, costs, and liabilities should all be covered. Although an insurance representative may be a good resource, the student might better study specific policies presented to them by representatives of local associations of insurors.

Other units that can contribute to the students' understanding of their work and living demands can be:

1. *You and Your Boss.* This should treat the problems of employer-employee responsibility in terms of what each should expect from the other and what to do when a misunderstanding arises. An employer can be an excellent resource person.

2. *Etiquette.* How to make introductions, how to make small talk, proper behavior in a restaurant, movie, or at a dance can be demonstrated through role playing and movies.

3. *Science.* Everyday application of scientific principles for practical problems from levers to insulation are included in magazines such as *Home Mechanics*, and newspaper columns. One or a series of units that demonstrate easy ways things may be done can be most illuminating. If the students pose problems and then set about finding solutions, this lends realism to the study.

4. *Application Form.* Using a variety of forms from many different businesses allows the youngsters to practice on the various forms until they can design their own card with specific information to be carried with them for reference purposes.

5. *Job Interviews.* The telephone company will furnish a telephone hookup with an amplifier-speaker that can be used by students to play roles in job interviews. The interjection of check questions can make this exercise entertaining and informative.

6. *Budgeting.* Inventing a family and then developing expenses for the week, month, or year can make this a worthwhile experience. By contrast, a budget for a single boy and girl often adds meaning to the study. Workbooks from the Fearon Company are available and can be used to support this unit.

7. *Community Services.* The practical matter of where to go and what to do to get water service, lights turned on, the gas connected,

or a telephone installed in a home or apartment can be given meaning through field trips to the offices and actually following the installers on the job.

8. *Gardening.* Where land is available, the making of a garden in the spring, followed by experience in canning in the fall, is a most rewarding sequence. The canned goods can then be used by the youngsters for gifts or special occasions.

Job analysis should be continued throughout the second year of the program with analysis of at least three different jobs. During the first year, the students learn how to analyze jobs. During the second year, another dimension is added—that of finding jobs. To facilitate this search, it is recommended that students make use of different sources for finding the jobs. First, the students should find a job in the want ads of the local newspaper. They can do an analysis of the job to see if it is suitable for them. A second source of finding jobs is the local employment agency. Registration and the taking of tests is part of the task of finding a job. The third source of possible jobs is friends and neighbors. As in other sources, the job identified should be analyzed for suitability. The sequence in the second year is specifically aimed at giving the students some job hunting skills in a systematic manner. The assumption is that most of the youngsters will change jobs during their adult lives and will need to have some notion of how to go about looking for suitable employment.[14]

During the third year of the vocational level work, it is assumed that the students will be engaged in either work experience or in full-time work. In either case, they will probably have only about a half-day available for related study. The units suggested are some that have been helpful to retarded youngsters in high school programs:

1. *Home and Family Living.* This unit is intended to explore the division of labor within a family setting. Of special concern is an analysis of jobs that are required to maintain a home and then a discussion of who does what, when, and how. Many youngsters have a queer notion of what is man's work and what is woman's work in a home. The theme of joint responsibility is the main emphasis.

2. *Credit.* The nature of charge accounts, credit cards, and installment buying can be explored by visiting a credit office or using a credit manager as a resource person. The traps in credit buying should be of special interest.

3. *Adult Finances I.* Record keeping, family reports, checks as re-

[14] Kolstoe and Frey and Peterson and Jones have examples of job analysis forms which can be used.

ceipts, medical and dental records, and the attitude toward records should be thoroughly illustrated and discussed. A household file system can be the medium through which this aspect of living is explored.

4. *Adult Finances II.* Income tax, social security, health, accident and life insurance, and local taxes can be studied through one or several units. Budgeting for taxes and insurance can be an important part of this study.

5. *Job Failure.* This unit can serve to identify sources of help in case of job failure. The analysis of the causes of failure may be a principal aspect of study with attention then focused on recourse. This includes unemployment benefits as well as agencies that can be of help in helping one secure another job or providing training that can lead to employment. Disability benefits and insurance can also be explored.

6. *Citizens' Behavior from a Legal Point of View.* The responsibility and recourse available to citizens for law violations such as parking tickets, traffic violations, arrest, and responsibilities toward neighbors can be explained and discussed. The function of the Legal Aid Society, lawyers, and the bar association can often be clarified by a visit to the office of the district attorney.

7. *Leisure.* Enjoyment from an esthetic point of view may be explored through exposure to different kinds of art, music, concerts, plays, and hobbies. Often the youngsters have an uncertain or negative attitude toward esthetic activities because they do not understand what the activities attempt to accomplish. One or a series of units that introduce them to these elements of culture can be pursued. Attendance at professional and amateur shows or performances lends viability to the study.

8. *Success.* The meaning of success in terms of need fulfillment as emphasized in the prevocational units can be applied to job and living to define success. A variety of examples of success may help to identify criteria other than those of material possessions and income. Service to others as well as service to self should receive major emphasis. A local guidance counselor may be an excellent resource person for this kind of discussion.

Job analysis should be continued throughout the third year, but with a different dimension added—that of interviewing. If the student is required not only to analyze a job, but also actually to go through the practice of applying for the job, he will add one more skill to his equipment for adult living.

Of special interest to the emerging adult are questions concerning morals, virtue, marriage, and parenthood. Gary Lawson has developed a workbook devoted to these problem areas which contains short stories that illustrate various dimensions of these problems in language and a manner understandable to the youngsters. They are part of the *Better Living* series available from Gary D. Lawson.[15]

The *Curriculum Guide for Teacher-Coordinators of E.M.H. Students*, prepared by the Oklahoma State Department of Education, Oklahoma City, in 1966, contains 78 units suitable for youngsters in the tenth, eleventh, and twelfth grades. The units cover a variety of subjects from alcohol to voting. One unusual unit covers funerals. The units are useful and appropriate.

[15] They can be sent for at 9488 Sara Street, Elk Grove, California 95624.

Part IV

SUMMARY

CHAPTER *13*

Summary and Projection

The concern of this book has been the presentation of an educational program that proceeds in a consistent fashion toward the objectives of developing the skills required for a retarded individual to live fully and work effectively in modern society. The specific behaviors identified by research as contributing to work and living effectiveness have been selected as guides for the program. These have been projected downward through five levels of development (vocational, prevocational, intermediate, primary, and preschool), so behaviors developed at each stage will be the building blocks upon which subsequent behaviors rest. Specific behaviors have been identified as outcomes to be achieved at each stage of development. These 513 outcomes have been classified into 7 broad areas for instruction: communication, arithmetic, social, motor, esthetic, health and safety, and vocational, then further arranged into 18 subareas. Instructional content, including both methods and materials, specific to each of the 18 subareas has been suggested. The foregoing is perceived as the curriculum that will lead to achieving the goals of independent living and vocational competence for educable retarded individuals.

In order to provide a usable way of describing the nature of the learner, this writing has combined the neurological organizational theory of Hebb with the behavioral theory of Miller, Galanter, and Pribram, so that mental retardation is conceptualized as:

> A diminished capacity for the formation of cell assemblies, and intercellular and superordinate associations, which results in restricted thought processes to determine standards for the formulation and evaluation of plans needed for appropriate adapting behavior.

Learning is presumed to take place within the context of the S-R model developed by behaviorally oriented psychologists. However, between the stimulus and response, it is assumed that mediation occurs. This recognition of the viewpoint of phenomenologists does not invalidate the S-R model, it only makes the model consistent with the subjective behavioristic theory of Miller, Galanter, and Pribram.

There are weaknesses in any approach to educating retarded children that are inherent in the point of view presented. Current research information on precisely which characteristics contribute to successfully adapting mentally retarded adults is far from complete. Basing an educational program on such incomplete information can, at the very least, be considered hazardous. The alternatives open, however, are not very attractive. Using historical practices, for example, carries the obligation of assuming that those practices that have emerged from past programs probably are the best ones that have been tried. "Best," however, is defined by the retention of the practice. It is not identified by comparing the practice with well-described program goals in any objective manner. Other possible procedures such as using a philosophical, definitional, or theoretical basis confine the program to logically projected goals. Of the alternatives indicated, it has seemed more realistic to accept goals that have been empirically identified as important even though those goals will be modified as society changes and as subsequent research identifies the effect of those changes on the living and working patterns needed for survival. Accepting empirically identified guidelines also obligates professionals to a continuing examination of the behavior patterns of successful adult retardates, to the necessary concomitant of discovering some method of insuring that all the required behaviors are identified, and to identifying the relative contribution of each behavior to successful living. Clearly, this calls for a long-range and continuing research program of no small dimensions.

Once the program goals have been adopted, the extension of those goals downward to the beginning of the school program is fraught with error possibilities. Whether the curricular areas are the ones that will contribute optimally is not sure. Whether the subareas selected are the best is not certain. Whether the outcomes projected for each level in each subarea are realistic is not demonstrated. Finally, whether the methods and materials suggested will contribute optimally is not sure. The alternative open, however, inspires even less confidence. To adapt the curriculum of regular classes in the public schools would be to accept that academic achievement is the vehicle best suited to developing skills of work and independent living. In view of the vast body of research that has failed to identify a reliable relationship between academic success and vocational success. This approach seems to hold only minimal promise.

Commitment to the specifying of behavioral outcomes expected at each level does provide some compensating advantages. First, the teacher at each level is provided a list of behaviors that are expected to be developed through the educational program provided. There is no need to wonder, "What shall I teach?" Furthermore, there is no need to wonder whether what is being taught at one level has any relevance to what will be taught at another level, or whether, indeed, it is related to the total program. It is, and in an easily identified manner. In short, the program has sequence.

Second, the outcomes lists can be used for educational planning for each child. By comparing the behaviors of a child with the outcomes listed in each of the subareas, it is possible to be quite exact about determining what the major educational needs of the child may be. From such a determination, it is but a short step to designing a program that will attend to the principal educational needs. In this manner, the outcomes lists can be used for educational diagnosis.

Third, an outcomes list provides a meaningful system for reporting the progress of each child. By using the 18 areas at each level for a report card, the teacher can evaluate a child's educational progress relative to specific behaviors. A rating system that identifies progress as "unsatisfactory," "satisfactory," "emerging," or "mastered," provides an understandable and realistic progress record that requires little explanation to be understood. Such a reporting system is a helpful guide when consideration for promotion to the next higher level is faced. Decisions for promotion always involve value judgments. It is easier to make these value judgments when the reporting system is based upon the goals of the program. In practice, the outcomes list makes a fine report card.

Fourth, many children in special classes come from families notable for their mobility. It is not unusual to find the children appearing in many different schools in any given academic year. When and if school records are forwarded to the new school, the records do little or nothing to help the receiving teacher continue a meaningful program for the transfer student. Using the outcomes list as the basis for a cumulative record file makes it possible for teachers to note not only the achievement status of the student, but also areas of strength and weakness and the educational program used in each area. Within children doubly handicapped by mental retardation and mobility, such record keeping seems an excellent method of minimizing the educational handicap inherent in mobility. The outcomes list, therefore, can be the basis of a useful cumulative file.

Given the behaviors desired to be developed, the suggesting of methods and materials that seem to contribute to achieving these behaviors is largely a judgmental matter. Virtually no evaluations have been done that clearly demonstrate the superiority of one set of materials and methods over another. This kind of classroom research suffers from many complications. Although the outcomes list can be considered the criterion against which methods and materials can be validated, teacher differences, procedure, programs, and a host of other variables must be accounted for if valid conclusions are to be drawn. Since teaching procedures seem to vary with individuals, it seemed prudent to present some model that might help to focus on teacher behavior. The S-R model does that. It allows teacher behavior to be viewed for stimulus manipulation or responses reinforcement. It does not allow for identifying the mediation that is presumed to take place between the stimulus and response. Any inferences concerning mediation must be made from observable behavior. Since mediation is believed to involve some kind of neural activity, a notion of the nature of neurological organization and its role in behavior seemed called for. This resulted in combining Hebb's theory with the theory of Miller, Galanter, and Pribram.

Theories are statements of relationships invented to explain facts. The S-R model is a theory just as is Hebb's explanation of neurological organization and the subjective behaviorism of Miller, Galanter, and Pribram. They have not been validated nor have they been disproved. Basing educational procedures on theories leaves one a long way from certainty. What it does provide is an orderly explanation that lends itself to systematic examination. The theories have been adopted not only to try to explain the consequences of mental retardation, but to encourage the scholarly investigation of their possible contributions to knowledge about the condition.

Projection

For a number of years, special educators have been the rugged pioneers on the scene of education in America. Until the early 1960s, when legislation and public awareness started to take note of and provide for the special educator, the law of classroom survival was footnoted by cutting pictures from magazines and adapting with dog-eared reading series. In the absence of commercial materials, the teachers were justifiably proud of their independent abilities to make do on their own.

Parallel with this, the need for special educators was growing. Not only were more handicapped children living after being born, but more sophisticated identifying procedures discovered individuals who had heretofore remained undiscovered. Training institutions have responded to such needs by turning out a more sophisticated, highly trained educator to deal with specific handicapping conditions.

These highly trained, specialized individuals cannot and should not be expected to revert to such antiquated patterns of behavior as magazine cutting to insure the success of their professional practice. But neither should they give up the flexibility of their creative independence. In the early 1960s, the task force teams from the President's Panel on Mental Retardation studied programs for handicapped children existing in Europe. Among other items, they reported strong emphasis placed on central depositories of instructional materials and the parallel training European teachers received in the use of these materials. Out of this report grew the recommendation to establish similar centers in the United States to serve teachers of handicapped children and youth. They were called Special Education Instructional Materials Centers (SEIMC).

In 1964, the United States Office of Education, Bureau of Handicapped Children and Youth, established two pilot programs—one at the University of Southern California and the other at the University of Wisconsin as repositories for instructional materials. The center at the University of Southern California established a working relationship with a large city school district, while the Wisconsin center worked in cooperation with a state education agency.

The success of these two pilot programs is measured by the fact that by the middle of 1967, almost every state in the Union was served by one of 15 of these regional instructional materials centers. The centers formed a national network so that their service to special educators was cooperative on a nationwide level. This, of course, does not presume or imply that each of the 15 centers engaged in the same types of activity. Their organization and philosophy were indeed similar —to store and make available materials for use by those individuals who serve handicapped children and youth. The methods by which this end was achieved was left to the creative independence of those individuals operating each center.

These regional centers, therefore, engaged in a wide variety of service activities particular to their respective regions in an effort to provide specific activities to educators working with handicapped children through instructional materials and methodologies. The first indication that these efforts were not sufficient probably came from the pilot evaluation of the two prototype centers conducted by the American Institutes for Research (Williams, Johnson, Smyke, and Robinson, 1968). Among the areas of concern identified in their report AIR discussed the need for diagnostic and prescriptive services to be offered in tandem with instructional materials services. The Bureau of Education for the Handicapped responded by establishing six pilot centers in 1969 that came to be known as Regional Resource Centers (RRC). Withrow (1968), writing for the Bureau, identified the basic posture of these new centers as one that would link instructional materials centers, research and training institutions together with local school systems and state education agencies.[1]

> There are a number of children whose handicaps are extremely complicated and pose major problems to local educational programs. These children present problems in diagnosis and the establishment of appropriate educational strategies. It is unreasonable to assume that every local educational facility will be able to maintain comprehensive diagnosticians and educational programmers in their systems; therefore, regional centers are being developed that will provide backup educational services to state and local services . . . The center will be designed to focus on long range plans and work with children, families, teachers, and school systems over a long period of time to assure that adequate follow-through is accomplished (p. 553).

The six Regional Resource Centers functioned as prototypes for their kind until late 1973 when the Bureau of Education for the Handicapped announced that all of their funded Special Education Instructional Materials Centers were to be phased out by mid 1974 but that all existing Regional Resource Centers would be reestablished by competitive bid. In place of the existing centers the Bureau planned

---

[1] Frank B. Withrow, "Enlarged Responsibilities for Educational Services to Handicapped Children," *Exceptional Children* (March 1968).

to establish thirteen Regional Resource Centers and a like number of new Area Learning Resource Centers (ALRC).

The United States was divided into thirteen service regions, each of which was designed to be served by a resource center and a learning resource center. An Area Learning Resource Center was directed to assist the states it served by helping to develop an intrastate ability to provide media services, instructional materials, and other appropriate technologies for use with handicapped children. The ALRC's were also charged with assisting pre- and inservice training programs to increase the capability of parents and teachers in the use of instructional materials. At the same time, each Regional Resource Center was directed to assist the states in developing an interstate ability to provide identification, diagnosis, and prescription services while also offering direct services to children for the purposes of demonstrating best practices and stimulating service development by each of the state agencies and their constituent local school systems.

The emphasis of both centers has shifted considerably from the early orientation of services being rendered directly to educators of the handicapped. Now any state desiring to establish or improve its capability to offer handicapped children and their educators the latest in diagnostic, prescriptive, and instructional material and media technology services may do so with the cooperative assistance of the RRC and ALRC serving their state. This arrangement not only recognizes state level responsibility for assisting with local program development and improvement but enhances the possibility that such programs, once established, could better survive any cutback or elimination of federal funds.

In an effort to facilitate the work of these regional centers and to focus more sharply the effect of federal funds earmarked for handicapped children, several specialty centers were established concurrently with the new RRC's and ALRC's. The Coordinating Office for Regional Resource Centers was funded to support the RRC's by providing them with technical assistance and organizing a national division of labor and resources to first identify and then solve common problems in areas like diagnosis and prescription. The National Center on Educational Media and Materials for the Handicapped was maintained to engage in research, demonstration, dissemination, and training activities in the areas of instructional material, media, and educational technologies. Such services are directed toward the regional ALRC's and other appropriate agencies engaged in designing or providing media and materials services for the handicapped.

Four national special offices were also established in each of the following areas: Visually Impaired; Hearing Impaired; Other Handicaps; and Instructional Materials Distribution. The first three specialty offices were charged with the responsibilities of obtaining and creating, as well as evaluating and disseminating information about materials designed for those three specific target areas of children. The Office for Materials Distribution was intended to provide, on a national level, the primary service once associated with the regional special education instructional materials centers: the loan of instructional materials for teacher examination and teacher training purposes, and in those instances where local and state resources are inadequate, for actual use in the classroom with children.

The committment of a significant number of federal dollars allocated for handicapped children and the establishment of a Bureau of Education for the Handicapped in the United States Office of Education are recent occurrences, recent enough that the rank and file of special educators across the country are still very much appreciative of this national recognition and support of their efforts to develop and improve the education of those children who were all but ignored not so many years ago. Such appreciation should not be construed as complete satisfaction with the present level of federal support and attention. Put succinctly, we've come a long way; but then we have a long way to go. If the previously discussed federally supported projects are to continue their evolution toward best practical solution to the continuing needs of special educators and the children they serve, then their support must increase and continue to be visible in the minds of federal, state, and local decision makers and resource allocators.

The commitment of the federal government to improving the lot of handicapped children has been demonstrated through its generous funding of research, training fellowships, and instructional materials centers. All of the cooperative efforts amount to little if teachers fail to exercise their own creative independence in their day-to-day contact with children. The final test of the effectiveness of all professional efforts is the degree to which those efforts aid the retarded to become effective citizens. All professionals bend their efforts in this direction, but the implementation of what is known and developed is in the hands of the teacher.

It seems apparent that teachers of the future will teach a much greater range of youngsters than teachers of the past. Furthermore, the range will not be in just one area. New programs supported by research funds or private agencies to help preschool children beginning in the first month or so after birth are being initiated almost daily. Thus public schools will probably have to face the question of the age at which their responsibility to the child begins. Likewise the frequency with which adults change not just jobs, but whole careers seems to foretell an increasing need for adult training programs in perhaps yet unknown vocational pursuits. Furthermore, advances in educational technology will probably reduce the amount of reading required by those people engaged in learning job skills. Much of this kind of instruction can and may be done by audiovisual machines in simulated job stations. This is likely to mean that functional illiteracy may not be a barrier to learning rather complex job skills, which in the past were solely dependent on reading and writing as instructional media. This continuing improvement in instruction will quite probably spread from purely vocational skills to the more academic areas so people of rather limited abilities will be able to participate in class work from which they had formerly been excluded. Many youngsters formerly considered trainable will probably begin to be seen in less restrictive programs and some will be able to participate in regular classrooms.

The foregoing simply projects that the days of the special education teacher laboring alone in his own little classroom may soon be gone. Instead the teacher will be working with others; child development specialists, adult vocational educators, regular classroom teachers, welfare, correctional and other public agency people in a host of roles and situations not yet fully imagined. As the world moves toward the reality of fully human experiences for all people and the equalizing of opportunities in all areas of living, opportunities that are indeed equal may someday be so much accepted that they become the rule, not the exception.

Quite probably the RRC–ALRC alliance may take a different form in the future, but it will probably continue to represent a major thrust of the federal and state governments in their cooperative concern for assuring equal opportunity among least restrictive alternatives to the handicapped.

Such a practical demonstration of help is to be applauded, but it is to be hoped that leadership in another area also emerges. Not much progress is made when only what is presently known is used. Progress occurs when new knowledge alters our perspective of something. So long as all our efforts are restricted to doing only those things that are considered practical we will probably become more efficient, but never more effective. To increase effectiveness we must do things differently. The cues that guide this departure from the tried and true come from research, not practical, conventional, applied research, but from creative, imaginative, impractical, research. This is an uncompromising examination of the variables that influence an event without any consideration of whether the outcome is good or bad or consistent with our wishes for a better world. The last half of the 1960s and the first half of the 1970s was a decade conspicuous for its tendency to treat efforts at basic research as foolish at best and insidious at worst. Federal support for basic research nearly disappeared as funds were channeled into activities and programs which could demonstrate that they were designed to help children. Accountability was designated as the criterion by which the effort was measured.

Apparently it never occurred to people that the practical aspects of operant conditioning came from research work with pigeons, that transistors evolved from studies by crystalographers, and that auto-teaching technology would not be possible without the contribution of each. As teachers we have been the beneficiaries of the discoveries of past generations each of which has probably made our work more effective. If such ongoing research is restricted much longer, we may very well be the victims of a pedagogy that continues to be efficient, but never becomes any more effective. That is a terrible price to pay for being practical, and certainly one which coming generations can ill afford. Perhaps, even if we may not wish to engage in that kind of work, we can advance civilization by verbal support, instead of imped-ing it with the real or implied criticism that comes from silence on the subject. If knowledge is truly the foundation of wisdom we would do well to support the search for knowledge, for special education is badly in need of all the wisdom it can get.

Instructional Outcomes for the Educable Mentally Retarded

Communication Skills

Oral Communication

PRESCHOOL LEVEL
1. Given a verbal question, the child can say his first and last name.
2. Given a verbal question, the child can say his/her age.
3. Given a verbal question, the child can say his house number and street name.
4. Given a verbal question, the child can say his home city and state.
5. Upon request, the child can formulate a verbal affirmative statement, e.g., this is a ball.
6. Upon request, the child can formulate a verbal negative statement, e.g., this is not a book.
7. Given a one-word cue, the child can identify polar opposites, e.g., big-little.
8. Given one end of a verbal proposition, the child can make simple deductions, e.g., if this is big, then it is not little.
9. Given a cue of one part of a statement, the child can formulate alternative statements, e.g., you may go or you may stay.

PRIMARY LEVEL
1. Returning from a field trip, the child can state five things he has seen.
2. Given a set of objects or pictures of five fruits, vegetables, people, or animals, the child will be able to name them correctly.
3. Given a call on the telephone, the child can answer correctly and sustain a simple conversation.
4. Upon request, the child can formulate a meaningful four-word sentence.

INTERMEDIATE LEVEL
1. When asked to relate specific incidents, the child can reply in clear and understandable speech.
2. The student uses complete sentences of five words or more in informal conversation with his peers.
3. When asked to make a formal introduction of a student to another student or a student to an adult, the child makes a correct presentation.
4. When asked to make an announcement to the class, the student can make the announcement in clear and precise speech.
5. When presented with a task, the student will ask for help on the details he does not understand.
6. When asked by the teacher, the student can give simple directions to the: fire exit; principal's office; rest room; library; cafeteria; gymnasium; nurse's office.
7. Given a telephone or pay telephone, the student can: call home; call the operator; call the fire station; call the police; call an ambulance.

PREVOCATIONAL LEVEL
1. When presented with the task of criticizing another student's oral expression, the student will be able to state at least one strength and one weakness.
2. When called upon to make a report to the class, the student can demonstrate his ability to organize his thoughts and present them in an understandable manner.
3. In a group meeting, the student demonstrates a knowledge of simple parliamentary procedure as a participant.
4. In a group meeting, the student demonstrates a knowledge of simple parliamentary procedure by properly conducting the meeting.
5. Given a telephone, the student can demonstrate proper etiquette in answering, taking messages, leaving messages, and making long distance calls.

VOCATIONAL LEVEL
1. Given a list of items, the student can place an order for the items.
2. Given an interview, the student can correctly respond to questions of

identification, experience, and qualifications for a job.
3. When questioned about a job with which he is familiar, the student uses vocabulary appropriate to the equipment and the job.
4. Given a social situation, the student participates in the conversation using the appropriate vocabulary and responses to other participants' comments.
5. Given a real or simulated need for household repairs, the student can demonstrate the ability to contact the proper artisan, clearly explain the nature of the problem, and negotiate the proper time, place, and responsibilities of the repair.

Listening Skills

PRESCHOOL LEVEL
1. After having heard a story or song, the child can tell the name, gist, or theme.
2. Given the following verbal commands to: close; open; hand up; put on; take off; put away; take out, in reference to a particular object, the child will complete the command.
3. After the teacher presents two rhythm patterns, the child will identify whether they are similar or different.
4. Given a rhythm pattern of tapping, the child will be able to reproduce it by tapping on his desk.
5. The child responds correctly to words like "stop," "go," and "look out."

PRIMARY LEVEL
1. Given four words, the student will be able to repeat them.
2. Given two directions, the student will be able to follow them.
3. Given a short message, the student will be able to restate the main points correctly.

INTERMEDIATE LEVEL
1. Given one line of a two-line rhyme, the student will be able to finish the next line with a rhyming word.
2. Given the short vowel sounds, the student will accurately associate each with the correct letter.
3. Given three words, the student will correctly identify two that start with the same sound.
4. Given the individual sounds of a four-sound word, the student will correctly identify the whole word.

PREVOCATIONAL LEVEL
1. After listening to a story, the student will be able to retell the story in his own words.

2. Given a record to listen to, the student can accurately identify the type of music played.
3. Given descriptions of three tasks to perform, the student will perform the tasks in the correct sequence.
4. Given a three-point lecture to listen to, the student will be able to recall the points correctly.

VOCATIONAL LEVEL

1. Given a verbal work plan, the student will be able to follow the plan correctly.
2. Given a group discussion, the student will be able to relate his comments to those of the other participants.

Written Communication

PRESCHOOL LEVEL

1. Given paper and crayons, or pencils, the child can use them correctly.
2. Given paper, scissors, and paste, the child will be able to cut out simple shapes and paste them on the paper.
3. Given a picture outline of dots, the child can connect the dots to complete the picture.
4. Given a picture of an animal missing a significant part, the child can draw in the missing part.
5. Given a paper containing four letters of the alphabet, two of which are the same, the child can draw a line connecting the two identical letters.
6. Given elementary manuscript paper, with one label word written in manuscript, the child can correctly copy the word.
7. Given a strip of paper on a child's desk on which his first and last name have been printed, the child can correctly print his name on a piece of manuscript paper.

PRIMARY LEVEL

1. Given four label words such as: water, desk, door, and crayons, printed in manuscript on the chalkboard, the child can correctly copy each word on manuscript paper.
2. Given instructions to write his name, the child can accomplish the task.
3. Given headings, dates, and time, the child can copy them correctly.
4. Given a sentence to copy, the child will begin the sentence with a correctly made capital letter.
5. Given a sentence to copy, the child will end the sentence with the proper punctuation.

INTERMEDIATE LEVEL

1. When presented with a paper written in manuscript, the student will be able to rewrite the paper in cursive writing.
2. Given an address, the student will properly place the address, the return address, and a stamp.
3. Given a reason for writing, the student will be able to write a friendly, coherent note.
4. Upon request, the student can define orally the abbreviations of: Mr.; Mrs.; Ms.; Dr.; Miss; St.; Blvd.; Rd.; and Ct.

PREVOCATIONAL LEVEL

1. Given a job application blank, the student can correctly fill in his name, date, address, telephone number, age, parents' names, etc.
2. Given a job application form, the student will be able to write the date two ways (January 1, 1978 or 1-1-78).
3. Given a topic to discuss or describe, the student will be able to write a paragraph using complete sentences.
4. Given a reason for writing, the student will be able to write a correct business or friendly letter.
5. Given a mail order form, the student will fill it out correctly.

VOCATIONAL LEVEL

1. Given a job application, the student can fill in the blanks, including the education and experience sections, accurately and legibly.
2. Given a situation, the student will be able to formulate and write an invitation or a note of condolence, congratulations, or regrets.
3. Given a need for shopping, the student will be able to formulate a meaningful shopping list.
4. Given banking forms, the student will be able to fill out the forms correctly.
5. Given an inventory record, the student will be able to fill it out correctly.

Reading

PRESCHOOL LEVEL

1. Given the letters of the alphabet, the child can tell the names and the sounds of the letters.
2. Given the letters of the alphabet, the child can identify the similar and dissimilar letters.
3. Given a list of meaningful words like: stop; men; women; caution, the child recognizes the words.

PRIMARY LEVEL

1. Given initial consonant blends, the child can read the correct sounds for each blend.

2. Given words with common endings, the child can say the correct ending sound.
3. Given word families, such as et, at, etc., the child can read the correct family sounds.
4. Given simple stories that the child has helped develop, the child can "read" the story on request.

INTERMEDIATE LEVEL
1. Given the first 100 words of Dolch or a similar word list, the student is able to read the words.
2. Given simple labels on drugs, household goods, groceries, and tools, the child is able to read them correctly.
3. Given a consonant letter, the student can associate it with the correct sound of a key word.
4. Given a compound word, the student will be able to read both little words in the big word.
5. Given a prefix or suffix, the student will be able to explain what it does to change a word.
6. Given a work sheet with missing words, the student will be able to fill in the missing word.
7. Given a newspaper, the student can identify on request, the different sections of the paper.

PREVOCATIONAL LEVEL
1. Given a familiar book, the student will be able to demonstrate: the use of the table of contents; the use of the index; the use of the glossary; how to use bold print; how to scan for information.
2. Given a newspaper, the student will demonstrate that he can find specific information in the paper when requested to do so.
3. Given a dictionary, the student can demonstrate how to use it.
4. Given free time in school, the student will voluntarily choose material to read that is of interest to him.

VOCATIONAL LEVEL
1. Given a bill and/or statement, the student will be able to interpret the information needed and respond with an action to fulfill his obligation to the bill.
2. Given a sales contract, the student will be able to identify the sales conditions, cost, interest, time, and penalties.
3. Given the need to look up information, the student will demonstrate the application of the alphabet system to the dictionary, telephone book, and catalog index.
4. Given an uncomplicated set of directions for a work task, the student will demonstrate his understanding by following the directions.

5. Given free time and a selection of popular magazines to choose from, the student will select a magazine appropriate to his/her interest and skill.

Arithmetic

Facts and Processes

PRESCHOOL LEVEL
1. Upon request, the child will be able to respond with the proper meaning of such quantitative terms as all, more, less, big, little, and some.
2. Upon request, the child will count up to ten.
3. Upon request, the child will count ten things.

PRIMARY LEVEL
1. Upon request, the child will group objects according to color, size, and shape.
2. Upon request, the child will count up to 100.
3. Upon request, the student will tell how many objects are represented by any given number up to 20.
4. Upon request, the child can state what number comes before or after a given number less than 100.
5. Given single digit numbers, the child will be able to add them correctly.
6. Given single digit numbers, the child will be able to subtract them correctly.
7. Upon request, the student will be able to point to objects in the correct ordinal position from first to tenth.

INTERMEDIATE LEVEL
1. Upon request, the student will be able to count by twos, fives, and tens to 100.
2. Given a picture or object, the student will be able to divide them in half, thirds, or quarters.
3. When the student is given the symbols $+$, $-$, $\times$ or $\div$, he will be able to name them correctly.
4. Given a number with a zero, the student will be able to explain its value in the number.

PREVOCATIONAL LEVEL
1. Given a number up to 1 million, the student will be able to read it on request.

2. Given numbers in which a carrying function is required, the student will carry to the second and third columns.
3. Given columns of numbers in which borrowing is necessary for subtracting, the student will be able to perform the operations correctly.
4. Given problems in which rate, ratio, interest, and percent are used, the student will be able to demonstrate the meaning of each.

VOCATIONAL LEVEL
1. Given an example of an income, the student will be able to prepare an uncomplicated budget.
2. Given an example of a paying job, the student will be able to determine the income earned.
3. Given an example of withholding tax, the student will be able to fill out simple tax forms.
4. Given a work task that uses numbers, the student will demonstrate his competence in using them.

Money

PRESCHOOL LEVEL
1. The child can verbally state that money buys things.
2. The child can verbally state that people are paid for work.
3. Upon request, the child can identify a penny, nickel, dime, quarter, half-dollar, and dollar.

PRIMARY LEVEL
1. Upon request, the child can verbally identify: @; ¢; and $.
2. The child can verbally state that: 5 pennies equal 1 nickel; 2 nickels equal 1 dime; 2 dimes and 1 nickel equal 1 quarter; and 4 quarters equal one dollar.

INTERMEDIATE LEVEL
1. When asked to select a coin or bill through $5.00, the child can select the appropriate one.
2. Given a list of money numbers, the child will read them correctly.
3. Given a series of items of differing prices, the child will be able to compute the correct total cost.
4. When asked to describe verbally the function of a bank, the child will respond appropriately.
5. When requested to make change for $1.00, the child can correctly use any combination of coins available.

PREVOCATIONAL LEVEL
1. Given an item of purchase, the student can make change up to $100.00.

2. Upon request, the student can offer two reasons why social security taxes are withheld from pay.
3. Given a signature card to open a checking account, the student will be able to: print his full name; print his address; print the name of the place of employment; and sign his full name.
4. Given a deposit slip, the student will correctly fill it out.
5. Given a check, the student will fill it out correctly.
6. Given a check stub, the student will record the check number, date, payee, amount, purpose, and effect a balance.

VOCATIONAL LEVEL
1. Given a menu, the student will be able to list the items needed and compute the cost for a meal, a day, or a week.
2. Given a newspaper, the student will be able to identify ads of homes and apartments and compute the yearly costs.
3. Given a newspaper, the student can discriminate the difference between two brands of food on "special" to determine the best buy.
4. The student can explain verbally the cheapest way to get to work and compute the daily and weekly costs.
5. Given a problem of maintaining an appliance, the student can compute the difference between maintenance and repair.
6. Given a problem of buying an appliance, the student can compute the cost including interest and carrying charges.

Time

PRESCHOOL LEVEL
1. Upon request, the child can state verbally whether the present time is morning, afternoon, or night.
2. Given the name of a scheduled activity, the child can state whether is takes place in the morning, afternoon, or night.
3. Upon request, the student can verbally name the days of the week.
4. Given a clock, the child can verbally describe its function.

PRIMARY LEVEL
1. Upon request, the child can verbally state what day of the week it is and tell what day comes before and what day after.
2. Given a calendar, the student will be able to use it to count, to tell how many days are in the month, and how many weeks are in the month.
3. Given a calendar, the child will be able to locate the present day and date.
4. Upon request, the child will be able to name the months of the year.
5. Upon request, the student can verbally state what the letters A.M. and P.M. represent.

6. Given a clock or clock face, the child will be able to state the time by the hour and half hour.

INTERMEDIATE LEVEL
1. Upon request, the child will be able to name the seasons of the year.
2. Given the name of a month, the child will be able to associate it with a season of the year.
3. Upon request, the child will be able to state the correct month, day, and year.
4. Given the room schedule, the child can tell when it is time for school to begin, go to the library, physical education, or lunch.
5. Given the room schedule, the child will be able to tell when to begin certain blocks of academics or go to other rooms without being reminded by the teacher.
6. Given a clock or clock face, the child will be able to tell time in relation to past, before, after, noon, midnight, by the quarter hour.

PREVOCATIONAL LEVEL
1. Upon request, the student can state three reasons why punctuality is important on a job.
2. Given a job situation, the student will be able to use the time of work and rate of pay to compute the weekly pay.
3. Given a situation, the student will be able to develop a daily schedule of activities around the job demands.
4. Given a situation, the student will be able to develop a daily, weekly, and monthly schedule around household chores.
5. Given a recipe, the student will be able to compute the total cooking and preparation time required.
6. Given a projected travel destination, the student will be able to compute the trip time using time tables, schedules, and maps.

VOCATIONAL LEVEL
1. Given a series of time cards for a week, the student will be able to determine the number of hours worked per day and for the total week.
2. Given a projected task, the student will be able to determine the amount of time necessary to complete each part of the task and the total task.
3. Given a pay check statement, the student will be able to identify gross and net pay and verbally explain the difference.

Measurement

PRESCHOOL LEVEL
1. Upon request, the child will be able to respond correctly to elements that are long or short, big and little, near and far, heavy and light, few and many, and all and none.

2. Given a yardstick, the student can identify an inch, a foot, and a yard.

PRIMARY LEVEL

1. Given a measuring container, the child will be able to fill it with the appropriate amount of liquid for one-half cup, 1 cup, 1 pint, 1 quart, or 1 gallon.
2. Given a weight scale, the child will demonstrate the use of the scale.
3. Given a weather thermometer, the child will be able to read the temperature correctly.
4. Upon request, the student can select from a large number of objects the correct number to equal one dozen.
5. Given a large number of geometric forms, the child will be able to sort by shape the circles, squares, rectangles, and triangles.

INTERMEDIATE LEVEL

1. Given a 12-inch ruler, the student can correctly measure the length and width of a room and convert them to yards.
2. Given a ruler, the student will correctly measure to one-eighth of an inch.
3. Given an identified building, the student will determine the distance in blocks, miles, and time.
4. Given a standard recipe, the student will correctly use the measures called for.
5. Upon request, the student will identify the directions of left, right, up, down, north, south, east, and west.
6. Given a thermometer, the student can take his own temperature.
7. Given a large number of three-dimensional objects, the student will be able to sort by sphere, cylinder, cone, cube, and pyramid.

PREVOCATIONAL LEVEL

1. Given the symbols of feet (′), inches (″), and degrees (°), the student will correctly identify each.
2. Given a yardstick or tape measure, the student will be able to find the numbers of specific feet and inches.
3. Given a tape measure, the student will be able to measure the height of a classmate and convert it into feet and inches.
4. Given a road map, the student can identify specific symbols and verbally state their meaning.
5. Given a road map, the student can demonstrate the route to be taken from one point to another.
6. Given the route on a road map, the student can determine the mileage between points.

VOCATIONAL LEVEL

1. Given clothing sizes, the student can identify his own sizes correctly.
2. Given a statement of miles traveled and gallons of fuel used, the student will compute the ratio.

3. Given a three-dimensional item, the student will correctly determine the height, weight, and width.
4. Given a statement of comparison, the student will be able to state verbally what kind of standard was used for the measurement.
5. Upon request, the student can verbally describe the kinds of measurements involved in his job.

Social Competencies

The Self

PRESCHOOL LEVEL
1. On request, the child can say his full name and age.
2. On request, the child can identify objects that belong to him and those that belong to others.
3. On request, the child can identify those other children who are taller, shorter, heavier, or lighter than he is.
4. When greeted by another person, the child will respond to the greeter either verbally, by gesture, or facial expression.

PRIMARY LEVEL
1. Upon request, the child can say his home address and telephone number.
2. In a verbal discussion, the child can name each member of his family and tell two facts about each.
3. Given a self-help task such as putting on boots, brushing teeth, working zippers, buckling, buttoning, or tying, the child will respond correctly.
4. Upon request, the child will be able to wash his face, neck, ears, hands, arms, feet, and legs.
5. Upon request, the child will participate in the selection of games, food, clothing, and friends.
6. Given a task to perform, the child can determine when the task has been completed.

INTERMEDIATE LEVEL
1. Given a youngster with whom he is unfamiliar, the child will be able to make at least one acceptable gesture to become acquainted, such as being able to name the child, play a game with him or engage in conversation.
2. Given five pictures labeled as showing the emotions of anger, sadness, happiness, hostility, or fear, the student can identify the pictures.

3. When discussing abilities, the child will be able to choose from a list of descriptive words those that describe his feelings when he performs well and those that describe his feelings when he performs poorly.
4. Given a law at his level of experience, the child will be able to state why it is important to obey it.
5. In a role-playing situation, the student can verbally state the difference between satisfactory and unsatisfactory behavior in the antagonists.
6. The child can participate in group discussions without arguing.

PREVOCATIONAL LEVEL
1. When verbally given the sentence starter "I can," the student can tell five things he is able to do.
2. When verbally given the starter sentence "I like" or "I do not like," the student can name five things for either sentence.
3. Given a situation involving the belongings of others, the student returns the property intact after every use.
4. When given a compliment, the student will respond positively with "Thank you," or a smile.
5. Given a situation in which the student is involved in a fight or becomes angry, the student will be able to verbalize what alternative actions might have been possible.
6. Given a situation involving a disagreement with another person, the child will be able to accept the situation as evidenced by his willingness to talk to or work with the other person.
7. Given a situation in which he is confronted with constructive criticism the student will be able to respond without arguing or denying the criticism.

VOCATIONAL LEVEL
1. When someone offers to assist him, the student accepts the offer in an appropriate manner.
2. When shown pictures of interaction among people, the student will be able to identify those that exhibit cooperative behavior.
3. Given a task in which he has previously made errors, the student will be able to identify the errors and the reasons for the errors.
4. When in a social dance situation, the student can demonstrate the proper behavior for the situation.

In the School

PRESCHOOL LEVEL
1. After demonstration, when asked by the teacher, the child can pour liquid into a glass or cup and drink when asked.

2. After demonstration, the child can put food into a bowl and use either a fork, knife, or spoon when asked.
3. After demonstration, the child can feed, water, and clean the home of classroom pets whenever asked.
4. On request, the child can verbally state the basic classroom rules and give reasons for them.
5. In a structured classroom activity, the child will accept the decisions of the person in authority without leaving the activity.
6. Within the school environment, when the teacher exhibits a positive verbal or physical response toward the child, the child's attempts to cooperate will increase.

PRIMARY LEVEL

1. Given a new situation, the child will respond with a behavior commonly acceptable in the situation.
2. Given a daily assigned chore at school, the child will be able to perform the task without complaining or having to be reminded.
3. Given the responsibility of checking out a library book, the child will return the book at the stated time to the stated place.
4. Given adequate previous training or experience in a specific exercise, the child will be able to lead others in the exercise.
5. In an unstructured situation, the child will demonstrate that he identifies the rights of others by allowing them to make choices and decisions and to express themselves.
6. During free time, the child will join an activity of his own volition and/or invite other children to join him in a play activity.
7. When shown ten pictures showing interaction among people, the student can differentiate those that show cooperating behavior from those that do not.

INTERMEDIATE LEVEL

1. The student can participate in a group project without arguing or fighting.
2. Upon request, the student can verbally state five ways school experiences help people prepare for everyday living.
3. Upon request, the student can verbally state five reasons why he should practice good health habits.
4. Upon request, the student can verbally state five reasons why he should practice good habits of grooming.
5. Upon request, the student will be able to say the names of the school principal, teacher, nurse, and secretary.
6. Given an academic task that the child fails, he will not physically or verbally abuse or disrupt others but rather will seek assistance in an acceptable manner.
7. Upon receiving a reasonable request for help from a peer for a classroom task, he will fulfill the request.

PREVOCATIONAL LEVEL

1. Given a situation in which the rights of another are being violated, the student will recognize that the rights are being violated, be able to determine an appropriate course of action, and take definite action which will defend those rights.
2. Given a set of school rules he is capable of following, the student will be able to abide by them without having to be reminded of them more than once.
3. Given a classroom situation where other students are involved, the student will be able to demonstrate an interest in the activity of others as demonstrated by taking part in the activity wihout distracting or disrupting those involved.
4. In group discussions and gatherings, the student will voluntarily contribute at least one idea, thought, or feeling during the time of the meeting.
5. Given an assigned work task involving two or more students, they will work together until the task is completed.
6. During a structured situation in which two students who have expressed a dislike for each other must work next to each other, the student will be able to work without teacher correction.
7. Given a competitive situation, the student will be able to contribute as a member of a team by demonstrating his ability to follow the rules of the game.

VOCATIONAL LEVEL

1. Given a social situation, the student will be able to select the clothing proper for the occasion and verbally offer two reasons to support the selection.
2. Upon request, the student will be able to state verbally five principles of grooming and relate them to employment or social situations.
3. In a given social situation, the student will be able to state verbally the appropriate graces called for and defend his selection of the behaviors named.
4. Upon request, the student will be able to define honesty, truthfulness, and tolerance, and cite examples of each.
5. Upon request, the student will be able to state a set of moral standards and explain and defend them.
6. Upon request, the student will be able to explain and demonstrate his understanding of the need for sharing in maintaining good relations with fellow employees.
7. Upon request, the student will be able to explain verbally the differences between the role of leader and worker in an employment situation.
8. Given a situation, the student will be able to set up committees and other groups necessary for organization in order to accomplish a goal.

Home, Neighborhood, and Community

PRESCHOOL LEVEL

1. Given an assigned home task that he can perform, the child will accomplish it to the satisfaction of the parents and will be able to state when he has done it well.
2. Given a written note or a verbal message, the child will deliver them to the designated person.
3. Upon request, the child will be able to state verbally three things about the work of his father, mother, or surrogates.

PRIMARY LEVEL

1. Upon request, the child will be able to tell the location of stores and public buildings with reference to his house.
2. Upon request, the child will be able to prepare a simple breakfast of cereal, milk, and toast.
3. Upon request, the child will be able to use a vacuum cleaner, dust pan and broom, can opener, dust cloth, mixer, mop and scrub brush, and stove.
4. Upon request, the child will be able to state reasons for starting work on time and putting things away when home chores are finished.
5. In role playing, the child will be able to ask a stranger for directions while maintaining a cautious distance and cordial behavior.
6. Upon request, the child will be able to state verbally two behavior rules that apply to each situation of being at the movies, riding on a bus or subway, in a restaurant, swimming pool, or library.
7. Upon request, the child will be able to describe at a simple level the need for each of the community helpers: police, firemen, garbage collector, bus driver, or subway conductor.
8. Upon request, the child will be able to describe at a simple level the need for each of the family service persons: doctors, dentists, nurses, clergymen, druggists, welfare worker.

INTERMEDIATE LEVEL

1. Upon request, the student will be able to find the telephone numbers of the Police Department and Fire Department in the local telephone book.
2. Given a public transportation system, the student will be able to describe which bus or subway he would use to go from his home to a downtown shopping area.
3. Upon request, the student will be able to name five local businesses, five occupations, and five different jobs people perform.
4. Upon request, the student will be able to name five historical figures and describe the contribution of each.

5. Upon request, the student will be able to name the mayor, governor, and president.

PREVOCATIONAL LEVEL
1. Upon request, the student can verbally state three responsibilities of a wage earner in a family.
2. Upon request, the student can verbally state five responsibilities of a homemaker in a family.
3. Upon request, the student will be able to supply three effects companions have on each other.
4. Given a map of the state, the student will be able to identify and briefly describe each of the major geographical areas.
5. When a state government division is named, the student will be able to tell its major function.
6. Upon request, the student will be able to identify each of the major utilities that serve houses.

VOCATIONAL LEVEL
1. When questioned, the student will be able to state his obligations as a family member and cite examples.
2. Upon request, the student will be able to differentiate between benefits and nonbenefits of neighborhood life.
3. Given either pictures of traffic signs or the signs themselves, the student will be able to describe their meaning.
4. Given a road map, the student will be able to identify the directions North, South, East, and West.
5. Given a road map, the student will be able to produce a route from any given point to another.
6. Upon request, the student will be able to identify agencies providing help in cases of specific family emergencies and describe how to secure the help.
7. Upon request, the student will be able to cite examples of behaviors that reflect the responsibilities, duties, and rights of citizens.
8. Given the request, the student will be able to plan and prepare a proper breakfast, lunch, or dinner.
9. Given a bundle of dirty clothes, the student will be able to sort and wash the clothes, using the appropriate settings for kinds and colors.
10. Given a basket of newly washed clothes, the student will be able to iron them, using the proper settings for each item of clothing.

Motor and Recreational Skills

PRESCHOOL LEVEL
1. Given a row of children standing one behind the other, the child will make a verbal indication of his presence within 10 seconds of the time the person in front of him has verbalized his presence.

2. Given a ball 6 inches in diameter, and thrown from a distance of 5 feet, the student will catch the ball so that it does not touch the floor.

3. Given a ball 6 inches in diameter, the student will throw the ball with an overhand motion a distance of 8 feet.

4. Given a 20-inch bat and a 4-inch ball thrown from a distance of 5 feet, the student will hit the ball while it is still in the air, causing the direction of the ball to be altered.

5. Given toys appropriate to the child's functioning level and time to play by himself, the student will play without making a fuss for a period of 20 minutes.

6. Given a model and a simple finger play, the child will imitate the finger movements of the model.

7. Given a ball 12 inches in diameter and a smooth solid floor, the student will throw the ball down and proceed to catch it as it comes back up to him.

PRIMARY LEVEL

1. Given a set of vertical climbing bars, the student will climb up one side of the bars, cross over, and climb down the opposite side from the one he started on.

2. Given a set of "hand over hand" bars 5 feet off the ground, the student will hang by both hands from the first rung, reach one hand forward to the next rung, and bring his second hand forward, without falling.

3. Given the direction to do a forward somersault, the student will perform the task without falling to either side.

4. Given a stable floor, the student will stand on one foot for a period of 10 seconds, without putting down his other foot.

5. Given a balance beam 4 inches wide and 6 feet long, the student will walk along the balance beam, placing one foot in front of the other, heel to toe.

6. Given a weight of at least 5 pounds with a handle, the student will bend at the knees to grab the weight, keeping his back straight, then pick up the weight by straightening his legs, until he has reached a vertical standing position.

7. Given only the level ground, the student will jump with both feet together so that both feet reach a level of 2 inches off the ground.

8. Given either the left or the right foot, the student will move from a position of standing on one foot and hop forward, landing on the same foot, without falling over.

9. Given the direction to move in a sliding movement, the student will step forward with one foot, then slide the second along the ground to meet the first.

10. Given an object thrown or rolled toward him from a distance of at

least 8 feet, the student will move so that the object does not hit him.

11. Given a prostrate position with arms at the sides and legs together on the floor, the student will roll over in either direction at least four times, keeping his hips centered along a straight line.

12. Given a ball 3 inches in diameter, or a beanbag, and a target 1 foot in diameter at a distance of 8 feet, the student will toss the ball or beanbag with an underhand motion, so that the ball or beanbag hits the target.

INTERMEDIATE LEVEL

1. Given a ball 12 inches in diameter and a smooth solid surface, the student will bounce the ball at least three times, so that his hand hits the ball between each time it hits the ground.

2. Given a 10-inch ball, thrown from a distance of 5 feet, the student will catch the ball using only his hands and fingers.

3. Given a 10-inch ball, being rolled from a distance of 8 feet, the student will step forward and kick the ball so that it returns in the general direction of delivery.

4. Given simple folk dances, with distinct verbal "calling," the student will follow the steps and directions called for in the dance.

5. Given structured games with up to five rules, the student will participate in the games in accordance with the rules.

PREVOCATIONAL AND VOCATIONAL LEVELS

1. Given clubs appropriate to the student's interests and open to him, the student will join and participate in such clubs and organizations.

2. Given the opportunity, the student will voluntarily participate in sports activities on both the individual and team level.

3. Given bingo, simple card games, and checkers, the student will demonstrate his ability to play and verbalize how he could become involved in such games.

4. Given the basic dances appropriate for the geographical area, the student will demonstrate his ability to perform the dances appropriate to the music provided.

5. Given the games baseball, football, hockey, and basketball, the student will explain the scoring system of each.

6. Given a supine position on the floor, with knees bent and feet flat on the floor, the student will bend from the waist, raising his head to a position where he can touch his chin to his knees, then return to the starting position a total of (x) number of times (sit-ups).

7. Given a supine position on the floor, with arms extended out along the floor and perpendicular to the body, and with legs pointed in the direction of the ceiling, the student will move his legs together,

from side to side, touching the floor on each side and always keeping his legs perpendicular to his body (hip twist).
8. Given a supine position on the floor with elbows propped against the floor and hands under hips, the student will raise his legs to a position above his body and move his feet and legs in a pedaling motion (bicycle).

Esthetics

Art

PRESCHOOL LEVEL
1. Upon request, the child will be able to select the primary colors of blue, red, and yellow.
2. Upon request, the child will be able to select the secondary colors of green, orange, and purple.
3. Given a request to use colors to express an emotion, the child will select dark colors for anger and light colors for joy.
4. When shown a picture in which lines are used to express emotion, the child will be able to associate (select) heavy lines for boldness and zigzagged lines for action.

PRIMARY LEVEL
1. Given a choice of symmetrical and nonsymmetrical art objects or pictures, the child will be able to select those which are symmetrical from those that are not.
2. Given finger painting materials, the child will be able to express an idea or emotion by a picture representation.
3. When shown pictures in which geometric shapes are used, the child will be able to point to and identify the different shapes.
4. Given a choice of different sized art tools such as brushes, scissors, etc., the child will select those that are appropriate for the task to be done (e.g., picture painted).
5. When presented with different kinds of textured materials, the child will be able to select those that are rough, smooth, sticky, wooly or furry.

INTERMEDIATE LEVEL
1. Given the proper materials, the child will be able to draw a picture of a simple subject such as a tree or a vase.
2. When presented with the following art materials, the child will be able to demonstrate at least one use for each: charcoal, pencil, tempera paint, print blocks, clay, and yarn.

    3. When shown a picture in which perspective is used, the child will be able to state verbally two ways in which perspective is achieved.

PREVOCATIONAL AND VOCATIONAL LEVELS
    1. Upon request, the student will be able to identify an example of balance in a piece of art work.
    2. Given a picture in which balance is achieved by apposition (offsetting line with color, etc.), the student will be able to identify the elements used.
    3. Given an art object in which rhythm is dominant, the student will be able to pick out the pattern in the art object.
    4. When asked to distinguish between repetition and variety, the student will be able to identify examples of each.
    5. Given a display of art work done by his peers, the student will be able to select the best work and verbally explain the reasons for his choice.

Music

PRESCHOOL LEVEL
    1. When records of different time are played (march, waltz, rock) the child will be able to keep time to the music by clapping his hands or marching.
    2. When clapping to a tune, the child will be able to sing or whistle along.
    3. When asked, the child will be able to identify songs or tunes he prefers over other songs or tunes.

PRIMARY LEVEL
    1. Upon request, the child will be able to identify simple musical terms such as note, rest, staff, and time.
    2. Given an accompaniment of a record or instrument, the child will be able to sing the words of at least three different kinds of songs.
    3. Given a record player and record or a tape deck and tape, the child will be able to play them properly.

INTERMEDIATE LEVEL
    1. When two songs are played, the student can distinguish major from minor melodies.
    2. When songs are played, the student can recognize soft rock, country and western, soul, and acid rock.
    3. Given a tune played for him, the student can distinguish between pop, salon, and classical music.
    4. Upon request, the student can verbally explain the difference between brass and stringed instruments.

5. Given some practice, the student will be able to play in a rhythm band.

PREVOCATIONAL AND VOCATIONAL LEVELS
1. Upon hearing a musical number, the student will be able to identify brasses, strings, percussions, and tell which group has the lead.
2. Upon hearing a vocal musical number, the student will be able to tell whether the number is a solo or group and distinguish between a small group and choir.
3. Given a vocal solo, the student will be able to identify a ballad from rock and soul.
4. Upon request, the student will be able to indicate verbally his preference in music and defend the choice.

Health

PRESCHOOL LEVEL
1. Given the need to go to the bathroom, the child will indicate his need, complete the task, flush the toilet, and wash and dry his hands.
2. Given a sink, toothbrush, and toothpaste, the child will brush his teeth after each meal.
3. Given a sink, soap, and washcloth, the child will wash his hands and face before and after each meal.
4. Given a class of boys and girls, the child will separate the class into groups according to sex.

PRIMARY LEVEL
1. Given the task of dressing himself, the child will put on clean socks and underwear each day.
2. Given the instruction to go to bed, the child will proceed to his bedroom and get into bed.
3. Given only a verbal command, the child will point to the major parts of the body.
4. Given the need to blow his nose and a box of tissues, the child will remove one tissue, blow his nose into it, then throw the tissue in the wastebasket.
5. Given the need to cough or sneeze, the child will place at least one hand over his mouth during the actual cough or sneeze.
6. Given pictures of sloppy and neat appearances, the student will verbalize five characteristics of a neat appearance and five characteristics of a sloppy appearance.
7. Given three different weather conditions and a variety of clothing, the student will choose the appropriate clothing for each condition.

8. Given a variety of food items, the student will verbalize whether the item is usually eaten at breakfast, lunch, or dinner.
9. Given an empty sink, dirty dishes, soap, and a washcloth, the student will put soap in the sink, add hot water, place the dishes in the water, use the washcloth to wash the dishes, rinse the soap off the dishes, and place them into the drying rack.
10. Given a personal problem, the child will verbalize the problem to the teacher to a degree that the teacher understands what the problem is.

INTERMEDIATE LEVEL

1. Given the question, "Why do we brush our teeth?" the student will verbally state five reasons why teeth should be brushed.
2. Given a comb and mirror, the student will comb his hair.
3. Given the question, "Why is bathing important?" the student will verbalize five reasons why it is important to take a bath.
4. Given a can of deodorant, the student will apply the deodorant to the appropriate body parts.
5. Given a scale graded in pounds, the student will read the scale and distinguish between lighter and heavier weights.
6. Given a thermometer measured in degrees Fahrenheit, the student will read the thermometer and verbalize whether the reading indicates warm or cold weather.
7. Given a picture of five major vital organs, the student will name the organs and verbalize the function of each (heart, lungs, brain, kidney, stomach).
8. Given the question, "Why do we need rest?" the student will verbally state three reasons why rest is important to our health.
9. Given pictures of many different foods, the student will choose five specific foods that should be eaten every day.
10. Given a question concerning the preparation of specific foods, the student will include in the answer the process of cleaning or washing that food.
11. Given several pictures of foods, the student will identify those foods that require refrigeration.
12. Given several pictures of foods, the student will separate them into categories of fruits, vegetables, and meats.
13. Given the proper ingredients and verbal instructions, the student will prepare a simple meal.

Personal Hygiene

PREVOCATIONAL LEVEL

1. Given a thermometer, another student, and a watch with a second hand, the student will place the thermometer in the second student's mouth and leave it there for 2 to 3 minutes, and read it to the nearest whole number.

2. Given a schedule of bathing every two days, the student will independently adhere to the schedule.
3. Given the question, "When should we call the doctor?" the student will verbalize three cases that would warrant calling a doctor.
4. Given examples of burns, cuts, and broken bones, the student will verbalize what medical attention is needed.
5. Given the question, "How are babies born?" the student will verbalize the basic process of human reproduction.
6. Given the question, "What is meant by good personal hygiene?" the student will verbalize that good personal hygiene involves the proper care of teeth and hair, and keeping the body clean and well fed.
7. Given a list of health agencies, the student will verbalize how often the services should be used, and what service is provided by which agency on the list.
8. Given a list of eating habits, the student will distinguish which are appropriate to his individual needs.
9. Given a self-recording chart, and a list of eating habits, the student will record his own eating habits.
10. Given the eating habits recording chart, the student will verbally relate the data to his own body needs.
11. Given a chart of the four basic food groups, the student will indicate the proper number of servings required daily for each group in order to maintain a well-balanced diet.
12. Given a list of foods the student has eaten for a given week, the student will classify them according to food group, compare this to the chart of required daily servings, and indicate which areas his diet was deficient in.
13. Given a recipe and necessary equipment, the student will read the recipe and follow the directions in order to produce the expected food product.
14. Given a question concerning physiological changes of the body during puberty, the student will verbalize three changes that occur during this period.
15. Given a list of parents, siblings, peer group, other adults, employer, and other employees, the student will verbalize the type of role or relationship he would have with each person or group.

VOCATIONAL LEVEL

1. Given a list of foods the student has eaten for a period of two weeks, the student will classify the foods according to the four basic food groups, and give reasons for the choices made.
2. Given a schedule of bathing every one or two days, the student will maintain the bathing schedule and keep a record of it.
3. Given a period of two hours per day for leisure time activities, the

    student will plan activities of rest and recreation to fill those two-hour periods for an entire week.

4. Given a question concerning the care of children, the student will verbalize five basic elements of child care.
5. Given a model of appropriate dress for a specific occasion, the student will produce a similar effect from his own clothing.
6. Given soap, bandages, ointment, and a minor cut, the student will clean and bandage the wound.
7. Given a complete meal, the student will demonstrate his ability to eat properly.
8. Given the need for immunization shots, the student will keep and follow a record of when the shots should be given.
9. Given a question concerning the dangers of contagious diseases, the student will verbalize what those dangers are.
10. Given a question concerning the proper use of drinking fountains and rest rooms, the student will verbalize the proper use of each.
11. Given a question concerning the disposal of trash and garbage, the student will verbalize at least three procedures.
12. Given a question concerning self-medication, the student will verbalize the dangers of its use.
13. Given a problem of health, the student will verbalize where the problem is located, when it began, and what caused the problem.
14. Given a question concerning the dangers of smoking, alcohol, and drugs, the student will verbalize three dangers of each.
15. Given a question concerning the importance of liquid to a diet, the student will verbalize two reasons for drinking fluids.
16. Given four different situations, the student will verbally identify the person or agency to approach for guidance or counseling.
17. Given an emotional state such as fear, joy, loneliness, and sorrow, the student will expound on this feeling verbally.
18. Given contact with peer group, teachers, and other adults, the student will demonstrate his ability to establish acceptable personal relationships.

Safety

PRESCHOOL LEVEL
1. Given the teacher, bus driver, and crossing guard, the child will follow the directives given by these persons.
2. Upon hearing a fire alarm in school, the students will follow the teacher out of the building and stay within 5 feet of the teacher.
3. On the school bus the child will remain seated from the time he gets on to the time he is supposed to get off.

4. Given household dangers such as knives, pins, matches, medicines, and poisons, the child will leave all such items alone.
5. Given a tricycle and the freedom to ride, the child will ride only on the sidewalk or within his yard.
6. Given a body of water, the child will stay away from the water when not accompanied by an adult.
7. Given the offer of a ride or candy from a stranger, the child will refuse any such offer.
8. Given an animal unfamiliar to the child, the child will remain physically separated from the animal.

PRIMARY LEVEL

1. Given a question concerning the danger of streets and alleys, the child will indicate at least one danger of each.
2. Given the traffic signals appropriate to the area, the child will indicate under what conditions he must wait.
3. Given the words, "STOP, CAUTION, GO, DANGER, FIRE EXIT, POISON, WALK, FLAMMABLE, and DO NOT ENTER," the child will read the words and verbally indicate an understanding of each.
4. Given a question concerning the dangers of lakes, pools, and rivers, the child will verbalize one such danger.
5. Given a question concerning bike safety rules, the child will verbalize five rules.
6. Given a bodily injury, the child will name four persons he could approach with the problem.
7. Given a question concerning the dangers of medicine, the child will verbalize at least one such danger.
8. Given scissors, ruler, saw, screwdriver, hammer and nails, pliers, pins, tacks, paper clips, staples, record player, and cassette, the child will demonstrate the appropriate use of each.
9. Given pictures of safe and dangerous situations in the home, the child will identify those which are safe and those which are dangerous.
10. Given a designated set of school behaviors, the student will play in accordance with those rules while at school.

INTERMEDIATE LEVEL

1. Given pictures of safe and dangerous situations in the home, the student will indicate which situations are safe and which are dangerous.
2. Given the conditions of overloaded electric outlet, bare electric wire, clutter on a stairway, broken step ladder, frying pan unattended on stove, can of gas near a fire source, and a young child near an unattended power saw, the student will take the steps necessary for correcting each situation.

3. Given a role-playing situation, the student will demonstrate the proper procedure for reporting a fire or accident.
4. Given the signals of a yellow, red, and green traffic light, the student will verbalize the meaning of all possible combinations of the traffic light.
5. Given a bicycle, the student will indicate the proper hand signals for a right and left turn while riding the bicycle.
6. Given a street diagram, the student will locate and mark the proper side of the street to ride a bicycle on.
7. Given the situation of being lost, the student will verbalize which agency he would call for help.
8. Given a car parked parallel on the street, the student will demonstrate the proper procedure for getting in and out of the car.

PREVOCATIONAL LEVEL

1. Given a question concerning the proper care of tools, the student will verbally state three reasons why tools must be kept in repair.
2. Given a question concerning the care of appliances, the student will verbally state three reasons why appliances must be kept in repair.
3. Given a question concerning the care of furniture, the student will verbally state three reasons why furniture must be kept in repair.
4. Given a question concerning the proper use of appliances, the student will verbally state three reasons why appliances must be used only for their designed purpose.
5. Given a variety of inflammable materials, the student will properly demonstrate their use.
6. Given a model of an electrical fuse box, the student will properly remove the old fuse and install a new one.
7. Given a question concerning the dangers of a power lawn mower, the student will verbally state five such dangers.
8. Given a request to call the police or fire department, the student will demonstrate his ability to complete the task.
9. Given a question concerning common fire hazards in a home, the student will verbally state five common examples of fire hazards.
10. Given a hypothetical example of an accident, the student will demonstrate his ability to keep the injured warm, keep crowds away from the scene, and contact the police.
11. Given a body of water large enough to support a person, the student will float or tread water for two minutes.
12. Given a Red Cross dummy, the student will properly demonstrate the method of artificial resuscitation.
13. Given a picture or model of poison ivy and poison oak, the student will identify which is which.
14. Given pictures of plants or snakes common to the locality, the student will identify those that are poisonous.

VOCATIONAL LEVEL
1. Given a hypothetical case of a fire, the student will discuss and demonstrate methods of putting out a fire.
2. Given an example of a hazardous situation, the student will describe ways to eliminate the hazard.
3. Given the heavy equipment and power tools of the school, the student will describe the hazards to be avoided in using this equipment and tools.
4. Given a motor vehicle, the student will demonstrate his ability to drive safely on any given course in traffic and to obey the traffic laws.
5. Given an accident report form, the student will fill out the form to meet the standards of the insurance or police agencies.
6. Given a car maintenance manual and car, the student will verbally state when the car should be brought to a garage for care.
7. Given a swimming pool and the Red Cross Swim Test, the student will pass the test to the level of beginning swimmer.
8. Given a situation of a drowning person, the student will describe the appropriate life-saving measures.
9. Given a job involving machinery, the student will keep his hair covered.
10. Given a question concerning safety rules of a specific plant, the student will list the rules.
11. Given a specific occupation, the student will explain the danger signals and symbols of that occupation.
12. Given a question concerning the qualities of his friends, the student will explain what the qualities of his friends are that led to that friendship.

Vocational Competencies

Analysis of Occupations

PRESCHOOL LEVEL
1. When questioned, the student will be able to state the occupation of his mother or father.
2. When questioned as to what his parents receive for working, the student will indicate or state that it is money.
3. When asked, the student will be able to identify two people outside his immediate family who work.
4. When questioned, the student will be able to name three different jobs performed by school personnel.
5. When questioned, the student will be able to name three different types of jobs.

PRIMARY LEVEL

1. When asked, the student will be able to name three occupations of the helping professions.
2. When asked, the student will be able to state verbally how the helping professions help people.
3. When asked, the child will be able to describe two chores performed in the home and tell who is responsible for them.
4. When asked, the student will be able to name three businesses operating in his community.
5. When questioned, the student will be able to name three kinds of stores and tell what they sell.
6. When questioned, the student will be able to name two community utility services.

INTERMEDIATE LEVEL

1. When asked, the child will be able to name two ways in which people help others through their work.
2. When questioned, the student will be able to describe the tasks performed by different members of the family.
3. Given pictures of a fireman, policeman, electrical worker, nurse, doctor, or factory worker, the student will correctly identify the occupation of each.
4. Given pictures of a police worker, factory worker, store clerk, gas station attendant, mail carrier, and farmer, the student will be able to name three things each worker does as part of his job.

PREVOCATIONAL LEVEL

1. When asked, the student will be able to discuss the differences between leisure time and work time.
2. Given ten labeled pictures of various work situations, the student will be able to match them correctly with ten pictures of different kinds of dress.
3. In a verbal discussion of various occupations, the student will be able to identify one occupation he would like to engage in and one he would not like to work at.
4. Given an uncomplicated job application form, the student will be able to fill in all the blanks correctly.
5. When questioned, the student will be able to tell about opportunities for jobs that are peculiar to his locality.
6. When questioned, the student will be able to discuss two services of the Employment Agency.

VOCATIONAL LEVEL

1. When questioned, the student will be able to name two skills needed for the successful performance of a given job.

2. When presented with a given job, the student will be able to fill out a job analysis form.
3. When questioned, the student will be able to name three sources of information about employment opportunities.
4. Given a role of job interview, the student will be able to conduct himself properly.
5. When questioned, the student will be able to name the major provisions of the wage and hour law.
6. When questioned, the student will be able to state verbally the provisions of unemployment compensation.
7. When questioned about fringe benefits, the student will be able to name the benefits of hospitalization, insurance, vacations, and social security.
8. When questioned, the student will be able to discuss the requirements for union membership and name two advantages of belonging.

Occupational Skills

PRESCHOOL LEVEL
1. Upon request, the child will be able to discriminate between his belongings and those of other children.
2. Given a group of common objects, the child will be able to categorize them by use.
3. Given three different instructions, the child will be able to follow them.

PRIMARY LEVEL
1. When given a group of different kinds of objects, the child will be able to sort them by shape, color, or size.
2. When asked, the child will be able to explain warning and direction signs.
3. Upon request, the child will be able to verbalize classroom rules of conduct.
4. Given an assigned classroom chore, the child will carry it out without being reminded by the teacher.

INTERMEDIATE LEVEL
1. Given an assortment of hand tools, the child will be able to name them on request.
2. Given a task to do in a group activity, the child will be able to complete his assignment in a satisfactory manner.
3. Upon the completion of a task, the child will be able to describe two reasons for taking pride in a job well done.
4. Upon request, the child will be able to name three activities of a good worker.

PREVOCATIONAL LEVEL
1. Given the opportunity, the child pays for his lunches and transportation from his earnings.
2. Upon request, the child will be able to recite his vital statistics.
3. Given a problem involving wages and hours worked, the child will be able to explain the relationship.
4. When criticized for poor work, the child can explain the reason why the criticism is warranted.
5. Given a job to do, the student will be able to function without supervision.

VOCATIONAL LEVEL
1. Given a job situation, the student can converse with fellow workers using the correct vocational vocabulary.
2. Given a job assignment, the student will be able to work alongside other employees without interfering with the work of his peers.
3. Given a job assignment, the student will be able to work a full day with no appreciable drop in production.
4. Upon finishing a task, the student will be able to start a new task without having to be directed to do so by his supervisor.
5. Given a task that requires a sequence of movements for completion, the student will be able to perform successfully each of the acts in the correct order.
6. Upon request, the student will be able to describe the appropriate dress for each of three different occupations.
7. Upon request, the student will be able to name three advantages of working for the company or business for which the student works.
8. Upon request, the student will be able to explain three job requirements of a supervisor.
9. Upon request, the student will be able to describe verbally what a worker must do to be promoted in his job.

Index

A

Abacus:
  finger, 129–131
  Oriental, 130–131
Achievement tests, 73
Adaptive behavior, 13
Aloia, G. F., 48–49
American Association for Health,
    Physical Education, and Recreation
    (AAHPER), 165
American Association on Mental
    Deficiency, subcommitte on
    nomenclature, 11–15
Area Learning Resource Centers (ALRC),
    265
Arithmetic skills, 119–141
  diagnosis of, 139–141
  intermediate level, 132–135
  measurement, 138–139
  money, 136–137
  new math, 135–136
  outcomes, 120–121, 275–280
  preschool and primary, 127–132
  prevocational and vocational, 135–136

Arithmetic skills *(cont.)*
  teaching methods, 126–136
  time, 137–138
Art, 173–176
  elements of, 173–174
  outcomes, 177–178, 288–289
Aukerman, R. C., 113–114
Axline, V. M., 102
Ayers, D., 53

B

Balance, in art, 175–176
Baller, W. R., 50
Baumgartner, B. B., 168
Beacon Primer, 101
Becker, R. L., 204
Beckham, A. S., 34
Bennett,   ,50
Benoit, E. P., 22
Bereiter, C., 79n, 80, 88, 115
Binet, A., 6, 7, 16, 20
Biological background, units on, 189–190,
    247
Blackburn, D. B., 180
Blackman, L. S., 127

Blatt, B., 4, 51
Bond, G. L., 102
Bone, R., 174n
Booth, A., 135
Boy Scouts of America, 167–168
Brain damaged, defined, 8
Britton, A. L., 53
Burdett, A. B., 203–204
Bureau of Education for the Handicapped,
    264–266
Buris, W. R., 57
Bush, W. J., 118
Buswell, G. T., 101

C

Camping, 168–170
Capobianco, R. P., 127
Career education, 199–205
    compared to vocational education, 199
Carroll, A. W., 48
Cell assembly theory, 22
Central nervous system inefficiency
    theory, 22–23
Cephalo-caudal principle, 158
Chaffin, J. D., 50, 157n
Chall, J., 103n
Charles, D. C., 50
Charney, L., 82n
Child:
    units on, 224
    work of, 225–226
City government, 236–237
Clark, A. D. B., 35
Clausen, J., 15, 20
Cobb, H., 33
Coghill, G. C., 103, 158
Cognition, 223
Cognitive change, levels of, 40–41
Collins, G., 132–133
Collman, R. D., 34
Color, in emotional expression, 174–175
Communication, oral (*see* Oral
    communication)
Communication, written (*see* Written
    communication)
Communication skills, 85–118
    developmental approaches, 113–118
    outcomes, 86–87, 269–275
    remedial approaches, 115–118

Community:
    outcomes, 284–285
    units on, 235–238
Concrete operations stage, 18
Conger, J. J., 77n
Conley, R. W., 28n, 29
Connolly, A. J., 139n
Conry, J., 31
Consequating, 70
Contingency management, 71
Convergent thought, 223
Copeland, R., 128
Corder, W. O., 158
Count-A-Ladder, 132
Count-A-Line, 132
Crasson, J. E., 31n
Cratty, B. J., 157
Cromwell, R., 79n
Cruickshank, W. M., 126
Cuisinaire rods, 131

D

Davis, E., 159, 163–164, 166–167
Davison, R., 50n
Dearborn, W. F., 101
Delacato, C. H., 115–117, 156
Deno, E., 54
Dever, R. B., 31
Dilling, H., 52
Dinger, J. C., 31
Disability, defined, 9
Distar (Direct Instruction System for
    Teaching Arithmetic and Reading)
    115
Divergent thought, 223
Dolch, E., 111, 135
Dolch games, 111
Driver training, 252–253
Dunn, L. M., 49, 51, 52, 89
Dye, H. B., 30

E

Educable mentally handicapped, 9–10
Education:
    career, compared to vocational, 199
    criticisms of programs, 46–57
    goals of, 32–36
    grouping for, 62–67

Education *(cont.)*
  instructional methods, 67–71
  instructional outcomes, 38–41, 44
  intermediate program, 42
  preschool program, 41–42
  prevocational program, 42–43
  primary program, 42
  program goals, 36–38
  vocational program, 43
Educational programming, 26–27
Elkema, C. E., 57
Ellis, N. R., 20n
Endogenous retardation, 8
Englemann Cognitive Maturity test, 88–89
Englemann, S., 79n, 80, 88, 115
Eskridge, C., 198
Esthetics, 171–183
  implementing, 182–183
  outcomes, 288–290
Evaluative thought, 223
Evans, R. N., 200n
Exogenous retardation, 8
Experience charts, 221–222
Extinction of behavior, 69

F

Facts and processes, 127
  outcomes, 275–276
Falender, C., 31n
Family, units on, 224–225
Farber, B., 24n, 28n, 47
Fernald, G. M., 102
Findley, W. L., 29, 36
Fitzgerald Key, 99
Flavell, J. H., 17–19
Formal operations stage, 18–19
Francis, R. J., 157
Franklin, C. C., 166
Frey, R. M., 13n, 35n, 202n, 250n
Friends, units on, 228
Frostig, M., 95–97
Fudell, S., 251

G

Galanter, E., 23–24, 82, 260
Garber, H., 31n
Gestalt psychology, 102–103
Getzels, J. W., 17

Giant word syndrome, 88
Giles, M., 118
Gillespie, P. H., 113
Girardeau, F. L., 68n
Goals:
  compared to objectives, 75
  program, 260
Goldstein, H., 50, 154, 218n
Gordon, E. K., 101
Grammar, teaching of, 99–100
Gray, W. S., 102
Grouping of children, 62–67
Guilford, J. J., 17, 19, 23, 222–223
Gunderson, A. G., 131–132

H

Hamerlynck, L. A., 31n
Handicap, defined, 9
Hanna, J. B., 136–137
Haring, N., 68n
Harrington, S., 31n
Hayball, H., 52
Hayes, B. H., Jr., 174n
Health, 184–191
  outcomes, 184–188, 290–293
  teaching of, 188–191
Hebb, D. O., 22, 24, 115–117
Heber, R. F., 11n, 20n, 31, 218n
Hegge, T. G., 98, 109–110
Heller H. B., 53
Henderson, C. N., 39
Hermelin, B. F., 35
Hewett, F., 69n
Hirsch, D., 24–26
Hirst, W., 120n, 159n
Hodges, R., 114
Hoffman, C., 31n
Hollister, G. E., 131–132
Home:
  economics of, 243–244
  functions of, 226–228
  management of, 244–245
  mechanics of, 245–246
  outcomes, 284–285
  preschool units on, 224–229
Homme, L. E., 70n
House, B. J., 41
Howe, C., 157
Hoyt, K. B., 199–200

Hudson, M., 250
Hueffle, K. M., 96
Hydrocephaly, 30

I

Iano, R. P., 53
Identification, with models, 77–78
Idiot, 6
Illinois Index of Self Derogation (IISD), 48
Illinois Test of Psycholinguistic Abilities (ITPA), 117
Imbecile, 6
Individual development, and vocational competency, 211–213
Individual program of instruction (IPI), 71–81
Inhelder, B., 24
Initial Teaching Alphabet (i/t/a), 114
Initial work experience, 205–207, 240–241
Instruction, individual programs of, 71–81
Instructional methods, 67–71
Instructional unit(s):
  on community, 235–238
  defined, 218
  on home preschool level, 224–229
  on neighborhood, 229–235
  plans for, 219–220
  prevocational level, 239–249
  vocational level, 249–256
Intellectual processes, 222–223
Intelligence:
  developmental stages, 17–19
  measures of, compared, 19–20
  and sensory deficiency, 16
  as test performance, 16–17
  tests of, 7, 16–17
IQ (Intelligence quotient), 12–13
  and minority groups, 14
  and socioeconomic level, 59
Intermediate level, 65–66
Intuitive thought, 18
Itard, J. M., 16, 21

J

Jackson, P. W., 17
Jacobson, L., 49
James, W., 101

Jewish Employment and Vocational Service (JEVS), 202–203
Job analysis, 254–255, 296–298
Job tryout, 207
Johnson, G. O., 9–10, 49–50, 51–52
Johnson, L., 113
Johnson, C. F., 264
Jones E. M., 34, 35n, 159, 242
Jones, M., 251n
Jones, R. L., 48–49
Jordan, L., 50
Jordan, T. E., 15, 52, 85–88

K

Kagan, J., 77n
Kahn, C. H., 136
Kahn, H., 203–204
Kennedy, R. J. R., 47, 50
Kephart, N. C., 40–41, 116–117, 156, 158
Key Math test, 139–140
Kirk, S. A., 9–10, 14, 29, 30–31, 47n, 52, 98, 103–105, 109–110, 117, 158, 218n
Kirk, W. D., 98, 109–110, 117
Kolstoe, O. P., 12n, 13n, 24–26, 34, 35, 39, 158–159, 202n, 250n, 251
Kottmeyer, W., 118

L

LaCrosse, E., 82n
Language:
  tests of, 74–75
  uses of, 90–91
Language Master, 93
Lawson, G. D., 250, 256
Learning characteristics, 67–71
Learning paradigm, 81–82
Lewis, E. O., 47
Lindsley, O. R., 69
Line, in emotional expression, 174
Linguistics, phonemic, 113–114
Listening skills, 91–93
  outcomes, 91–92, 271–272

M

McCarthy, J. J., 117
McGettigan, J. F., 53
McGuffey reader, 100–101

Mackin, E. F., 200*n*
MacMillan, D. L., 48–49
Mainstreaming, 51–53
Malpass, L. F., 157
Mangum, G. L., 200*n*
Massed-differentiated-integrated theory, 103–105, 158
May, L., 132
Measurement, 138–139
  outcomes, 125–126, 278–280
Mediation, 262
Memory, 222–223
Mental age, 12–13
Mental defective, defined, 8
Mental deficiency, defined, 8
Mental retardation:
  and age, 46–48
  attitudes toward, 3–6
  behavioral classification of, 6, 11
  causal classification of, 8, 11
  characteristics of, 20–21
  as concept, 15–20
  conceptualized, 260
  definition of, 24–26
  diagnosis of, 58–62
  educational classification of, 9–10, 11–12
  educational programs (*see* Education)
  era of education, 4
  era of normalization, 5
  as generic term, 13
  identification of, 57–58
  intervention, need for, 28–32
  psychometric classification of, 6–8, 11
  theories of, 21–24
Mercer, J. R., 14, 59
Merrill, M. A., 7*n*, 16
Metamessages, 153–154
Methods and resource materials:
  arithmetic, 126–136
  communication skills, 113–118
  reading, 106–113
  social competency, 151–155
  written communication, 95–99
  See also Resource materials
Metric Center, 135
Metric system, 133–135
Meyrowitz, J. H., 48
Michal-Smith, H., 34
Miller, E., 23–24

Miller, E. L., 82
Miller, G., 260
Millslagle, W., 39
Minority groups, and IQ tests, 14
Mobility:
  teaching of, 163–167
  testing of, 159–160
Molloy, J., 165–166
Money, 136–137
  outcomes, 121–123, 276–277
Monroe, M., 102
Moron, 6
Moss, J., 50
Motor and recreational skills, 156–170
  mobility, teaching of, 163–167
  mobility testing, 159–160
  outcomes, 160–163, 285–288
  swimming, 166–167
Music, 179–182
  outcomes, 179–180, 289–290
Mussen, P. H., 77*n*

N

Nachtman, W., 139*n*
National Center on Educational Media and Materials for the Handicapped, 265
Neighborhood, 229–235
  outcomes, 284–285
New math, 135–136
Newlyn, D., 34
Normalcy, 7
Normalization, 5, 51–53

O

Objectives, compared to goals, 75
Occupational information, 241–242
Occupations:
  analysis (*see* Job analysis)
  outcomes, 298–299
  resource materials on, 250–251
O'Connor, N., 35
Ocvirk, O. G., 174*n*
Oliver, J. N., 158
Operant conditioning, 68–71, 76–77
Oral communication, 85–91
  outcomes, 269–271
Osgood, C. E., 117

Outcomes:
  arithmetic skills, 120–121, 275–280
  art, 177–178
  communication skills, 86–87, 269–275
  esthetics, 288–290
  health, 184–188, 290–293
  listening skills, 91–92
  measurement, 125–126
  money, 121–123
  motor and recreation skills, 160–163,
    285–288
  music, 179–180
  reading, 105–106
  safety, 191–194, 293–296
  social competency, 280–285,
    in school, 146–149
  outside of school, 149–151
  time, 123–124
  use of lists, 261–262
  vocational competency, 209–210, 211–
    212, 296–299
  written communication, 93–95

P

Pangle, R., 158
Parnicky, J. J., 203–204
Peabody Language Development Kit, 89–
  90, 93
Peck, J., 251
Permissiveness, in classroom, 78–79
Personal hygiene, 291–293
Pertch, C. F., 50
Peterson, R. C., 34, 35n, 159, 242
Phenylketonuria (PKU), 30
Phonics, 101, 109–110
Physical education, 242–243
Piaget, J., 17–19, 24, 25, 40
Pinpointing behavior, 69–70
Pitman, I., 114
Pitman, J., 114
Precision teaching, 69
Prehm, H. J., 31n
Preschool level, 63–64
President's Panel on Mental Retardation,
  263
  report of (1962), 11
Prevo, H., 251n
Prevocational program, 66–67, 239–249
Pribram, K., 23–24, 82, 260

Primary level, 64–65
Pritchett, E. M., 139n
Proximal-distal principle, 158
Psycholinguistics, 73–74
Pugh, B. L., 99n
Punishment, 80
Pygmalion in the Classroom, 49

R

Rainey, D. S., 251
Rarick, L., 157
Rathbun, M. C., 174n
Reading, 100–113
  outcomes, 105–106, 273–275
  teaching of, 106–113
  theories on, 103–106
Recreation, 167–170, 242–243
  camping, 168–170
  organizations for, 167–168
Reflex arc, 23
Regan, C. E., 50n
Regional government, units on, 237
Regional Resource Centers (RRC), 264–
  265
Reichard, C. L., 180
Remedial Reading Drills, 98, 109–110
Resource materials:
  art, 178
  occupational information, 242, 250–251
  for units on the neighborhood, 234–235
  vocational level, 202–205, 255–256
  See also Methods and resource
    materials
Reward reinforcement, 68–71
  and punishment, 80
Richards, M. H., 180n, 182
Robbins, M. P., 116
Robinson, J. H., 264
Role switching, 152
Rosenthal, R., 49
Rynbrandt, D. M., 35

S

Saenger, G., 35
Safety:
  methods and resource materials, 194–
    196
  outcomes, 191–194, 293–296

Schiefelbusch, R., 68*n*
School:
  as family, 228–229
  social competency in, 281–283
Schurr, E. L., 160
Seguin, E., 16, 22, 156
Seigel, D., 218*n*
Self, 247–248
  outcomes, 280–281
Self-concept, 144–146
  and esthetics, 171–173
  and special class placement, 48–49
Self-management, 152
Sensory deficiency, 16
Sensory deprivation, 21–22
Sensory impairment, 58–59
Sensory-motor stage, 18
Shape, in art, 175
Shop (*see* Home, mechanics of)
Shotwell, A., 34
Simon, T., 6, 16
Skeels, H., 30
Skinner, B. F., 68
Skodak, M., 30
Slow learners, 9
Smith, J. O., 89
Smith, R., 251
Smyke, P. H., 264
Social competency, 142–155
  outcomes, 149–151, 280–285
  resource materials, 154–155
  in school, 146–149
  self-concept, 144–146
  teaching of, 151–155
Social studies, 246–249
Sociodrama, 151–154
Space, in art, 176
Spearman, C., 17
Special class(es):
  assignment to, 59–62
  effectiveness of, 49–50
  legality of, 52
  management of, 77–81
  screening for, 57–58
  and self-concept, 48–49
  future of, 263–268
Special Education Instructional Materials
  Centers (SEIMC), 263
Spellman, C. R., 50*n*
Spradlin, J. E., 68*n*, 87–88

Stalacker, L., 202*n*
State government, units on, 237
Stein, J. V., 157
Stein, J. U., 158
Stephens, W. B., 24
Stern counting blocks, 131
Stevens, H. A., 20*n*, 218*n*
Stinson, R., 174*n*
Strauss, A. A., 8
Stroud, J. B., 100, 102*n*
Subjective behaviorism, 23–24, 260
  as teaching model, 82
Sullivan Reading Series, 110–111
Sund, R., 25
Suppes, P., 136*n*
Sweeter, W., 25
Swimming, teaching of, 166–167

T

Teachers:
  effect on achievement, 49
  future prospects for, 266–268
  and learning paradigm, 81–82
Tentative identification, 60
Terman, L. M., 6–7, 16
Test Operate Test Exit (TOTE), 23, 68
Tests:
  achievement, 73
  auditory efficiency, 74
  Englemann Cognitive Maturity, 88–89
  of general ability, 72–73
  intelligence (*see* Intelligence tests)
  Key Math diagnostic, 139–140
  language, 74–75
  motor, 74
  psycholinguistic, 73–74
  visual efficiency, 74
Texture and light, in art, 176
Theory, role of, 262
Thorndike, E. L., 101
Thorndike, R. L., 49
Thurstone, L. L., 17
Time, teaching about, 137–138
  outcomes, 123–124, 277–278
Tinker, M. A., 102
Tizard, J., 35
Totally dependent child, 10
Trainable mentally handicapped, 10
Traxler, A. E., 102

U

University of Southern California program, 263–264
University of Wisconsin program, 263–264

V

Valett, R., 163
Vath, W. R., 30n
Vaughan, T. D., 39
Vocational competency, 197–213
    outcomes, 209–210, 211–212, 296–299
Vocational Education Act (1963), 198
Vocational level, 67, 249–256
von Hilsheimer, G., 129, 135–136

W

Walker, V. S., 53
Wallin, J. E. W., 6n
Warren, F. G., 34, 157n
Watkins, E., 108–109
Watson, J. B., 101
Wechsler, D., 19–20
Weiner, B. B., 47

Wertheimer, M., 102
Wigg, P., 174n
Williams, C. F., 264
Wilson, R. J., 53
Withrow, F. B., 264
Work, concept of, 199–200
Work experience:
    initial, 206–207, 240–241
    permanent placement, 207–208
    tryout of, 207
Work-oriented program, 50, 79
World image, 23
Written communication, 93–100
    cursive writing, 98
    manuscript writing, 97–98
    outcomes, 93–95, 272–273
    teaching of, 95–99

Y

Yoakum, G. A., 101n, 108–109

Z

Zeaman, D., 41